*Literature and the Pastoral*

# Literature and the Pastoral

## ANDREW V. ETTIN

Yale University Press

New Haven and London

Designed by James J. Johnson
and set in Goudy Old Style type.
Printed in the United States of America by
Edwards Brothers, Inc., Ann Arbor, Michigan.

*Library of Congress Cataloging in Publication Data*

Ettin, Andrew V., 1943–
    Literature and the pastoral.

    Bibliography: p.
    Includes index.
    1. Pastoral literature—History and criticism.
I. Title.
PN56.P3E87  1984      890'.93321734      83–26052
ISBN 0–300–03160–2 (alk. paper)

10  9  8  7  6  5  4  3  2  1

*For Johanna and for Anna*

Warum muss einer dastehn wie ein Hirt,
so ausgesetzt dem Übermass von Einfluss,
beteiligt so an diesem Raum voll Vorgang,
das er gelehnt an einen Baum der Landschaft
sein Schicksal hätte, ohne mehr zu handeln. . . .
Hat nichts als Welt, hat Welt in jedem Aufschaun,
in jeder Neigung Welt.

RAINER MARIA RILKE

[Why must one stand there like a shepherd, so overwhelmed by the over-
flowing of influence, appointed to a place so full of example that he who
leans against a tree in the landscape receives his fate, with nothing more
to do. . . . He has nothing other than the world, the world each time he
looks up, each time he lowers his gaze, the world.]

# Contents

# Acknowledgments

A WORK AS LONG IN THE MAKING AS THIS HAS BEEN BECOMES DEBTOR TO MANY. THE longest-standing obligation is to five then-graduate students—Gerald Johnson, Ann Rosalind Jones, Daniel Marrone, Barbara Pavlock, and Anne Posell—who joined me for a seminar on classical and Renaissance pastoral literature, gladly sharing their knowledge, ideas, and impressions, helping me to pick my way through some forming thoughts and too many texts during uncommonly halcyon autumn afternoons in 1974, while the hills around Ithaca affirmed that the green fields were not gone. Their acumen, diligence, and, perhaps most of all, their enthusiasm, had much to do with the genesis of this book.

Others read portions of the text at a very early stage and offered valuable advice and encouragement: Winthrop W. Wetherbee, Ralph W. Johnson, Charles Levy, Herbert Lindenberger, Louis L. Martz, and Maurice Charney, who has continued to offer wisdom and gracious support to his former student over the years. More recently, the reader for Yale University Press gave helpful editorial recommendations; I also appreciate the assistance of Ellen Graham and Barbara Folsom.

A grant from the Research and Publications Fund, Graduate School, Wake Forest University, paid for typing the final draft.

I also want to record here my gratitude for the kind interest and encouragement from my colleagues in the Department of English, Wake Forest University, shown in so many ways during the past six years.

Translations from Theocritus come from *The Poems of Theocritus*, Translated with an Introduction by Anna Rist (Chapel Hill: University of North Carolina Press, 1978). Unless otherwise indicated, other translations are my own.

# Introduction

Yeats's pronouncement at the beginning of his career that "The woods of Arcady are dead" has proven premature.[1] Arcady is still with us, because "pastoral forms and attitudes" (in Harold Toliver's phrase) are still with us. Indeed, they are part of us all. The pastoral tradition stretches beyond the grove of works using characters and motifs that Theocritus, Vergil, and Longus introduced. Like the terms *tragedy* and *comedy*, the term *pastoral* denotes experiences and ideas that are permanent parts of our thinking and writing.

In this book I analyze some of the major formal and thematic characteristics of pastoral literature and show how the pastoral's artistic and cultural ideas extend into other writing. Surveying pastoral literature has long been an enormous undertaking, because the whole story cannot be told through the writings of the handful of most renowned pastoral poets.

> Beside all these yet finde I many mo
> Which haue employed their diligence also,
> Betwene Shepherdes, as it were but a fable,
> To write of matters true and profitable.
> But all their names I purpose not to write,
> Which in this maner made bookes infinite.[2]

These words of Alexander Barclay strike a sympathetic response from anyone who has even partly traversed the pastoral tradition recorded in works like W. Leonard Grant's *Neo-Latin Literature and the Pastoral*, which cites literally thousands of pastoral poems written in Latin between the times of Dante and Milton. Accurately defining pastoral literature may seem almost impossible once one goes beyond the broad sort of definition appropriate for a handbook of literary terms. W. W. Greg, writing in a critical era far simpler than our own, introduces his *Pastoral Poetry and Pastoral Drama* (1906) by saying that the subject is so diverse that little could be gained by trying to offer a generic definition; instead he hopes that his book will supply the reader with an implicit definition. I have tried to keep in mind these two cautions: do not purpose to write of "bookes infinite" and do not let the urge to define get in the way of the texts' own complexity.

Prudent words notwithstanding, some attempt to define as well as describe the realm of pastoral literature will always be necessary. If no one definition quite satisfies everyone, perhaps we can learn something from each attempt. As must be the case with any form of art that survives through time and appears in many languages and cultures, pastoral literature as a whole has acquired a richness, vitality, and variety of style and matter that one might not suspect in perusing (for example) Vergil's *Eclogues* or a collection of English Renaissance pastoral lyrics. As pastoral elements are used in epics, plays, and novels, the contours of the form become even more elusive. The further we get from shepherds and nymphs, fields and groves, the less sure we can be that we are still in the pastoral world; but the more we try to adhere to those restrictions, the less certain we can be that we are telling all that must be said about the limits of the pastoral mode and the influence of the pastoral genre on literature as a whole. Writing about a literary kind always means mediating between the description too inclusive to be a definition and the definition too exclusive to be a description.

It is, after all, hard to find the starting point in an interpretive circle: to describe pastoral literature, one needs to define the canon; to define the canon, one needs a description of the category. And as it happens, what one sees depends on where one stands. For example, one of the most influential of Vergil's eclogues is the Fourth, often called the "Messianic" eclogue because it foretells the birth of a child who will bring the new golden age; yet this was one of three of Vergil's ten eclogues cited by the editor Servius in the fourth century as outside the proper range of pastoral poetry. It is difficult to define the canon when the basic proof-texts are pulled away. If Vergil's *Eclogues* are not all "pastoral," if many of Theocritus's *Idylls* are even more remote from the pastoral environment and attitudes, what precisely is pastoral?

Michael Drayton, in the epistle prefatory to his *Pastorals*, lists a select company for his work. He acknowledges the Greeks as progenitors of the form and meticulously awards the crown to Theocritus as the *best* writer of pastorals. Next comes Vergil; and though Drayton admits that some of the *Eclogues* perhaps violate the decorum established by Theocritus, he confesses that (according to what had become the standard Christian typological reading) the messianic prophecy of Christ's birth particularly endears Vergil to him; furthermore, the angels' song to the shepherds at the nativity consecrates pastoral poetry itself, Drayton adds. Sannazaro he acknowledges for the innovation of piscatorial eclogues. As for English poetry, he praises the *Shepheardes Calender* as the masterpiece and makes the judgment that still seems beyond dispute: "Spenser is the prime Pastoralist of England."[3] This neat little group, comprised (except for the angels) of poets who had published volumes of eclogues, looks conventional. All of the authors mentioned by Drayton would be mentioned immediately by any modern critic writing of the pastoral. Drayton may be proceeding in a merely commonsensical way, citing those poets most often identified as pastoral. His common sense, however, seems preferable to attempts to prove that such-and-such is not "really" pastoral, even though readers and writers have always assumed that it is.

Less conventional to modern eyes, but quite so to Renaissance readers (and indeed stemming from the earliest annotations on Vergil), is the idea that the pastoral is an allegorical genre with ethical purposes. This was not merely a notion held by critics and mentioned in due course in the introduction to books; it was a powerful formative principle for pastoral writers. Barclay approaches the idea tentatively when writing of Theocritus' handling of his shepherds,

> Which in playne language, according to their name,
> Had sundry talking, sometime of mirth and game,
> Sometime of thinges more like to grauitie,
> And not exceeding their small capacitie.          [Prol., 23−26]

That is, the *Idylls* are primarily entertainment, and even poems touching on serious matters are restrained by a strict decorum. More recent pastoral poets, he goes on to say, have used pastoral motifs "as it were but a fable," a fiction masking the true subject, "matters both true and profitable." For the writer who thinks this way, the formal trappings of the pastoral genre are merely attractive or protective ways of presenting real nourishment. So Barclay hopes that his work will not be scorned "Because it maketh only relation / Of Shepherdes maner and disputation" (Prol., 93−94). The attentive reader, he claims, will find

> That it conteyneth both laudes of vertue,
> And man infourmeth misliuing to eschue,
> With diuers bourdes and sentences morall,
> Closed in shadowe of speeches pastorall,
> As many Poetes (as I haue sayde beforne)
> Haue vsed longe time before that I was borne.          [Prol., 97−102]

Here Barclay completes the progression from the approximations of gravity that he finds in Theocritus to the determined moral allegorizing of his own poetry.

Barclay, I should point out, was far more cautious than others had been about closing their meanings in shadows of speeches pastoral. Though Petrarch describes his *Bucolicum carmen* as a product of a time when he was unable to settle his thoughts for more sustained compositions, he also claims that pastoral poems are inherently so well masked that they are incomprehensible ("omnino non possit intellegi") without glosses.[4] Indeed, the allegories in his pastorals were sufficiently cryptic that he found it expedient to offer detailed glosses of some of them to his correspondents, a courtesy for which subsequent readers have been grateful. (We are not so favored in the case of Boccaccio.)

It is true that Barclay is more moralist than poet. It is also true that, even in the Renaissance, the conviction that pastoral was an allegorical form was seldom pursued with the maddening determination to be obscure that characterizes many eclogues of Petrarch and Boccaccio. But Drayton seems to have been above all else a writer of supple craft, whose chief pleasure lay in handling the implements of art, and whose own *Pastorals* have all the appropriate trappings of pastoral poetry that we recognize from his predecessors; yet he nonetheless declares,

> The subject of Pastorals, as the language of it ought to be poor, silly, & of the coursest Woofe in appearance. Nevertheless, the most High, and most Noble Matters of the World may bee shaddowed in them, and for certaine sometimes are: but he who hath almost nothing Pastorall in his Pastorals, but the name (which is my Case) deales more plainly, because *detracto velamine*, he speakes of most weightie things.

Drayton's poetry is more directly accessible than that of Petrarch, more pleasurable and more directly comprehensible; but Drayton himself claims that if one sees only the surface of the text, one does not see the whole poem. Though the veil has been drawn back, the concern for weighty matters has not been put aside. Our own age has generally lost its taste for what might be called extrinsic allegory—that is, a consciously constructed set of equivalences applied to an artistic pattern that can stand on its own. Nonetheless, modern critics are still finding allegorical relevance in the poems of Theocritus and Vergil, as well as those of Renaissance writers, and furthermore finding that the allegory does not detract from but enriches the poem's artistic resonance.

I do not mean to claim that the pastoral is necessarily or primarily allegorical. However, I do think it important to temper the common notions that pastoral is escapist or simple or nostalgic or epicurean. There are works that will fit these descriptions, of course, and the pastoral as a whole may tend to favor the values implied in these terms. However, neither the critical tradition nor the close reading of individual texts will support the supposition that there is nothing more to be said than this about the pastoral artistic heritage.

Why has this artistic tradition lasted so long and turned out to be so complex? To put the question in another way, why have those who have chosen a veil chosen one coarse-spun? Puttenham's brief but interesting commentary on pastoral poetry takes up the questions. He considers the theory that this is the earliest form of poetry and that it proceeds naturally from the conversations, courtships, and quarrels of real shepherds. In so doing he allows as not unreasonable the possibility that pastoral poetry might stem from a genuine oral literature that developed out of the shepherd's life. He recounts what is included in such an idea:

> the shepheards and haywards assemblies and meetings when they kept their cattell and heards in the common fields and forests, was the first familiar conuersation, and their babble and talk vnder bushes and shadie trees, the first disputation and contentious reasoning, and their fleshly heates growing of ease, the first idle wooings, and their songs made to their mates or paramours either vpon sorrow or iolity of courage, the first amorous musicks, sometime also they sang and played on their pipes for wagers, striuing who should get the best game, and be counted cunningest.[5]

This is in fact a good summary of the subjects found in most pastoral poems. Puttenham, however, distinguishes between these earlier forms of pastoral folk art and the later (and higher) forms of artistic composition represented in works like Vergil's eclogues. The Renaissance critic, certain that creation is a conscious act of the will, is certain that the pastoral was purposefully devised:

> the Poet diuised the Eglogue long after the other drammatick poems, not of purpose to counterfait or represent the rusticall manner of loues and communication: but vnder the vaile of homely persons, and in rude speeches to insinuate and glaunce at greater matters, and such as perchance had not bene safe to haue beene disclosed in any other sort, which may be perceiued by the Eglogues of *Virgill*, in which are treated matters of greater importance than the loues of *Titirus* and *Corydon*. These Eglogues came after to containe and enforme morall discipline, for the amendment of mans behauior, as be those of *Mantuan* and other moderne Poets.

So Puttenham rejects the plausible idea that the pastoral was the first kind of poetry on the grounds that it is really a sophisticated, not primitive, form. He also discards the notion that it looks wistfully toward the past—toward lost innocence, simplicity, or any of the other great and misty specters that beckon us backward. Instead, he sees it as pointing forward, toward moral reformation. Further, although he believes a rustic style to be characteristic of the pastoral, this is only to serve artistic and political strategies. Pastoral humility justifies the writer's candor while also admitting his vulnerability and therefore his need for indulgent protection.

What looks low, then, is really high but disguised, like those shepherds and shepherdesses (in, for example, *Daphnis and Chloë* or *The Winter's Tale*) who turn out to be disguised nobility. As Renaissance critics were aware, the pastoral is neither inherently nor exclusively a medium for verbal entertainments, emotional posturing, and wistful evocations of a lost and innocent past. Of course, many pastoral texts fit these stereotypical notions of the genre. In so doing they express a view of pastoral life and art well enunciated by neoclassical writers, who were particularly interested in restricting the experiential and stylistic dimensions of the form. Pope, in the Discourse prefacing his own *Pastorals*, writes,

> The complete character of this [kind of] poem consists in simplicity, brevity, and delicacy; the two first of which render an eclogue natural, and the last delightful.
>
> If we would copy Nature, it may be useful to take this idea along with us, that pastoral is an image of what they call the Golden age. So that we are not to describe our shepherds as shepherds at this day really are, but as they may be conceiv'd then to have been; when the best of men follow'd the employment. . . . what is inviting in this sort of poetry proceeds not so much from the Idea of that business, as of the tranquillity of a country life.
>
> We must therefore use some illusion to render a Pastoral delightful; and this consists in exposing the best side only of a shepherd's life, and in concealing its miseries.[6]

With this critical theory goes an interpretation rather different from Drayton's of "the only undisputed authors of Pastoral," Theocritus and Vergil; and from the notion that pastoral is connected with "that age which succeeded the creation of the world" emerges the conviction that it should portray an ideal way of life.

Through the divergent opinions of Puttenham and Pope we see how pastoral literature can comment on and even criticize contemporary events as well as express visions of a perfectly sheltered world of pretense having little to do with contemporary existence. The differences are found not only in subject and purpose but in style as well: to Puttenham, pastoral diction is characterized by "rude speeches," but to Pope, by "delicacy."

How, then, does one frame a definition of pastoral literature? One purpose of a definition is exclusionary, to permit a direct answer to the question of whether a particular example fits the category. The other purpose is inclusive and addresses the slightly different question of how a particular example might fit the category. The difference between the two questions marks a difference in attitudes toward the phenomenon. If one believes a given phenomenon to be single in its internal characteristics and stable through time, then one should find it possible and proper to posit a narrow definition. If, however, one believes the phenomenon to be internally complex (that is, divisible into parts that can be detached from the main body and used separately as components in other contexts) or to be mutable through time, then the most appropriate definition is broader, more permissive. One cannot, of course, work with a definition that defines nothing; this book therefore offers some general guidelines for understanding what pastoral literature is and how it is related to other literary forms that seem close to it. However, my main purpose is to trace out what I believe to be the rather shady borders of a complicated and seasonally changing body of literature that is not always neatly marked off from the literary terrain that adjoins it.

To return to the questions raised earlier: the pastoral has been useful to allegorists and attractive to writers from widely different points of view because it is inherently multiplicitous. Sometimes it fools us and proves to be quite as simple as it appears. But one can never be quite certain without taking a close look.

# I

## *The Nature of Pastoral Literature*

THE ORIGINS OF PASTORAL POETRY ARE LOST IN THE INACCESSIBLE REACHES OF prehistory. We cannot even be certain with what literary context Theocritus was working when, early in the third century B.C., he seems to have invented the pastoral lyric poem, though surely, as Emerson wrote of *Leaves of Grass*, it "yet must have had a long foreground somewhere, for such a start." Whether in the immediate "foreground" to the *Idylls* there were genuine folksongs actually made and sung by herdsmen, or an already mature literary tradition cultivated by educated artists, remain open questions.[1] However, pastoral motifs appear in much earlier works, notably the poems of Homer and the Hebrew Scriptures. In brief passages of these writings we can see many of the seedlings of a subsequently bountiful pastoral literature that has constituted a major, continuing tradition within Western art and significantly shaped our cultural understanding for close to three thousand years.

Surely among the earliest images of pastoral life to impinge on the cultural consciousness of the West are these from the *Iliad*, in which we can see that, from the very beginning, pastoral motifs have had diverse implications.

> And the renowned smith of the strong arms made on it a meadow
> large and in a lovely valley for the glimmering sheepflocks,
> with dwelling places upon it, and covered shelters, and sheepfolds.
>
> [Book 8]

> As when rivers in winter spate running down from the mountains
> throw together at the meeting of streams the weight of their water
> out of the great springs behind in the hollow stream-bed,
> and far away in the mountains the shepherd hears their thunder;
>
> [Book 4]

> now the strong rage tripled took hold of him, as of a lion
> whom the shepherd among his fleecy flocks in the wild lands
> grazed as he leapt the fence of the fold, but has not killed him,

8

but only stirred up the lion's strength, and can no more fight him
off, but hides in the steading, and the frightened sheep are forsaken,
and these are piled pell-mell on each other in heaps, while the lion
raging still leaps out again over the fence of the deep yard;
such was the rage of strong Diomedes as he closed with the Trojans.

[Book 5][2]

In the first passage Homer shows the warm aesthetic appreciation of pastoral
pleasures that will later characterize so many familiar idyllic spots, like Milton's
Paradise: "Betwixt them lawns, or level downs, and flocks / Grazing the tender
herb, were interpos'd" (*Paradise Lost*, IV, 252–53).[3] But Homer's scene is idyllic
when it is stilled for a moment by art in a gilded place of security on Achilles'
shield. In other sections of the shield, and in most of the poem's pastoral similes
(typified by the third passage), the poet seems impelled by his theme to show the
shepherd's vulnerability in the face of greater and terrifying forces, unable to
protect his flocks, forced to take cover to save his own life. Homer's shepherd does
rise above the ignoble "cowherd" fear (the pun is Spenser's) that Renaissance
writers saw as concomitant with pastoral seclusion and unambitiousness; nevertheless, he quickly becomes merely a victim and a powerless observer.

Between these two extremes is the equanimity of the middle passage. Here
the trope carries us away from the horror of battle to a purely sensory experience of
its sound, joining the poem's auditor and the shepherd in the commonality of
wonderment. In this passage the solitary figure of the shepherd is neither poignant
nor vulnerable; he is simply an isolated man suddenly moved to take notice of
something greater than himself, something imposing but not threatening to him.
And both the shepherd and the thundering waters provide points of perspective
for one another. That is, we comprehend each within the context established by
the other. In his characteristically paratactic fashion, Homer gives us the double
scene by switching perspectival locations from the torrents to the shepherd on the
mountainside, so that neither point of view exclusively commands our own. Both
are appreciated for what they separately contribute to this moment, as well as what
they mutually express.

In this passage we see the pastoral image naked of moral meaning. Within
the literary context this pastoral image is a unit of measurement, affording a scale
to the panorama. The shepherd's pastoral experience is a simple yet profound
meditative engagement with something outside the flow of ordinary experience.
Homer has made his auditor a shepherd because the solitary, isolated, insignificant, and powerless figure of the shepherd is precisely the right foil for the
tumultuous torrent, and because the shepherd need give nothing more than a

recognition of nature's magnitude. The great scene itself takes place far from his eyes; but without seeing it he can appreciate its significance.

In Hesiod (perhaps contemporaneous with Homer), the multiple possibilities for interpreting pastoral experiences become fused into a suggestive, ironic ambiguity. In the *Theogony*, Hesiod writes of his own artistic initiation by the Muses.

> The Muses once taught Hesiod to sing
> Sweet songs, while he was shepherding his lambs
> On holy Helicon; the goddesses
> Olympian, daughters of Zeus who holds
> The aegis, first addressed these words to me:
> "You rustic shepherds, shame: bellies you are,
> Not men! We know enough to make up lies
> Which are convincing, but we also have
> The skill, when we've a mind, to speak the truth."
> So spoke the fresh-voiced daughters of great Zeus
> And plucked and gave a staff to me, a shoot
> Of blooming laurel, wonderful to see,
> And breathed a sacred voice into my mouth
> With which to celebrate the things to come
> And things which were before. They ordered me
> To sing the race of blessed ones who live
> Forever, and to hymn the Muses first
> And at the end.[4]

The Muses express their disdain for mere shepherds, gross fellows without the spark of imagination or sophistication. Nonetheless, the Muses also grace one of these clods, presumably because they find in him a humble and receptive conduit through which to give human voice to their eloquence. Here the shepherd is less than "a man," lacking those parts that distinguish us from beasts; yet for that very reason—we might say, because of his lack of an ego—he can speak with divinely inspired wisdom. As he is too low for respect in his own right, "his" art (more a divine loan) makes him divinely privileged.

The range of pastoral motifs in the Bible sets a pattern for subsequent moralistic uses of pastoral imagery. Homer's divergent views of pastoral experience have religious and ethical equivalents in the Bible. The opposition between Abel and Cain, shepherd and farmer, faithful man of peace and grasping man of violence, is particularly suggestive; for the shepherd gratefully accepts what he receives and, like a good pastoral literary character, gives a properly bountiful offering to the deity in thanks, while the tiller of the soil struggles against man and

God as much as he struggles against nature. Those who do not remember that "The Lord is my shepherd" (Psalm 23 : 1) will learn that we are all vulnerable, like the most helpless of beasts; "like sheep they are laid in the grave" (Psalm 49 : 14).[5] Isaiah promises that God "shall feed his flock like a shepherd" (40 : 11); on the other hand, "they are shepherds that cannot understand" (56 : 11). Jeremiah also sees the shepherd as the divine exemplar of attentiveness—"I will set shepherds over them who shall feed them" (23 : 4)—but also as the image of those who fail in their responsibilities—"their shepherds have caused them to go astray" (50 : 6).

The identification, here and elsewhere, of God as a shepherd will later join with classical myths of pastoral deities (like Pan) or pastoral characters who have been deified (like Daphnis). These references will combine with allegorical and typological readings of the biblical and classical texts so as to produce multi-faceted pastoral images. For example, the Geneva Bible of 1560 glosses Ezekiel 34 : 2, a denunciation of shepherds who feed themselves rather than their flocks, "By the shepherds he meaneth the King, the magistrates, Priests, & Prophets."[6] In the next verse, however, "He describeth the office and duetie of a good pastor, who ought to love and succor his flocke and not to be cruel toward them." This duty is fulfilled perfectly by the shepherd who is to tend all the flock, even the shepherd David himself: "He promiseth the true shepherd Christ and with him peace." Such lines of interpretation figure prominently in a poem like "Lycidas" and certainly are not confined to that work. So pastoral images are traditionally accepted as metaphors for more elevated topics. Furthermore, those images acquire a range of possible external references that might look self-contradictory or internally inconsistent but which in fact merely attest to the wide evocative range of pastoral motifs: not just shepherd versus king, but shepherd as king and minister and God and, of course, merely as shepherd.

In the most languidly idyllic pastoral descriptions, such as the large meadow and lovely valley of the first passage from Homer, we will feel that the pastoral life is sequestered and protected. The pastoral world will seem, indeed, to be a safely contained and self-contained haven from the hazards of public places and the flow of ordinary time. Even in this case, though, the idyll may take place within an explicit or implicit unidyllic context, like Homer's Trojan War or raging rivers, that gives the bucolic pleasance a meaning beyond that indicated by its internal formulation. The idyll is what it is because it is clearly set apart from something different.

In other forms of the pastoral we are made to realize that the appearance of being separate and different from the rest of the world is indeed merely an appearance. Much as the Homeric sheepfold can pen the sheep in but not hold the lion out, the pastoral setting is simultaneously a place both safe and vulnerable. If it is a spot for containment, that containment signifies an awareness of the menacing power outside. If it is blissfully simple, its simplicity may be ignorance or helplessness.

The pastoral is an ironic form, based on a perceivable distance between the alleged and the implied. It lets us know either that its point of view is significant largely because it contrasts with some other point of view, or that its real subject is something in addition to (or perhaps even instead of) its ostensible subject. The pastoral impulse toward containment involves holding contraries together in apparent unity, forged by art out of discordant emotions and perceptions. Pastoral ironies express cultural values, which influence and are shaped by art. Vergil, for example, makes it quite clear in his eclogues that the Roman world is a different one from the one in which his pastoral characters reside. They feel the impact of Roman decisions on their lives; but to the herdsmen themselves, involved with their own affairs, the grand schemes of imperial Rome (like those of "the federal government" today to those people who, rightly or wrongly, feel that they are at the mercy of a distant power) are remote and totally different from their little world. Spenser, however, sees no anomaly in describing Queen Elizabeth as the queen of shepherds and portraying her court as a coterie of nymphs and herdsmen with names like Neaera, Daphnaida, Harpalus, and Amyntas. The queen herself was interested in cultivating such an image of her reign, in contrast to Augustus's vision of conquering, subduing, and civilizing by nonpastoral arms and laws.

The desire to find a principle of harmony can be seen not only in pastoral's relationship with the society at large but also within the imagery of pastoral literature itself.

> Where are my bay-leaves? Bring them, Thestylis.
> And where are my love-charms? Come,
> crown the bowl with purest purple wool
> that I may cast a spell on my cruel love
> and bind him to me. . . .                    [Theocritus, Idyll II][7]

> Here no night Rauens lodge more black then pitche,
> Not eluish ghosts, nor gastly owles doe flee.

> But frendly Faeries, met with many Graces,
> And lightfote Nymphes can chace the lingring night
> With Heydeguyes, and trimly trodden traces,
> Whilst systers nyne, which dwell on *Parnasse* hight,
> Doe make them musick, for their more delight:
> And *Pan* himselfe to kisse their christall faces,
> Will pype and daunce. . . .                    [Spenser, "June," 23–30][8]

These typical descriptive passages combine several elements. They attest to our emotional reliance on nature; the soothing power of music, which in turn is linked to the harmonies within nature; our longing for a secure love, even if achieved through the workings of the imagination. In these passages the trappings, entertainment, and natural luxuriance show the tangible vibrancy and bounty of the bucolic world. Furthermore, all these elements are held together by a common centripetal motion, as they are gathered in by the controlling figure at the center, whose spell-weaving poems are created in despite of mutability. How appropriate and natural it is, then, that this figure at the center be represented so frequently by someone who tends a herd. Indeed, the herd itself, sometimes endearing, sometimes vulgar, sometimes pitiable, sometimes merely a presence in the background to remind us that we are not all that exists, is a fitting metaphor for the complex experiences and attitudes penned together in the pastoral.

The pastoral poet's artistic role is also complex. As Sidney writes, "My sheepe are thoughts, which I both guide and serve."⁹ Guide and serve: the poet's double function expresses the dichotomy at the heart of the pastoral. The pastoral poet's guidance is regulation, not the autocrat's imposition of will. The poet has limited powers over the material and is as much bound by that material as the material is by the poet. The shepherd in literature may be literally a bondsman, like Moeris in Vergil's Ninth Eclogue or Corin in *As You Like It*; in figurative ways as well, the pastoral singer acknowledges limitations on the independence of the creative imagination.

> Prima Syracosio dignata est ludere uersu
> nostra nec erubuit siluas habitare Thalea.
> cum canerem reges et proelia, Cynthius aurem
> uellit et admonuit: 'pastorem, Tityre, pinguis
> pascere oportet ouis, deductum dicere carmen.'          [VI, 1−5]¹⁰

> [First my muse thought it proper to play with Syracusan verse, and was not ashamed to dwell in the woods. When I tried singing of kings and wars, Apollo plucked my ear and warned, "What is right for a shepherd, Tityrus, is to fatten his sheep but sing a taut song."]

The adjective *deductus* ("taut") means both "carefully made" and "modest." So this passage sets in opposition the values of grand Apollo and of Thalia (muse of both comedy and pastoral poetry). The well-made song, the slender perfection that contains riches, can be its own reward. Apollo's tweak of the ear keeps the singer in his place. Thalia may romp freely in the woods but must not forget what does and does not belong to her. In contrast to the epic poet's conscious sense of personal inadequacy and need for the assistance of the deities through invocation, the pastoral poet may run the risk of straying too far or daring too much and hearing the inverse of an invocation, the admonitory voice of the cautioning deity. Taking care of one's sheep requires restraining one's own ambitions: guide and serve. Or to put it in another way, only by refining one's ambition for mastery into a willingness to guide can one enjoy the freedom to play and the satisfaction of seeing one's literary sheep properly nourished. Art comes from a union of freedom and restraint. Pastoral irony and pastoral containment thereby help to perfect art while offering it a semblance of liberty. Some subjects are beyond the pastoral poet's proper grasp; indeed, the pastoral poet professes not to have rule over his or her own thoughts and emotions, though capable of enough artful control over them that they may be penned. The pastoral poet is free of that vice of bad shepherds, selfish pride. The restrictions in the pastoral genre relieve the poet of burdens that will come with greater public responsibilities in "higher" literary forms, like the epic.

So the poet at least professes to shed these responsibilities by writing verse that needs to be carefully limited to its proper scale. Yet in this way the poet also gains freedom: those who claim only the desire and ability to say a bit about private feelings and concerns will be excused some passing observations about public matters. Meanwhile, by celebrating those values that are implied by their art, the pastoral poets affirm the value of the pastoral ethos.

Theocritus's Seventh Idyll is a rich text for probing the pastoral because it is explicitly about the nature of art in general and of pastoral art in particular.[11] In fact, it is surely the earliest extant commentary on pastoral aesthetics. The poem's opening splendidly illustrates Gombrich's thesis that art creates an illusory world through gestures in the direction of the conventional one. Against the "factual" background of Demeter's story and the spring of Bourina are set the characters of the poem, perhaps identifiable to the poet's audience but at the very least presented here wearing fictive masks.

> It chanced one time that we left the city and hied
> to the Haleis, Eucritus and I and Amyntas our third.
> A harvest home was being held for Demeter
> by Phrasidamus and Antigenes, sons of Lycopeus—
> a noble line, if ever there was one, sprung
> from ancient worthies, Clyteia and Chalcon himself,
> who grappled well the rock with his knee, and well
> drew out Bourina Spring with a blow of his foot—
> whereon elm and poplar, beginning rear
> luxuriant crests aloft of green-leaf hair,
> all over-wove, of shadow threads, a grove. . . .           [1–11]

Referring allusively rather than directly to the poet's own society, the poem shapes a culture that seems to function independently and have its own relevant heritage. The origins of Bourina can stand metaphorically for the origins of this artistic world, brought into being by one push, giving rise to a veritable grove that makes its own sheltering place.

Characters similarly seem to appear as if by magic at the margins of this pastoral world:

> We met with a wayfarer,
> thanks to the Muses, a noble fellow, by name
> Lycidas, of Cydonia, and you could tell at a glance
> he was a goatherd; he fitted the part completely.

We do not know whether there was a Cydonia on Theocritus's Cos, or whether this refers to some other Cydonia mentioned in ancient texts; but Lycidas the Cydonian appears oddly here, looking like a denizen of the locale and yet referred to as if he is known to be an outsider. In Milton's poem about another Lycidas, characters similarly come forth out of some presumed space beyond the poetic world and step back into the shade when their roles are finished, like Saint Peter, who "Last came, and last did go" (108). They come as if they were deities themselves, or were sent by the pastoral divinities, who have garbed them to define precisely the role they are playing: Theocritus's Lycidas is outfitted exactly like a goatherd, while Milton's "Pilot of the Galileean Lake" bears the two keys that identify him as Peter. Their appearances define the nature and limits of their pastoral milieu; they tell us their purposes in the poem. At the same time they are presented as if they were not purely fictive, not only characters enclosed within a poetic universe, but emerging from an independently existing social or metaphysical context. The pastoral fully develops the tensions between artifice and what we normally call reality. Through that tension the pastoral urges us to accept its pretended realism while leaving us uncertain about how much is really pretended. Lycidas is the very model of a goatherd; but is the curiously emphatic statement that he looked exactly like a goatherd meant to imply that he really was or was not one?

The pretended realism carries over into the allusions to the literary context. The speaker of the idyll, Simichidas (generally taken to represent Theocritus himself), professes his limitations when measured against two masters of lyric poetry, both contemporaries or near-contemporaries of Theocritus, cited by their real names and referred to by pastoral standards:

> I am not, in my own conceit, a match as yet
> for the noble Samian Sicelides, nor Philetas.
> I should rival their song as a frog vies with cicadas!

Lycidas subsequently recalls the lyric achievements of the legendary goatherd
Comatas.

> Would, in my day, you were numbered among the living;
> then would I herd your fine goats on the hillsides
> and listen to your voice, as you lay and warbled sweetly
> under the oaks or pines, divine Comatas!

By defining its literary context and generic heritage, the pastoral circumscribes its
literary world. For the pastoral poet, the history of poetry is the history of pastoral
poetry. That is all the singer knows and all the singer needs to know. Such history,
complete with its legendary authors, extends the pastoral memory from the
present day through deepest antiquity and, through those legends, opens the
pastoral world to wonderworking, magic, and romance. It also constitutes a significant ethical gesture. These allusions to other poets suggest that pastoral poetry
thrives on emulation, healthy challenge, and a continuing community of shared
aesthetic values. To a considerable extent the pastoral "world" is located in the
literary memory of the pastoral poet. It is peopled by the real or fictitious poets who
inspire and challenge each new singer. And though the new poet may feel, even
acknowledge, some anxiety about their influence, the poet acknowledges that
influence as a generative principle. The forebears give warrant for the poetry and
provide the pattern and the standard. Each pastoral work is new, but the poet still
says, "Yet once more . . .".

The pastoral poet's explicit creation of a generic heritage within the text
itself is particularly important because, as the passage from Vergil's Sixth Eclogue
suggests, the pastoral poem takes shape in the face of an implicitly or explicitly
contrasting form of poetry. The stylistic antithesis may be left latent in a given
poem and hinted at only through the poet's claim to be satisfied with generic
limits. Surprisingly often, however, it is acknowledged indirectly, as the poet
takes note that the verse has gone beyond the usual limits of the pastoral:

> Sicelides musae, paulo maiora canamus.                    [Vergil, IV, 1]

> [Sicilian muses, sing a rather loftier song.]

> O fountain Arethuse, . . .
> That strain I heard was of a higher mood.
>                                    [Milton, "Lycidas," ll. 85, 87]

Or it is directly referred to, so that the poet can shy away from it or reject
it directly. So, in Idyll VII, Lycidas (the pattern of the goatherd) in praising

Simichidas alludes to the contemporary dispute between the followers of Apollonius, who cultivate the grand epical voice, and those of Callimachus, who pursue the lyrical and pastoral.

"I shall present you with my olive stick," said he,
"For a young sprig fashioned by Zeus, with no pretensions!
How I hate the builder who seeks to raise his house
as high as the peak of Mount Oromedon there,
and the Muses' cuckoos, with their eye on the bard of Chios!
In vain they labor . . . !"

The epic is a constant challenge for the pastoral poet, an implicit rebuke to the lyricist's "slender" song, which is its diametric opposite, in much the same way as the heroic life is a challenge to private leisure.

The antithesis is interpreted from the pastoral poet's viewpoint in the first stanza of "The Garden" by Andrew Marvell. The opening lines evoke the various forms of public achievement and, indirectly, the nonpastoral literary forms in which such achievements are conventionally celebrated.

How vainly men themselves amaze
To win the palm, the oak, or bays,
And their uncessant labors see
Crowned from some single herb or tree,
. . . . . . . . . . . . . . . . . . . . . . . . .
While all flowers and all trees do close
To weave the garlands of repose.                    [1–4, 7–8][12]

This tension is not ignored by epic poets, many of whom began their careers (in keeping with Vergil's pattern) by writing pastorals. The epic poet also finds the pastoral inset an important part of the poem, using it to develop a definition of the heroic life and a judgment of that life. However, the pastoral poet, even when not actually alluding to the looming mountain of the epic, develops an aesthetic to set beside the epic's. For in pastoral, although we meet with ambition, effort, victory, and the will of the deities, the pastoral poet gives these to us in a different scale. It is not a "reduced" or "smaller" scale, for such terms imply that the standard for judging must be the epic. Rather, the pastoral scale (like the Cotswolds contrasted with the Alps) is that of the individual, personal life and the immediate natural environment.

In Lycidas's song of Idyll VII Theocritus affords a splendid demonstration of pastoral's human, nonepical scale. Having just scorned the imitators of Homer, a group headed by Apollonius, whose major work was the epic on Jason's voyage with his Argonauts, Lycidas offers his *melodrion* (his "little tune") which pointedly begins with a carefully conditional prayer for his beloved's safe voyage.

> Fair sail shall Ageanax have to Mitylene
> when the wet sou'wester chases the waves to where
> the Kids set in the evening, and Orion
> in the morning plants his feet on the ocean floor. . . .
> Fair sail shall Ageanax have to Mitylene—
> so he but save Lycidas from Aphrodite's oven,
> For the love of him is the hot blast that consumes me!            [53–59]

Several points should be made about this passage. First, though the astronomical details point to an autumn crossing and may be biographically significant, they also function poetically within the pastoral framework of the poem. The ruling constellation is Eriphoi, "the Kids," a most appropriate reference-point for Lycidas, the epitome of a goatherd. Also, Orion is twice mentioned in the *Odyssey* by "the bard of Chios," both times in contexts relevant to Theocritus's passage. First, Calypso in Book V cites Orion's death as an instance of divine resentment directed against those loved by other immortals. Second, Odysseus sees Orion himself in the underworld, "in the meadow of asphodel, rounding up and driving together / wild animals he himself had killed in the lonely mountains, / holding in his hands a brazen club, forever unbroken" (XI, 573–75).[13] That is, Orion (according to Homer) is not merely a hunter but a slain lover who, after death, becomes an otherworldly hero-herdsman. Theocritus therefore manipulates his allusions. He does not imitate Homer or Apollonius, but his references have special pastoral meanings for those familiar with these authors' works. In contrast to Apollonius, Theocritus makes the seemingly daring voyage a lover's bargaining point.

Further, in this passage we see that the prayer, the voyage, and the allusions to other (and more imposing) literary works are all put in service of Lycidas's private desire. The entire sentence in fact turns on the word *if* (*ai*) with which line 55 begins: "if he will be kind to me." Pastoral poems are generally about private desires, and love in particular; there are good reasons why that should be so. As this passage indicates, love is desire. It directs all experience toward one object, totally absorbing the attention of the lover, who becomes isolated from other emotions, as well as other ways of viewing experience. Spenser's Colin Clout affords a striking example of the lover whose absorption by love completely cuts him off from the rest of life, though in his case the suffering is not so much a burning as a freezing to death:

> Thou barren ground, whom winter's wrath hath wasted,
> Art made a mirror, to behold my plight.     ["January," 19–20]

"Thou barren ground . . . art made a mirror": here too we see the pastoral tendency to make all external reality function on behalf of a private experience. Personal concerns and subjective understanding are the stuff of the pastoral.

Silenus's mythographic song in Vergil's Sixth Eclogue demonstrates how the pastoral aesthetic shapes nonpastoral material. It is virtually a miniature version of the *Metamorphoses*, a metonymous overview of mythic history in a length and form appropriate for one singer to offer in one evening of song. Further, although the attentive and informed reader will find pastoral relevance and thematic significance to the poem's treatment of the myths, these myths are touched on so briefly and in such number that they are likely recalled more as an elaborate texture of poetry than as a series of dramatic events and pictures. Their "substance" therefore seems less important than their cumulative aesthetic effect. Finally, the eclogue's narrator repeatedly reminds us that we are listening to one person's narration: "tum canit . . . tum canit . . . ille canit" ("then he sings . . . then he sings . . . he sings"), the narrator continually interjects. Silenus's song is not merely a retelling of old truths; nor—for all its energy and breadth—is it an epically ambitious survey of imagined life. It is a bravura individual performance that embodies the mythic material for poetry, along with demonstrations of its poetic uses. So the poem's coda makes clear, through its reference to the originator of poetry.

> Omnia quae Phoebo quondam meditante beatus
> audiit Eurotas iussitque ediscere lauros,
> ille canit, pulsae referunt ad sidera ualles,
> cogere donce ouis stabulis numerumque referre
> iussit et inuito processit Vesper Olympo.     [82–86]

[Every tale that Phoebus used to recite, when happy Eurotas heard and told his laurels to learn by heart, he sings—the vales reverberate and the stars resound!—'til Vesper bade the shepherd fold and count his flock, and rose against the unwilling sky of Olympus.]

The cluster of verbs—*meditante, audit, ediscere, canit, referunt, referre*—asks us to imagine the historical and cosmological pattern of the world as a sequence of telling, learning, remembering, and retelling, one singer to another. In what sense is this the "taut song" that Phoebus cautioned our narrator to sing? Precisely in its concentration of this mythic energy into the single voice of the intoxicated old satyr Silenus, echoing in his brief song the ancient mythopoeic lyric of Apollo, the pastoral god. Notwithstanding its subject, the poem remains one singer's time-honored and succinct display of art, a pastoral response to the desire for an epic.

If, then, the songs of Lycidas and Silenus can be accommodated within the pastoral style, the far more modest effort of Simichidas fits even more comfortably.

> The Loves have sneezed for Simichidas. Poor wretch,
> Myrto I love, as the goats love the spring.                    [96–97]

Coming hard on the heels of Lycidas's apostrophe to *theie Komata* (89), "divine Comatas," this is cozily homely in its language, much more clearly deserving the stylistic labels of *humilis* ("humble") and *sceleris* ("slender") that the pastoral has borne from the time of Vergil onward. But even as the language of the Bible manages to be variously earthy, sonorous, and reportorial, while keeping within a recognizable stylistic mode, so the pastoral can modulate its tones without violating its own nature. It can expand (for example) to embrace a passage that gestures toward another genre and still avoid being taken over by that other genre. We can speak of pastoral moments in the epic; but no one would claim that the lines of Lycidas or Silenus quoted above are epic moments in the pastoral. A genre like the epic is capacious enough to admit the pastoral "in its own person," so to speak. The pastoral, confined willingly or resistantly to its slender dimensions, watches its borders far more cautiously and self-consciously. It understands its own fragility. It appreciates the implications of limits, which can stimulate internal development while marking off a space for safety.

> caper tibi saluos et haedi:
> et, si quid cessare potes, requiesce sub umbra.                [VII, 9–10]
>
> [Your goat and kind are safe:
> so if you can rest, relax in the shade.]

The pastoral impulses toward containment and simplicity have structural analogues as well. It is true, of course, that the monologue, the dialogue, and the various forms of binary literary structure are not limited to the pastoral. Yet it is also true that the pastoral particularly cultivates the dramatic, ironic, or harmonic effects possible in a poem that is a monologue or has a two-element structure. Vergil's Sixth Eclogue depends for its effect largely on the interplay between two speakers: the poem's narrator (who first admits to his ambitions, notes Apollo's warnings, and subsequently reminds us of his controlling narrative presence) and the vatic singer, Silenus. In Theocritus's Seventh Idyll, Simichidas provides the narrative and partly lyrical framework for two songs, Lycidas's and his own, which are set in different keys but are perfectly compatible with one another. The pastoral song contest is another type of duality, in which the two singers alternate verses, each varying what the other has just said. Though it sometimes becomes a real contest, with a winner and a loser, it often ends with the singers exchanging gifts, each one a winner. And even when someone loses, it is on the basis of subtle differences in essentially similar presentations, not radical challenges or disagreements about basic aesthetic principles. In this way the pastoral world holds together its internal tensions.

Even poems not strictly dualistic in form can be dualistic in structure. Setting aside the five introductory lines that set the dramatic context, Vergil's Second Eclogue is a monologue. However, Corydon's realization that he has been a fool and ought to try to do better really divides the poem into two movements: the first, a yearning lament on his love for Alexis; the second, his partially successful mental struggle against his emotions. Obviously a binary movement will not necessarily resolve into supportive melodies or neatly balanced or reconciled antitheses. It does mean that the work's structure is basically simple, or at least plausibly simplifiable. It also means that the structure typically works out a simple pattern of event and response or sets forth a contrast between two views of experience.

Emotions become intense when constricted by the boundaries of the fictive pastoral world and the presumptive boundaries of action and expression within it. Using these boundaries, the pastoral writer may suggest that the problems are after all limited, local, personal, and perhaps even small; but the writer may also suggest that they are internal, intense, private, and seemingly inescapable. By the same token, pastoral joys may be all the more pleasurable for their easy accessibility, without requiring any special effort; for this same reason they may also be, as Dr. Johnson would have it, easy and vulgar. They may be there for the taking because they are all around us.

Nature, after all, is one of the few phenomena that we can "possess" only by our love for it. We cannot exactly own it, but we do not have to own it in order to enjoy it or feel that it is ours to enjoy. Nature also remains always bountiful and always passive in some respect; even when it seems actively harsh, it can do nothing to define itself, but merely remains accessible to our definition. We still maintain some power over it through our power to interpret it. It stands, one might say, as an ideal substitute lover when we feel that human lovers are perversely independent of our wills. In pastoral literature the natural world does not always constitute the highest value; but it is a high value against which all others are measured.

Pastoral works are not always about nature; indeed, they usually are not primarily concerned with nature directly. The natural world in pastoral writing can be primarily a backdrop (as it usually seems to be in Theocritus, for example), a solace, or an outward expression of an emotional condition. In the last situation it serves a particularly potent function because, as an external embodiment, it appears more objective than the narrator's or speaker's judgment of human emotions and circumstances; it seems to be an emotionally and psychologically plausible revelation of truth.

Not all nature writing, conversely, is pastoral. What makes a work pastoral are its attitudes toward the natural world and human experience. In pastoral literature, experiences and emotions are contained within finite limits. Those limits are implied by the patterns revealed within the natural world and within the pastoral way of life, consonant with the patterns of the natural world. The containment is necessitated by the fragility or delicacy of the experiences and emotions, or by tension between pastoral and nonpastoral experience.

Unamuno's poem "En un cementario de lugar castellano" shows how a number of pastoral motifs and traditions may join in a work of art to become essential parts of its expressive power.

> Corral de muertos, entre pobres tapias,
> hechas también de barro,
> pobre corral donde la hoz no siega,
> sólo una cruz, en el desierto campo
> señala tu destino. [1−5][14]

> [Sheepfold of the dead, closed within poor mud walls, also made of clay, poor sheepfold where the sickle does not reap, only a cross in the deserted plot marks your mission.]

The first phrase contains complex pastoral implications. The cemetery, as a sheepfold for the dead, encloses those who are passive and powerless; it is not only their place of interment but also their safe home. It may also recall the Psalmist's phrase, "like sheep they are laid in the grave," with its implication of helplessness before a greater force. The poverty of the rural setting underscores that idea, familiar from pastoral contrasts with urban or courtly life, that the pastoral life is secure because it is too humble to be envied, and yet insecure because powerless to defend or sustain itself. Poignantly, pastoral sympathy between human and natural life extends here to the physical being of the "sheep," themselves turning to clay within their clay enclosure surrounded by its clay walls. The sickle's absence implies that they are sheltered now from the threat of death, having faced it already; it also implies that the spot is barren of life-giving energy. The cross, signifying that this pastoral world can be defined in the terms of Christian pastoralism, may also remind us that, to a Christian, the scythe has no dominion under the cross's protecting arms.

> Junto a estas tapias buscan el amparo
> del hostigo del cierzo las ovejas
> al pasar trashumantes en rebaño,
> y en ellas rompen de la vana historia,
> como las olas, los rumores vanos.

> [By these walls the sheep that pass in a flock shelter themselves from the bitter north wind, and on them break empty rumors—like waves—of empty history.]

These walls shelter not only the sheep who lie within but also those living sheep who pass by (reminders of mortality and humility); and further, they are a barrier against the turmoil of the outside world and the environment itself. Under the protection of this sanctified pastoral enclosure, all the business of the world and the sweep of grand affairs seem, in the words of Ecclesiastes, a "vanity of vanities." As Sir Calidore says in *The Faerie Queene,*

> All this worlds gay shows, which we admire,
> Be but vaine shadowes to this safe retyre
> Of lyfe, which here in lowlinesse ye lead.                    [VI, ix, 27]

Their environment, however rough and windy, is not hostile. Indeed, it is a sort of retreat sheltered from epic turmoil and strife, coming into its own in the quintessential ideal month of pastoral glory.

> Como un islote en junio,
> te ciñe el mar dorado
> de las espigas que a la brisa ondean,
> y canta sobre ti la alondra el canto
> de la cosecha.

> [Like an island in June, you are bound by the golden sea of grain waving with the breeze, and over you the lark sings her song of harvest.]

Furthermore, it is an island in a fabulous sea of gold, brightened even more by the bird's cheerful harvest song, indicating the full richness of nature at its peak, nature that continues with its cycle of ever-renewing life even amidst death.

> Cuando baja en la lluvia el cielo al campo
> baja también sobre la santa yerba
> donde la hoz no corta,
> de tu rincon ¡pobre corral de muertos!,
> y sienten en sus huesos el reclamo
> del riego de la vida.

> [When the sky descends to earth in rain, it falls too on your sacred grass where the sickle does not cut, on your little plot, poor sheepfold of the dead, and they feel in their dry bones the enticement of the waters of life.]

Of course there is pathos here too. For though nature is ever-renewing, in the bones of the dead it can only stir a life that they are powerless to live. They are one with nature and as moved to growth as the grass around them; yet within this "pinfold" (as the Attendant Spirit in Milton's Ludlow Castle masque calls Earth) they must remain as they are. The sentiments here are close to those in Gray's "Elegy Written in a Country Churchyard," where the bucolic sleepers remain unroused in their earthen beds amid stirring nature.

> Salvan tus cercas de mampuesto y barro
> las aladas semillas,
> o te las llevan con piedad los pájaros;
> y crecen escondidas amapolas,
> clavelinas, magarzas, brezos, cardos,
> entre arrumbadas cruces,
> no más que de las aves libres pasto.

> [The mud and rubble of your walls save the winged seeds, or the birds reverently bring them to you; and there grow hidden poppies, carnations, camomile, heather, and thistles between the toppling crosses, no more than feed for the flightly birds.]

Their pastoral world, however, is after all a sheltered spot for nature to protect and pour forth her abundance upon, humble plants but well suited to the environment. This passage is the equivalent of the floral tributes to the beloved or to the departed one that appear often as set pieces for rhetorical display or for emotional effect (or symbolic significance) in pastoral poetry, a lyrical moment of beauty; here, however, it reminds us that the display is for the living, even the least of them, the birds, not for the departed or for their absent mourners.

Cavan tan sólo en tu maleza brava,
corral sagrado,
para de un alma que sufrió en el mundo
sembrar el grano;
luego, sobre esa siembra,
barbecho largo!

[They only dig in your splendid underbrush, holy sheepfold, to sow the grain of the soul of one who has suffered in the world. Then, over the sown seed, the fallowness stretches on.]

The dead are forgotten, gone into the great all-swallowing earth, with the fallen crosses over their graves as reminders of the neglected and distant hope of rebirth. Nothing is harvested from this field—not the dead, not even the crop of weeds waiting to be trimmed. The only harvest is the natural one, the process of change that affects all things that have ever lived. As in Thyrsis's lament for Daphnis in Theocritus's First Idyll, and Mopsus's lament in Vergil's Fifth Eclogue, death seems final.

Cerca de ti el camino de los vivos,
no como tú, con tapias, no cercado,
por donde van y vienen,
ya riendo o llorando,
rompiendo con sus risas o sus lloros
el silencio inmortal de tu cercado!

[Near you is the path of the living, not walled or fenced in like you; and there they come and go, laughing or crying, shattering with their laughter or tears the immortal silence of your walls.]

In the face of this, the outside world—well represented here by the unwalled road and those who pass by on it—seems cruelly vital and free. The pastoral dead, trapped in their enclosure, seem cut off not only from the world's vanities but also from its joys and sorrows, its full range of emotional vitality and human engagements, its ability to move and pass and change. The immortal silence is both outside of life and endless.

Después que lento el sol tomó ya tierra,
y sube al cielo el páramo
a la hora del recuerdo,
al toque de oraciones y descanso,
la tosca cruz de piedra
de tus tapias de barro
queda, como un guardián que nunca duerme,
de la campiña el sueño vigilando.

[After the sun has descended slowly to the earth and the plateau stretches toward the sky at the time of remembrance, at the bell for prayer and rest, the crude stone cross on your clay wall remains, like a guardian that never sleeps, vigilant over the sleeping countryside.]

With the coming of evening, the twilight moment that Vergil and Gray so effectively use for its suggestion of melancholy, and Gray in particular for the atmosphere of quiet and passing, the pastoral enclosure seems a guarded place, protected by a symbol of religious confidence that remains after the light of nature has faded; and the landscape seems altered by a shift in perspective that reminds us that the world of nature is untrustworthy and uncertain, capable of bringing tears as well as laughter. It is the world vulnerable to collapse and upheaval. For Vergil the fall of evening (almost literally a "fall" in Unamuno's poem) is uncomfortably ominous, a time for seeking the shelter of home. In Unamuno's poem the evening brings a new revelation. As the light of the sun fades from the earth, and the earth seems to loom higher to reach toward the sky, that sky itself attests to a power beyond nature.

No hay cruz sobre la iglesia de los vivos,
en torno de la cual duerme el poblado;
la cruz, cual perro fiel, ampara el sueño
de los muertos al cielo acorralados.
Y desde el cielo de la noche, Cristo,
el Pastor Soberano,
con infinitos ojos centellantes
recuenta las ovejas del rebaño!

[There is no cross over the church of the living, around which the village sleeps; the cross, like a faithful dog, protects the slumber of the dead in their divine sheepfold. And from the night's heaven Christ, the chief shepherd, with numberless sparkling eyes counts the sheep of his flock.]

"And when the chief Shepherd shall appear, ye shall receive a crown of glory that fadeth not away" (1 Peter 5 : 4). In this stanza the naturalistic and religious pastoral imagery merge in a vision that ties together the two worlds of the poem.

This is not the same as the apotheosis that enters the pastoral tradition in Vergil's Fifth Eclogue and illumines the poet's vision in Spenser's "November" eclogue and Milton's "Lycidas." Though in a sense "penned" in heaven, the dead are also asleep under the earth, part of both worlds and yet protected by the shepherd of all. Ironically, they enjoy a protection denied to those who are alive, though it is only in the realm of night that we can understand this. Their sleep is watched over by "the good Shepherd" who does not sleep but who is made manifest in the natural world itself, giving assurance that the process of life is not a mere wearing away of the living but a meaningful procedure through which the faithful sheep are made ready for their transcendent reward in a sacramental universe; under the watchful care of the greatest shepherd of all, the dead enjoy amid their humility and poverty a protection unknown to those who walk the paths of life, watched over by one not ashamed to take on their pastoral role and to set as his watchdog the sign of his own suffering.

> Pobre corral de muertos entre tapias
> hechas del mismo barro,
> sólo una cruz distingue tu destino
> en la desierta soledad del campo!

> [Poor sheepfold of the dead between walls made of the same clay, only a cross signals your service in the barren solitude of the fields.]

The final stanza, recalling the poem's opening, reasserts the experiential reality of the scene, while at the same time taking on an ironic coloration from the profound vision that has immediately preceded it. In this deserted solitude the dead silently attest, through the cross, to life and hope. The two worlds of the pastoral—the literally low, the figuratively high—are again separated but held in tension against one another.

In Unamuno's poem we see the particular quality of the pastoral expressing two very different attitudes toward an experience and two different modes of understanding experience fused into a statement that might be called ironic, if we understand irony to mean only the recognition of opposites having compensatory values or truths. The poem uses pastoral motifs to express pathos and elegiac sorrow as well as spiritual bliss. It uses pastoral motifs also to express the realities of seclusion, poverty, humility, harmony with nature, passivity before experience, independence from time and history, protection from life's vicissitudes, obedience to a cycle of life beyond the human scale, harmony with higher laws, natural or divine generosity toward human life; and to affirm a privileged spot within the world.

Of course this pastoral "world" is a world of the dead. And if that too is an idea fraught with ironies about the nature of pastoral experience and about the world's fitness for embodying an ideal, this is also part of the complex story of the functions of pastoral literature.

# 2

## The Functions of the Pastoral

THERE ARE, OF COURSE, TECHNICAL REASONS WHY THE PASTORAL HAS ATTRACTED so many authors, as there are for other literary forms like the sonnet, where the scale can be small and the generic characteristics easily indicated. The genre's artifices afford a handy textbook of devices to master and display. Such devices allow room for inventiveness while also providing ready-made structures, strategies, and principles for maintaining control. So pastoral poetry is convenient for young or inexperienced writers. Further, because pastoral poems are like miniature plays in which a small number of characters speak in stylized form, and because (following Vergil's example in imitating Theocritus) the situations and language are expected to consist in large measure of clever variations on some predecessor's patterns, the writer is under no obligation to show a personal voice or individual style. Again this is a benefit for the young writer, who may, like Vergil, indeed do something quite new and personal through those innovations, but who need not in order to turn a competent, pleasant verse. That is, the writer of a pastoral can show considerable literary sophistication without necessarily having developed artistic maturity.

There are larger artistic considerations as well. The first two great books of pastoral poetry contain many different kinds of literary expression. In them pastoral literature becomes a richly varied medium for addressing personal experience. The pastoral poem usually claims to be nothing more than a private reflection or emotional exclamation. Consequently it is a fitting means for those necessary functions of art. At the same time it is itself a small enclosed space, a kind of pastoral world in which a writer can explore within finite limits the potentialities of art and craft. Like the love elegy, which flourished in Augustan Rome at the same time as the pastoral eclogue, and like the sonnet, which flourished in Renaissance Europe at the same time as the pastoral eclogue, pastoral poetry is a way of expressing private concerns and emotional reactions to personal circumstances, especially love, within the disciplines of art. If the writer wants to do more, the pastoral style provides a useful disguise.

Pastoral also appeals to some broader desires to return to one's origins—for some writers, the roots of poetry itself, for others the golden age of literary culture. These are contradictory views of pastoral poetry, of course, but the form thrives on such contradictions; it is at once the simplest and most refined of art forms. On the one hand, Theocritus's *Idylls* in particular seem close to an imaginative recreation of genuine bucolic discourse and art, filled with vulgarity and casualness and all manner of seemingly trivial and incidental concerns, along with great energy, wit, beauty. This is a large step beyond folksongs and verbatim conversation, but Theocritus obviously values appearing natural. He provides a literary model of "genuine" folk art, rather akin to Beethoven's settings of Scottish and Irish ballads. Vergil, on the other hand, was for centuries the preeminent poet; and his book of pastoral poems, so obviously meticulous in their studied artistry, was the first stage in what came to be known as the *rota Vergiliana*, the sequence through poetic genres up to the epic, by which Vergil refined his artistry.

In still more general terms, the opposition between nature and nurture is one of the most basic in our culture. It is, in fact, one way of schematizing a vast body of cultural polarities: spontaneous versus planned, direct versus subtle, simple versus sophisticated, native versus foreign, ancient versus modern. These are in addition to the complex sets of oppositions that Harold Toliver neatly arranges in his book on the pastoral. (His list includes numerous antitheses within four general categories: nature versus society, nature versus art, idyllic nature versus antipastoral nature, and earthly nature versus celestial paradise.)[1]

Pastoral literature is well suited to address these antitheses, and it does so in two ways. One, of course, is by taking sides, setting the pastoral life against some other sort (heroic, for example, or industrial). The contrast might be developed in the sophisticated terms employed by Tasso in his *Jerusalem Liberated* (discussed in chapter 5) or in the deliberately cultivated artlessness of this eighteenth-century poem, the author of which was, not incidentally, a university graduate and minor government official:

Mir gnüget ein zufriednes Herze
Und was ich hab. . . .
Dies kleine Feld und diese Schafe,
Wo, frei von Unruh und Verdruss,
Ich singe, scherze, küsse, schlafe.[2]

[A happy heart's enough for me, and what I've got. . . . this little plot, and these sheep; where free from troubles and from grief, I sing and joke and kiss and sleep.]

The second way is to bind opposites—for instance, by joining nature with art, allowing the highly refined emotions and sophisticated literary compositions to come forth from ostensible countrypeople dwelling amid nature and yet clearly unrustic in their speech and manners. (It is this quality that Ben Jonson reacted against when he complained that Sidney violated decorum by having shepherds speak as well as himself.) Drayton's Tenth Eclogue, for example, reads in part:

> O Night, how still obsequious have I beene
> To thy slow silence whispering in thine eare,
> That thy pale Soveraigne often hath been seene,
>    Stay to behold me sadly from her Spheare,
>       Whilst the slow minutes duly I have told,
>       With watchful eyes attending on my Fold.      [31–36]

The Augustan and Renaissance periods were, after all, also eras of the villa, the comfortably rural home in which society and nature, elegance and simplicity, can be joined. In a style like Drayton's, sophistication and simplicity coexist.

The pastoral expresses attitudes as well as situations and in this regard has generally served two similar but distinguishable purposes. The first, which is the one most commonly associated with it, is to express an ideal or supposed ideal of life. Indeed, for many readers *pastoral* and *idyll* (a word really meaning "little picture") are almost synonyms, and *idyll* is generally thought to imply *ideal*. It is worth mentioning, though, that the idyll may be carefully circumscribed, falling short of perfection or shown to be fragile or limited when measured against the standards of the wider society. As Touchstone appraises life in Arden,

> In respect that it is solitary, I like it very well; but in respect that it is private, it is a very vile life. Now in respect it is in the fields, it pleaseth me well; but in respect it is not in the court, it is tedious. As it is a spare life, look you, it fits my humor well; but as there is no more plenty in it, it goes much against my stomach.     [As You Like It, III, ii, 14–22][3]

The pastoral world may look ideal in itself, or when measured against the immediate alternative; but in the long run, the pragmatic Touchstone observes, its shortcomings become clear. So through pastoral motifs the writer criticizes life as we ordinarily live it and also reconciles us to it. Through this process we see its faults more clearly and imagine what it would be like to live without them. We also see what it would be like to live without society's compensatory (and perhaps corresponding) virtues.

The other main function is to offer a model of all human life, distanced, estranged, and clarified through the literary artificing. The pastoral world presented in the work of art may not be a supposed or hoped-for ideal but rather a controlled, schematic version of ordinary life. This is not to say that such a pastoral version of the world will seem ordinary and everyday. On the contrary, it may be exaggeratedly artificial, just as Pope's mock-epical view of courtly frivolities in *The Rape of the Lock* seems flamboyantly "unrealistic," although we know the poem refers rather closely to a real situation.

In this version of the pastoral we may see more clearly, through pastoral fictions, the common concerns of humanity. The pastoral world in this sort of work is not a separate world but a microcosm: it is not set apart from some other way of life for purposes of comparison; it stands instead for ordinary life, magnified so that the scale of values and emotions differs from what we have become accustomed to. The troubles seem greater, the joys and pains more dramatic, the pleasures perfect. This sort of pastoral emphasizes our problems and pains, life's greater and smaller disappointments—or, sometimes, life's small disappointments that seem greater than they are in the long run. The scale of personal emotions in the pastoral thereby expresses our subjective experience of our most immediate personal concerns. This is how intense and large those concerns seem to us when we are in the midst of them, totally absorbed by them. If they appear "trivial" when set beside the vast issues of epic and tragedy, they are nonetheless the stuff of most people's emotional lives, compressed and shaped by art. The pastoral-as-microcosm can be an emotionally intense place in which to live. But beneath the pastoral images and masks, its characters and situations will look quite familiar to us.

Lorca's "El Lagarto Viejo" ("The Old Lizard"), for instance, treats pastoral life as exemplary of life in general. The old lizard, making his way through a daydream, is regarded with a mixture of wry, indulgent humor and affectionate appreciation by the narrator, who sees in him a paradigm of life's various little follies, losses, and satisfactions.

> ¿Venis quizá en la busca
> de la bella lagarta,
> verde como los trigos
> de Mayo,
> como las caballeras
> de las fuentes dormidas,
> que os despreciaba, y luego
> se fué de vuestro campo?
> ¡Oh, dulce idilio roto
> sobre la fresca juncia!⁴

[Have you come out in search of that lovely lizardress, green as the May wheat, green as the manes of dormant springs, who spurned you and left you in your field? Oh, sweet idyll broken amid the fresh sedge!]

Past joys are always slipping away and coming back to become the substance of our abstracted thoughts. That "sweet idyll" of young love is preserved in another idyll, the meditations of the aged. When all seems gone except quiet thought and the peace of a solitary home, then evening's fall seems to herald a final, fuller closure.

Ya se ha disuelto el sol
en la copa del monte,
y enturbian el camino
los rebaños.
Es hora de marcharse,
dejad la angosta senda
y no continuéis
meditando.
Que lugar tendréis luego
de mirar las estrellas
cuando os coman sin prisa
los gusanos.

[Now the sun has dissolved in the goblet of the mountains, and the flocks bustle along the road. It is time to depart. Turn from the narrow path and leave off meditating. Soon enough you will have the leisure to gaze at the stars while the unhurried worms consume you.]

In this poem the lizard, so like us in so many ways, bearing in his appearance itself the emblems of our intellectual and moral existence as well as our physical being, poignantly embodies our experiences of life. Grotesquely marked by his "studies" of life and nature, he remains wise and also deeply engaged with love and nature, even if that engagement is through the recollections of the past. This, too, marks him as *fortunate senex*, basking in the privileges of age.

As much as any other aspect of it, the tone of this poem carries its expression of pastoral emotion. The ending is characteristically Vergilian in its evocation of stillness and encroaching darkness, bringing to mind the endings of the First and Tenth Eclogues.

Ya está el campo sin gente,
los montes apagados
y el camino desierto;
solo de cuando en cuando
canta un cuco en la umbría
de los álamos.

[Now the field is unoccupied, the mountains fade and the road is deserted; only a cuckoo sings, now and then, in the poplars' darkness.]

Furthermore, the elegiac mood is combined with gentle affection for the good lizard ("buen lagarto"), who turns out to be surprisingly, comically, movingly human—so much so that the speaker at last breezily bids him "Buenas noches, amigo / Don Lagarto!" ("Good night, my friend Mister Lizard"). The poem expresses the deep kinship between human and animal life, and between animal life and all the other elements of the natural world. In this poem we are in the presence of complete harmony throughout creation. It is a harmony that embraces disappointment and death and survives the effects of time, religion, and indeed all of culture.

The pastoral image often seems to exist to be an element in a definition. There are, to be sure, a number of pastoral poems or passages from Theocritus onward that seem to be without ulterior intention, existing for the sheer satisfaction of the scene described, idylls untainted by internal complexity or external comparisons—idylls, we might say, written in an idyllic mood. More often, however, the pastoral confronts its opposition, sometimes losing in one fashion or another to that opposition.

> Clear water in a brilliant bowl,
> Pink and white carnations. The light
> In the room more like a snowy air,
> Reflecting snow. A newly-fallen snow
> At the end of winter when afternoons return.
> Pink and white carnations—one desires
> So much more than that. The day itself
> Is simplified: a bowl of white,
> Cold, a cold porcelain, low and round,
> With nothing more than the carnations there.[5]

This opening section of "The Poems of Our Climate" by Wallace Stevens sets forth the issue. This is not, narrowly speaking, a pastoral poem, being devoid of the conventional images of pastoral lyrics. Yet in it the flowers (cultivated carnations, pink and white, not wildflowers) and the bowl (plain white porcelain, not richly carved fragrant wood) are images of simplicity, freshness, and innocence that function the way pastoral images function in more traditional works, opposing clutter and corruption.

> Say even that this complete simplicity
> Stripped one of all one's torments, concealed
> The evilly compounded, vital I
> And made it fresh in a world of white.

Human nature, as Stevens sees it, cannot bear too much of this studied perfection. "The imperfect is our paradise." These images are, then, indeed pastoral images for Stevens because they function like pastoral images. They permit him to contrast real and supposed notions of perfection, in both life and art. For complex, "evilly compounded," and yet—and therefore—"vital" human beings, the neat, well-controlled, simplified, clearly defined ("brilliant-edged") pastoral world of perfection ("A world of clear water") cannot long suffice.

Pastoral artifice can also seem self-indulgent. Dr. Johnson's notorious complaint against "Lycidas" is not the only instance of this sort of opposition to pastoral poetry. As George Herbert phrased it in "Jordan" (I),

> Is it no verse, except enchanted groves
> And sudden arbours shadow coarse-spun lines?[6]

Herbert's objection is at once literary and ethical. The predictable artifice of pastoral imagery takes us away from poetry's communicative urgency and supple expressiveness. Tropes become conventions and then periphrasis.

> Must all be vailed, while he that reads, divines,
>     Catching the sense at two removes?

Herbert's splendid pun on *veil / vale* sharply draws our attention to the habitual association of pastoral and allegory, an association that links one form of artifice with another. Behind the complaint lies the implication that such veiling is dishonest, falsifying both the natural and artistic worlds.

> Shepherds are honest people, let them sing:
> Riddle who list, for me. . . .

Pastoral artifice, in other words, is not pastoral enough. It is a sort of cheat practiced by preying on the honest credit of plain country music. It makes riddles when what one expects and wants is straight talking: to "plainly say, *My God, My King*."

Stevens and Herbert posit two different sorts of limitations to the pastoral experience. For Stevens, in respect to complex human nature pastoral over-simplifies; for Herbert, in respect to truth's directness pastoral oversophisticates. These "limitations" of the pastoral are, of course, themselves artistic projections; neither is the final word on pastoral limits. Both critiques, however, identify the genuine limitations in some pastoral works; they also accurately represent at least the occasional moods of us all. We all feel, at least at times, impatient with both studied simplicity and labored elaborateness. Of course, in both these examples the pastoral image serves as the logician's "straw man," set up to be a convenient target for knocking down. Stevens and Herbert are sensitive enough, though, to acknowledge the pastoral's attractiveness; what they show us is not precisely straw, after all, but flowers.

Voltaire, in "Le Mondain," challenges head-on the pastoral view of earliest times, Eden or the Golden Age, as perfection-in-simplicity. Instead, he more contentedly apostrophizes to our own "fallen" world, "Ah! le bon temps que ce siècle de fer!"[7] ("Ah, what a fine time is this age of iron!") His description of Adam and Eve's prelapsarian life sardonically evokes those literary images of pastoral naturalness that praise the simple life.

> Dessous un chêne ils soupent galamment
> Avec de l'eau, du millet et du gland;
> Ce repas fait, ils dorment sur la dure.

> [Beneath an oak they elegantly sup on water, millet and acorns; their repast done, they sleep on the ground.]

To Voltaire this is a standard to despise, rather than long for.

> Admirez-vous pour cela nos aïeux?
> Il leur manquait l'industrie et l'aisance:
> Est-ce vertu? C'était pure ignorance.
> Quel idiot, s'il avait eu pour lors
> Quelque bon lit, aurait couché dehors?

> [Do you admire our ancestors for that? They lacked both industry and ease: Is this virtue? It is mere ignorance. What idiot, if he had a good bed, would choose to sleep outdoors?]

Each person's virtue may be someone else's folly. And as we can see, the pastoral experience may be simple or refined and attacked because it is not sufficiently sophisticated or because it is too artificial. Humble form that it is, the pastoral does not put up great resistance to authors' attempts to make of it what they wish.

The most interesting uses of the pastoral may be the most complex or the least predictable. For example, in contrast to Voltaire, Leconte de Lisle, in "Midi," uses pastoral motifs consciously but unconventionally.

> L'étendue est immense, et les champs n'ont point d'ombre
> Et la source est tarie où buvaient les troupeaux;
> La lointaine forêt, dont la lisière est sombre,
> Dort là-bas, immobile, en un pesant repos.          [5−8][8]

> [The land stretches on, the fields empty of shade and the spring dry, where the flocks used to drink. The far forest, dark at its edge, drowses motionless there in its listless rest.]

We expect the fields, the spring, the woodlands, the *repos*; but these fields offer not a drop of shade, the spring where the flocks once drank has dried up, and the woods do not resound with the name of Amaryllis but lie languid in a heavy hush. This is not only a description of a landscape but also a reply to the literary tradition of pastoral ecphrasis. However, it is not a direct reply: just as Leconte does not merely repeat familiar motifs, neither does he merely invert them; he does not say, with Yeats, "Gone are the woods of Arcady, / And over is their antique joy." Rather, he reconstructs the images of the pastoral setting.

This reconstruction takes place because Leconte is revising the "lesson" to be learned from nature—particularly from nature in its pastoral mood.

> Homme, si, le coeur plein de joie ou d'amertume,
> Tu passais vers midi dans les champs radieux,
> Fuis! la nature est vide et le soleil consume:
> Rien n'est vivant ici, rien n'est triste ou joyeux.
>
> Mais, si, désabusé des larmes et du rire,
> Altéré de l'oubli de ce monde agité,
> Tu veux, ne sachant plus pardonner ou maudire,
> Goûter une suprême et morne volupté,
>
> Viens! Le soleil te parle en paroles sublimes;
> Dans sa flamme implacable absorbe-toi sans fin;
> Et retourne à pas lents vers les cités infimes,
> Le coeur trempé sept fois dans le néant divin.          [21−32]

[Man, if you pass the radiant fields at midday with a heart full of joy or bitterness, Flee! Nature is empty and the sun consuming: nothing lives here, nothing is sad or happy. But if, free from the deceptions of tears and laughter, eager to forget this unquiet world, no longer knowing how to forgive or curse, you want to taste one grand, cheerless luxury, Come! The sun speaks to you in words sublime; enwrap yourself forever in its persevering flame, and return with slow steps toward the insignificant cities, heart seven times immersed in the nothingness divine.]

Not simply a landscape, the poem is an ethical address teaching "man" that only when he is empty of driving emotions (*désabuse*, *oubli*, *ne sachant*) is he ready for the lesson of nature's divine, dreaming, docilely intense emptiness. Furthermore, understanding this lesson prepares one to return, spiritually shielded, to urban frenzy, not to find a permanent home within the natural world. Indeed, that world everywhere declares its difference from us, its separateness from us.

Though it expresses "le néant divin," nature in Leconte's poem affords a moral after all. It teaches that all is subsumed by the sheer presence of existence itself. Nature, occupied with its own being, lost in its dreams—which are not dreams of *something* but merely dreams that go on and on without conclusion or fulfillment ("le songe intérieur qu'ils n'achèvent jamais")—gives us the image of life. Leconte knows that there is a difference between saying that nature is a blank page and saying (as he does) that nature is susceptible to false interpretations and true understanding. He knows, that is, that nature lies passive before us, available for us to impose on or to comprehend in all its apartness. He indicates that even in its most uncommunicative guises, even when it seems to hold forth nothing at all to the human observer, nature is expressive.

By revising the pastoral motifs, he revises our sense of nature and redefines pastoral tranquillity. Such a redefinition, he claims, is specifically vital for our understanding of nature and of all life, even within the turmoil of "ce monde agité," where *ce* suggests the social world in which a poet writes and publishes, as well as the world in which we all live and breathe. After the grand sweep of the natural world ("L'étendue . . . immense"), the insignificance of the cities ("les cités infimes") seems clear. The sheer fact of pastoral *otium* defies the city's implicit moral claims.

While revising our notions of pastoral experience, Leconte leaves his own redefinition of the pastoral experience intact. Nature, "empty," will be useless to the observer whose heart is already "full": that is, the natural world, here presented as a revised version of the pastoral world, will be able to say nothing to anyone who has no room to "absorb" its meaning. The value of emptiness, Leconte's version of pastoralism, is that in place of a narrow passion it permits an openness to full and automous existence, a flaming in the summer of life.

In *The Arraignment of Paris*, George Peele uses pastoral elements that are far more conventional than Leconte's, but he uses them with a virtuoso's love for complexity. Within the contexts of human history and divine values. Peele probes the merits and limitations of pastoral existence. He creates a bipolar universe, shepherds below and deities above; those two orders of beings define the world of his drama. Below, a series of unhappy love affairs among the pastoral characters culminates in the death of the shepherd-poet Colin, whose courtship has been spurned. This part of the play emphasizes the historically familiar literary association of shepherds and love, preparing us for the central event of the play, Paris's choice of Venus. We understand that this imprudent decision is the best we could expect from a mere shepherd, who here represents the simple, private man, subject to inflaming and irrational passions. We also understand that it must necessarily lead to disaster, for in this pastoral world love seems to have no other outcome.

Appropriately, then, Paris pleads at his arraignment before the council of the gods,

> Of tragic Muses shepherds con no skill;
> Enough is them, if Cupid ben displeased,
> To sing his praise on slender oaten pipe. [IV, i, 154–56][9]

Shepherds know about love; though their feelings may be intense, their attitude toward love is simple, direct, and uncomplicated. However, their judgment about absolute values is untrustworthy because their range of concerns and resources is so limited. Not being "men of the world," they cannot deal responsibly with complex problems and decisions. Using the shepherd Paris (and the pastoral world of which he is a part), Peele explores the consequences of mortal love. He traces through the problems such love causes in the private, public, and cosmic spheres.

The dispute amongst the goddesses is finally settled by Diana, who awards the prize to "This peerless nymph, whom heaven and earth beloves," Queen Elizabeth, who embodies all the virtues and so elevates her pastoral kingdom to divine purity and dignity, "peerless" as queen and nymph united in one being (V, i, 82). By thus revising the story of Paris, Peele gives his play two endings. The historical one concludes at the end of the third act with Paris's announcement that his choice has unfortunately made him the instrument of war; the mythical one concludes the play as the three Fates yield their responsibilities and free the queen from mortal destiny so that all the goddesses acknowledge her supremacy. Here the pastoral choice is the choice of the frail, impercipient, passion-torn; and it leads to that other form of life in which human passions are unbridled, war. The divine choice, informed by wisdom and an understanding of the higher virtues, leads to eternal devotion and peace. In this work the negative aspects of pastoral's emotional and moral attributes induce a coherent expression of unpastoral political principles. In terms of the two general purposes for the pastoral, in this case the pastoral life is indeed an image of our imperfect, mortal existence, and it is also set within a larger context for contrast; this contrast is not social but metaphysical and depends upon our recognizing a separation between ourselves and the higher divine natures.

In the pseudo-Theocritean Idyll XXV, an epyllion or miniature epic about Herakles' battle with the Nemean lion, we see another way of using pastoral motifs to define and pay tribute to a nonpastoral figure. In this instance, however, it is not a royal mortal deity who rises above mere pastoralism but a demigod who is valued for being able to descend to the pastoral level. The pastoral references give the hero the common touch. As the poem begins, an old cattleherd describes to Herakles the splendid rustic landscape of Augeas's farm. This homely opening praises a rustic set of values which Herakles warmly approves and to which he appropriately responds by saying that, although he is looking for Augeas, if the king is busy with affairs of state he will speak instead with one of the servants, the overseer of the fields. On the other hand, a certain dignity is maintained: while Augeas and Herakles tour the stables, the cleansing is not mentioned, only the vitality of the herd, with certain animals being singled out for their beauty. When, in a passage reminiscent of an epic, Herakles relates his adventures and focuses particularly on his heroic fight with the lion, he concludes by explaining that he conquered "the cause of many a sorrow to flocks and to men." So for Herakles victory over the lion is not simply a personal triumph but a defense of natural harmony against brutal wildness. The ease with which Herakles moves among the lower social orders and shows concern for their welfare, and his appreciation for the animals and the artifacts of rural life, mark him as truly noble in character, a popular hero who does not seek popularity but earns it because he is "natural" and has the "common touch."

By way of contrast we can think of Marlowe's Tamburlaine, who first appears dressed as a shepherd according to "my parentage," but quickly casts off his "weeds that I disdain to wear," showing beneath his real (not literary) pastoral garb "This complete armor and this curtle-axe" of a conquerer (I, ii, 35, 41−42).[10] Through pastoral costuming Marlowe makes a number of implicit statements about Tamburlaine. In contrast to the feckless royalty shown in the play's first scene, Tamburlaine is unspoiled, not decadent, not weak, not deceitful. He is an honest child of nature, naturally virtuous, tough and frank. Yet were he suitably cloaked in his pastoral garb, he would be a mere rustic, provincial in his abilities and ambitions. A Herakles can stoop to place himself on a level with a cowherd or an overseer of field work; a Tamburlaine must dissociate himself from rusticity.

Tamburlaine is a familiarly paradoxical character, who seems to embody pastoral virtues while transcending pastoral limitations. When Zenocrate addresses him, still in his shepherd's garb, as "my lord—for so you do import," Tamburlaine replies, "I am a lord, for so my deeds shall prove" (33−34). He is speaking metaphorically and proleptically here, declaring his nobility of nature rather than nurture; however, we could trace a long literary lineage for him of royal or well-born characters who are raised as pastoral people but show in their manners their genetic superiority to the natural rustic. Such a genealogy would reach back to Longus's Daphnis and Chloë and include the Pastorella of Spenser's

*Faerie Queene*, Book VI, as well as ahead to Perdita in *The Winter's Tale*. This guise of pastoral covert royalty marks the author's ambivalence toward the two worlds within the literary universe and the values they embody. On the one hand, pastoral virtues prove a necessary antidote to the illnesses of the great world; on the other hand, if those virtues are indeed indigenous to the pastoral world rather than to the world of power, education, wealth, and social complexity, then society as we know it is morally and experientially incoherent. We would have to take seriously the biblical and philosophical praises of humility, simplicity, generosity, and harmony, setting these values above those ordinarily taken to be the measures of worldly success. Therefore, it may be convenient to explain that the quintessentially noble-seeming pastoral character is not truly pastoral after all but secretly noble by birth—or, in Tamburlaine's case, by election of the will.

We have said that pastoral motifs are used generally in one of two ways: to express the ideal (which might also mean to challenge or test a notion of idealization), or to express and shape the world of conventional experience. We have also seen that these functions may be joined in complicated ways, and that even when one can neatly identify the function of the pastoral element, the entire work may be quite complex. For example, Horace's Epodes 16 and 2, while using pastoral elements in simple ways to represent unambiguous ideals of life, are not really simple poems.

The speaker of Epode 16, having begun by sketching the horrors of civil war once again tormenting Rome, suggests a plan. Take to the seas, he urges.

> nos manet Oceanus circumvagus: arva beata
>     petamus, arva divites et insulas,
> reddit ubi cererem tellus inarata quotannis
>     et inputata floret usque vinea,
> germinat et numquam fallentis termes olivae
>     suamque pulla ficus ornat arborem,
> mella cava manant ex ilice, montibus altis
>     levis crepante lympha desilit pede.
> illic iniussae veniunt ad mulctra capellae,
>     refertque tenta grex amicus ubera.         [41−50][11]

[For us, the encircling Ocean waits. Let us seek the fields, the happy fields, and islands of the blessed, where the unploughed land yearly yields corn, the unpruned vine blooms, and the olive branch unfailingly buds—where the black fig bedecks its own tree, honey seeps from the hollow oak, and from the tall hills a spring bounds lightly down. There the goats come without command to the milking pail, and the friendly flock returns with udders full.]

Eduard Fraenkel has observed that Horace, who had favored Brutus in the civil war, was careful not to offend the government that had at least allowed him to live. Nor could he openly advance a pragmatic program of civil disobedience. His scheme comes about in the poem through a fanciful, unrealistic political process.[12] So he registers his dissatisfaction through a transparently impossible scheme that has purely poetic validity.

Horace sees this voyage as an act of courage and defiance, not an opportunity for the meek to slip away quietly to a languid land of daydreams. It means detaching oneself from the familiar world: not just the physical world we have grown accustomed to but the world of pragmatic concerns, the world of fear, suspicion, and weakness. The fainthearted need not apply.

> . . . mollis et exspes
> inominata perpremat cubilia.                                    [37–38]

[Let the timid and hopeless cling to their ill-fated beds!]

It takes courage to cast aside the familiar ways and reach a green world devoid of ambition, strife, or want. But once there, one is safe, for the place is reserved for the pious. It is unspoiled by the great adventurer-conquerors, or by the terrors and struggles of tragedy (represented here by Medea) and epic (Ulysses).

> non huc Argoo contendit remige pinus
>     neque impudica Colchis intulit pedem;
> non huc Sidonii torserunt cornua nautae,
>     laboriosa nec cohors Ulixei.                                 [57–60]

[Never did a ship with Argive oarsmen come here, never did a shameless queen of Colchis set foot; no Phoenician sailors have turned their yardarms toward this spot, nor the toiling crew of Ulysses.]

This refuge, the fortunate isles, is a protected environment of plenty. Of course there is a poignant irony: in the iron age the refuge of the devout is necessarily in utopia. Horace has made the voyage there an undertaking of determination and faith.

Epode 16 is not a simple poem, but it depends on a simple notion of a pastoral refuge of peace and natural wealth, a place uncomplicated by fears, doubts, wayward passions, sophistications, or invasions. That fervently desired haven of moral perfection constitutes a rare, passionate indulgence by Horace, an uncharacteristic moment of fantasy to which he is probably moved by the intensity of his frustration and disgust.

Against this we can set his treatment of country life in Epode 2, a long encomium describing the satisfactions of both georgic labors (cultivating plants and enjoying their fruits, pruning, hunting, while a faithful wife raises the children and attends to the firewood, flocks, and winemaking) and bucolic leisures:

> libet iacere modo sub antiqua ilice,
>     modo in tenaci gramine:
> labuntur altis interim ripis aquae,
>     queruntur in silvis aves
> fontesque lymphis obstrepunt manantibus,
>     somnos quod invitet levis.                    [23 – 28]

[How pleasant it is to rest, now beneath an ancient oak, now on the matted grass, while the brook glides past between its high banks, and birds twitter in the woods, and the springs' surging waters splash, a sound summoning easy sleep.]

These are the pleasures of living a simple life without civilization and its discontents, a life in accord with first principles:

> Beatus ille qui procul negotiis,
>     ut prisca gens mortalium                    [1 – 2]

[Happy is he who, far from the concerns of business, like the earliest breed of the human race. . . .]

But the final four lines offer a new way of understanding the opening reference to *negotium*. This praise of rural living, all sixty-six lines of it, has been spoken by a most unpastoral character.

> haec ubi locutus faenerator Alfius,
>     iam iam futurus rusticus,
> omnem redegit idibus pecuniam,
>     quaerit kalendis ponere.                    [67 – 70]

[When the usurer Alfius had finished talking, ready to embark on the rustic life, he pulled in all his money on the Ides, to put to use again on the Kalends.]

The sardonic twist at the end of Epode 2 has led some critics to conclude that Horace "really" meant that even a usurer could be moved by love of the countryside, and others, that he is satirizing the vogue for pastoral poetry. Indeed, the poem contains both attitudes. The loving portrait of bucolic life is itself totally devoid of irony; but the conclusion unquestionably has a bite to it. Everything Alfius enumerates can be translated into wealth: so much property, so much livestock, so much produce. At least for him, the urge to live in the country is one more form of the urge to possess, and the usurer's vision of his homestead is also an excited reverie of his tangible profits. Appropriately for a greedy man, Alfius blends motifs of the pastoral and the georgic in his encomium; his country estate allows pastoral leisure for him, but for everyone else it involves constant toil to bring forth every bit of goodness that the land can yield.

In this poem the pastoral becomes a rich man's dream. He finds leisure, comfort, and innocent natural pleasure here. His values are right, but only wealth could make it all possible on quite so satisfying a scale. Horace (like Pope and Voltaire centuries later) knows that existence on a real farm is no idyll except for the gentleman-farmer, and that the pastoral life (as distinct from simply farm life) is reserved for poets' fantasies and for those wealthy enough to make dreams come true. Pope writes that "we are not to describe our shepherds as shepherds at this day really are, but as they may be conceived . . . to have been; when the best of men followed the employment." For him the pastoral recreates in literature the golden age. It is not and cannot be a record of the real life of real shepherds, for that is not satisfactorily pastoral but merely rustic. Fontenelle writes that since the rise of civilization "the Pastoral Life being grown the lot of the most wretched sort of People, no longer inspir'd any delightful Thought."[13] Horace's Alfius is neither a shepherd nor the best of men; but in his society he can come closest to making the ideal a reality.

Horace's two epodes show lavish spots offering natural bounty, innocent pleasures, peace of mind, and a simple (but far from austere) way of life akin to that conventionally ascribed in religion and poetry to the earliest stage of human society. Harmony reigns in the peaceable kingdom. These are traditional simple pastoral visions set into ironic and complex poems. Each place of peace, examined in isolation from the dramatic context of the entire poem, seems unequivocally pure. Its outward beauty and spiritual essence are perfectly consonant. Only when we see that spot within the framework of the poem's larger structure does our concept of the pastoral place change. Though it is used differently in each poem, the pastoral milieu allows the poet to define a set of values and to comment on the possibility for living within those values, given the characteristics of his society and human nature.

For Tibullus, writing at about the same time as Horace and Vergil, the pastoral expresses a time of past peace. His Tenth Elegy looks back to the Golden

Age before the invention of the sword, and also to his own youth, both of which afford images of what he hopes for his old age. Once upon a time,

> Non arces, non vallus erat, somnumque petebat
> Securus sparsas dux gregis inter oves. [9 — 10][14]

[There was no pomp of arms, no fortified camps; a leader only sought safe sleep amidst his mottled flock of sheep.]

As recently as his own childhood the gods who ruled people's lives were household gods.

> Hic placatus erat, seu quis libaverat uva,
> Seu dederat sanctae spicae serta comae. [21 — 22]

[Then were they happy enough with a libation from the vine, with a sanctified wreath of tufted wheat.]

Now war threatens life and land.

> Quis furor est atram bellis arcessere mortem?
> Inminet et tacito clam venit illa pede.
> Non seges est infra, non vinea culta, sed audax
> Cerberus et Stygiae navita turpis aquae. [33 — 36]

[What madness is it to summon black death to the field of war! He hovers over us anyway, and steals upon us with a silent step. No fields of grain grow below, no vines are cultivated; only threatening Cerberus, and the hideous boatman of the Stygian stream.]

He wants a pastoral old age.

In Vergil's First Eclogue the unfortunate Meliboeus, going into exile, addresses his friend Tityrus, who has been given freehold of a little property of his own, as "Fortunate senex" ("Lucky old man"). Such luck Tibullus's narrator also hopes for. Although the pastoral often seems a young man's game, it is frequently a dream-world for the elderly, who are privileged to live out their last long years in tranquillity, free from want. Tibullus shows us both sides, the pastoral life of the child and the hoped-for pastoral life of the *senex*.

> Quam potius laudandus hic est, quem prole parata
> Occupat in parva pigra senecta casa. [39 — 40]

[How much more worthy of praise to tend to your family, and age slowly in some little cottage.]

For Tibullus the pastoral life is the very image of personal satisfaction and social harmony. It is, furthermore, the original condition of human life, from which we have fallen by our uncontrolled meddling with the nature of things. Not only is pastoral peace our primordial condition, it was also the way of life for the preceding generation and for the narrator in his own childhood. (As Raymond Williams has observed, every generation imagines the golden age as a period that still existed in its own infancy.)[15] The pastoral images thereby link us to our earliest, purest, most natural condition, and to the protected and piously simple way of life that we imagine we remember from our own childhood. It ties together the times we think of as specially blessed. It gives us as well an image in which to embody our longings for our own future and that of humankind.

Vergil's Fourth Eclogue, roughly contemporaneous with Horace's Epode 16, uses pastoral images to describe a hope for the future also, but in ways less private than Tibullus and less socially divisive than Horace. Using the pastoral motifs of idealization, Vergil suggests not only the shape but also the shaping of the future.

The beginning of the poem shifts noticeably from one style of verse to another:

Sicelides Musae, paulo maiora canamus.
non omnis arbusta iuuant humilesque myricae;
si canimus siluas, siluae sint consule dignae.
  Ultima Cumaei uenit iam carminis aetas;
magnus ab integro saeclorum nascitur ordo.

[Muses of Sicily, let us sing something a bit more exalted! Hedgerows and the humble tamarisks do not please everyone. If we sing of the woods, let those woods be worthy of a consul.
  Now the conclusive age of Cumaean song has come; the great sequence of years is born anew.]

The opening three lines self-consciously declare that this work goes beyond the normal range of pastoral: at once a confession, a warning, and a boast. They also remind us that the poem is an artifact, a piece of inspiration and crafting, shaped by a writer who has to be alert to stylistic decorum, the capacities of metaphors, and the uses of myths. Out of this texture of artifice the prophecy leaps startlingly and not a little awkwardly, pushing against the preciosity of *paulo*, "a bit more." We sense that what follows is both greater than, and less real than, the preparatory vocal exercises of the poet's persona. It is greater because it deals with a larger subject than the poet's attempt to find the right voice for his intended topic and because it is unabashedly a vision of an as yet unevolved future invested with mythic action. The poem's two beginnings, the invocation and the start of the prophecy, thereby leave us unsettled, at least uncertain as to why the Sicilian (that is, pastoral) muses are evoked for this *loftier* song. Throughout the poem, a knowledge of the great world of public affairs, and the knowledge of human nature that goes along with our knowledge of the great world, constantly tug at the onrushing force of the unfolding prophecy, demanding revisions and corrections. These hold us back from the complete fulfillment of that elevated pastoral ideal implied in the invocation, the reconciliation of the realm of the consul and the realm of the woods.

The opening words of the prophecy are fraught with ambiguities that begin as seemingly temporal problems but evolve into historical and ethical problems as well. The word *ultima*, for example, denotes extremity, and can mean both first and last; so the allusion to the sibylline prophecies suggests simultaneously that the ages of history described therein are coming to an end and that the earliest stage has come again. Are we witnessing a new beginning or the repetition of the past? Is this indeed a break with the patterns of the past, or will we face again the strife and long decline that the myth of the golden age construes as the story of human history. At this stage in the poem, Vergil does not pause to raise, or to allow us to raise, such questions but rushes onward toward the poem's vision of transcendent pastoralism, the forthcoming golden age of peacefulness and generosity.

> At tibi prima, puer, nullo munuscula cultu
> errantis hederas passim cum baccare tellus
> mixtaque ridenti colocasia fundet acantho.
> ipsae lacte domum referent distenta capellae
> ubera nec magnos metuent armenta leones;
> ipsa tibi blandos fundent cunabula flores.
> occidet et serpens et fallax herba ueneni
> occidet; Assyrium uolgo nascentur amomum.          [4, 18–25]

[But for you, child, the untilled earth, as her first little offerings, will pour forth rambling ivy, foxglove everywhere, and colocasia mixed with the smiling acanthus. The goats will return home themselves, udders swelling with milk, and the herds will have no fear of the mightly lion. Even your cradle will sprout delightful flowers. And the serpent will perish; so too the deceptive poisonous weed. Everywhere Assyrian incense will grow.]

Nature responds as human life moves toward perfection; for both nature and humanity are bound together in sympathetic harmony by laws of the spirit. Taking on a divine existence (*deum uitam*), the child links divinity with all that lives. The process of restoring the primal harmony of things also purifies nature itself; the lamb need fear the lion no longer, and we no longer fear any of nature's dangers.

Vergil, however, takes a surprising tack following this compendium of pastoral glories.

> at simul heroum laudes et facta parentis
> iam legere et quae sit poteris cognoscere uirtus,
> molli paulatim flauescet campus arista
> incultisque rubens pendebit sentibus uua,
> et durae quercus sudabunt roscida mella.
>       Pauca tamen suberunt priscae uestigia fraudis,
> quae temptare Thetim ratibus, quae cingere muris
> oppida, quae iubeant telluri infindere sulcos.
> alter erit tum Tiphys et altera quae uehat Argo
> delectos heroas; erunt etiam altera bella
> atque iterum ad Troiam magnus mittetur Achilles.      [26–36]

[But just as soon as you can read the praises of heroes and of your father's achievements, and can understand the qualities required of an adult, the plains will wax golden with tender corn; from untended brambles empurpling grapes will hang, and dewy honey seep from the rugged oak. Yet a few traces of ancient delusions will remain, moving people to test the seas with ships, encircle towns with walls, cut furrows into the earth. There will come another Tiphys, and an Argo again to carry the chosen heroes. And there will be wars again, and again a great Achilles will be sent to Troy.]

Here the pastoral age seems to give way to the georgic and the epic.

Denying the earlier implication that the birth of the child will miraculously bring forth a change in the nature of the world, Vergil shows that we will still face the challenges of our own natures. Human impulses are represented in two ways: the will to cultivate, which is a desire to extend domination over the vegetative world by making it more productive; the will to reap, to extend domination over the earth by claiming it as one's own. It is that latter desire, identifiably different from the former but originating from a similar instinct, that leads to a new era of strife. These baser instincts, Vergil indicates, are antipastoral. They pull us away from the pastoral life, even when it is clear that this life is divinely sanctioned— indeed, divinely sent.

During the strong adulthood of the child, however,

cedet et ipse mari uector nec nautica pinus
mutabit merces; omnis feret omnia tellus.
non rastros patietur humus, non uinea falcem,
robustus quoque iam tauris iuga soluet arator;
nec uarios discet mentiri lana colores,
ipse sed in pratis aries iam suaue rubenti
murice, iam croceo mutabit uellera luto,
sponte sua sandyx pascentis uestiet agnos.                    [38—45]

[The trader will himself turn from the seas, the nautical pine no longer bear cargo; every land will produce everything. The ground will not have to endure the harrow, or the vine the pruning hook; and the sturdy ploughman will loosen the yoke from his oxen. Wool will no longer be taught to counterfeit many colors, for the ram in the meadows will change the color of his own fleece himself, now to a sweetly blushing purple, now to a saffron tint; spontaneously, scarlet will bedeck the feeding lambs.]

The grown child, become a godlike ruler, will expunge that contumacious spirit of humankind that leads to so much sorrow (though at times it does so much good, when human decadence corrupts the earth and we need to earn back nature's treasures). It is notable that this vision of spontaneous production mingles pastoral and georgic elements as it unites the natural and the cultivated. Not only will we get milk and honey; all things that human beings have decided they need in order to make life comfortable and gracious will come forth. The connectives, the insistent use of "now" and "himself," show the energy of the speaker's commitment to this fantastic vision; the negatives show that we can best understand such perfection through its differences from the life to which we have grown accustomed.

Since he is not writing a political treatise, Vergil does not attempt to posit how the youth will restrain our bad habits, our mortal desire for mastery, our struggle with one another and our environment. What he posits is that this child is the nexus of a mystical union between nature and civilization and that the union reaches fruition (as the child reaches maturity) when people allow nature to produce what they need and when nature does in fact give us what we want. But this fruition results from people's spiritual evolution to perfection. The divine youth need not do anything. Vergil can write of him reading (legere) about great deeds, and knowing (cognoscere) about adult responsibility, without necessarily attributing to him the labors of fulfillment: for a divine being, knowledge is sufficient because that is identical with power. So the two pastoral moments in the poem occur at the child's birth, when his newness and innocence are fittingly celebrated by one set of pastoral images, and in his maturity, when his influence drives away the vestiges of our mortal shortcomings and another set of pastoral images express the new golden age over which he will preside. The former shows us nature making itself miraculously pastoral, as plants and beasts respond instinctively to the child's sacred innocence. The opening invocation of the pastoral muses is therefore thematically appropriate, though it may seem odd for the poem's tone. The latter deals with the more difficult dimension of pastoral, the spread of pastoral virtues to amend human behavior. Vergil suggests that human nature changes only in the fullness of time, and so we drag with us into the future the baggage of the past.

The life of this child affords a small history of the human race; ontogeny recapitulates phylogeny. For a moment in human childhood we see the pure pastoral experience. But that experience is under the pressure of time, because childhood does not last forever. Here time is metonymous for the various forces that Vergil senses pressing in on the pastoral world, or pressing out from it because of human tendencies and desires. Anything that disrupts that integrity, Vergil indicates, disrupts the pastoral experience itself. Only at the end of time, in a maturity that takes the place of old age, does the pastoral experience return to us.

In the Fourth Eclogue Vergil uses the pastoral to transcend the pastoral. He creates visions of pastoral moments, but in a schematic view of history that allows—perhaps compels—him to consider the pastoral's relationship to human time and effort. The alert and knowing narrator, conscious of his audience and therefore of a public that is very much part of a social and political world, becomes a poetic visionary who has earned the right to deliver this vatic oration because his sensibility is sufficiently complex to receive and describe the patterned flux of history. What results is a dialectic movement between nature and civilization that is resolved by a fusion of antitheses into something unfamiliar; something basically pastoral in its external trappings and its attitude toward human effort, yet unpastoral in the vigorous abundance of its creative energy.

That energy extends to the poet himself, who perhaps implies that the result will not be a life of *otium* but of delight in work, for the work will become a kind of pastoral song, not strictly necessary but pleasurable in itself and rewarding because its inspiration is divine.

> o mihi tum longae maneat pars ultima uitae,
> spiritus et quantum sat erit tua dicere facta:
> . . . . . . . . . . . . . . . . . . . . . . . . . . . .
> Pan etiam, Arcadia mecum si iudice certet,
> Pan etiam Arcadia dicat se iudice uictum.          [53−55, 58−59]

[O may the last days of a long life linger for me, and breath long enough to tell then of what you accomplish! . . . Even Pan, were he to contend with me and Arcadia be judge, even Pan with Arcadia for judge would confess himself vanquished.]

The poet, instead of sinking back into complacency or languor, is inspired to new poetic heights; and the repetitions in lines 58—59 indicate his barely controlled excitement. As work becomes pleasure in a world purged of base instincts, freedom become productive. Pan's song is the artistic standard of judgment because only the pastoral song is appropriate to the pastoral vision that inspires the poet's imagination as both a writer and a person. What he sees, of course, is not "merely" pastoral. It is the perfection of life expressed in pastoral terms.

Certainly the expression is fantastic, and to the degree to which it is we can acknowledge that Vergil may find it impossible to imagine how else to express such a state of freedom from want or necessity; or we may believe instead that Vergil can imagine this state only as the fulfillment of wishes and not as a real condition that could come about in fact within the sensate world in which all human life exists. However, we can see, regardless of our interpretation of the poem, that Vergil has used the pastoral as a way of embodying his feelings about the nature of human life, ambition, and dreams. His use of pastoral images, and ideas associated with those images, has allowed him to write about our relationship with nature, with our own emotions, with one another. Vergil understands, and uses in this poem, the potential of the pastoral for expressing what we would like to be true.

Vergil also understands the complex possibilities that pastoral affords for expressing contrary perceptions. In his last—tenth—eclogue, he writes the lament that his friend Gallus, a love-stricken elegist, soldier, and politician, cannot write for himself because of his distress. In this poem he imagines Gallus's words.

Tristis at ille "tamen cantabitis, Arcades,"
   inquit
"montibus haec uestris, soli cantare periti
Arcades. o mihi tum quam molliter ossa
   quiescant,
uestra meos olim si fistula dicat amores!
atque utinam ex uobis unus uestrique fuissem
aut custos gregis aut maturae uinitor uuae!
certe siue mihi Phyllis siue esset Amyntas
seu quicumque furor—quid tum, si fuscus
   Amyntas?

et nigrae uiolae sunt et uaccinia nigra—
mecum inter salices lenta sub uite iaceret;
serta mihi Phyllis legeret, cantaret Amyntas.
    Hic gelidi fontes, hic mollia prata, Lycori,
hic nemus; hic ipso tecum consumerer aeuo."            [31–43]

[Sadly he says: "You will still sing of these thoughts amid your hills, Arcadians, you who best know how to sing, Arcadians. Oh, what rest my bones would find if one day your pipes told of my love. Would that I had been one of you, to tend your flocks or gather the fruits of the vine. Surely, whether Phyllis or Amyntas or some other passion were mine (what does it matter that Amyntas is swarthy? So violets and hyacinths are dark), we would lie together amid the willows, beneath the supple vine. Phyllis would wreathe garlands for me, Amyntas sing. Here are cool springs, here soft meadows, Lycoris, here the woods; here with you, only time itself would eat away at me."]

Tormented by his own love for Lycoris, which is complicated by the ways of the Roman world in which they live, Gallus romanticizes the pastoral world. The names of Phyllis and Amyntas send us back to Vergil's Third Eclogue, a pastoral song-contest in which these two fictive characters were cited as perfect patterns of pastoral lovers. Here Gallus longs for a real life simpler and happier than the one he endures, a life of amorous happiness, devoid of jealousy or want. He also wishes that he could be satisfied with the fictions of pastoral, as opposed to the apparently more realistic tribulations expressed in the love elegy. Albeit—indeed, because—the pastoral is more rustic, less sophisticated, less refined, less dramatic than the elegiac, it affords a safe and comfortable refuge from a culture in which the love of one's life (an actress and courtesan) is likely to run off with a dashing soldier. Desperate to flee from his torments, he wishes for both the quiet satisfactions of the pastoral and the violent distractions of the wilderness. The calm, poised, controlled voice of the poet composing this eclogue is in itself testimony to the justness of Gallus's wish: the pastoral poet who can write this poem is doing what Gallus is unable to do. He, despite his love for Gallus, remains in control of himself and his art. His pastoral song expresses a measure of spiritual peace and comfort unknown to the urbanized artist. When, at the close of this poem the pastoral poet refers to himself in the lines,

Haec sat erit, diuae, uestrum cecinisse poetam,
dum sedet et gracili fiscellam texit hibisco,            [70–71]

[This was enough, goddess, for your poet to have sung while sitting weaving a basket of slender hibiscus,] he indicates that, like weaving the basket, making the poem is a gentle craft, done in the quiet understanding of nature and her materials. His love, furthermore, is similarly attuned to the mild and peaceful ways of natural growth. Against Gallus's tormented exclamation of willing defeat, "omnia uincit Amor: et nos cedamus Amori" (69), "Love conquers all; so let us too give in to love," the pastoral poet expresses his love for Gallus.

> Gallo, quoius amor tantum mihi crescit in horas
> quantum uere nouo iridis se subicit alnus.                    [73—74]

> [To Gallus, for whom my love grows each hour like the green alder stretching upward in the early spring.]

The poem is like a basket woven of hibiscus; his love is like the sprouting alder: these images suggest that, in contrast to the animal passion of Gallus, the pastoral emotions are gently vegetative; and they furthermore suggest that for the pastoral poet art and love are unified and harmonized through his affinity with nature.

To this extent, then, Gallus's view of the pastoral life is accurate, as is his sense of the pleasures of pastoral art. However, this poem immediately follows one of the most poignant and disturbing poems in the collection. The Ninth Eclogue treats the effects of the land confiscations following the civil war. In it the herdsmen speak of their physical dangers, loss of property, and grief at the ruining of the land they have worked and loved. Their plight is expressed through the fragments of remembered songs they quote to one another, songs of love (to the likes of Galatea and Phyllis) that they can only recall in snippets, songs they cannot finish. When Gallus swears in Eclogue Ten,

> Ibo et Chalcidico quae sunt mihi condita uersu
> carmina pastoris Siculi modulabor auena,                    [50—51]

> [I will go, and the songs I made in Chalcidic verse play on Sicilian shepherd's reed,]

we must accept this as a fervent desire and yet also as a necessary but unwitting fictionalization of the pastoral experience. The pastoral eclogist who gives these words to Gallus understands in what sense they are true. For to a degree they are true. The pastoral lyric, as a formal structure of literary devices and as an expression of harmony with nature, affords ways of containing passions within bearable limits, or ways of transcending mortal torments. Compared with the life Gallus is living, what he says of the pastoral is right. At the same time, however, Vergil the pastoral eclogist (and farmer's son) knows a lot more than Gallus does about the realities of pastoral life. Vergil knows that the pastoral is what it seems to be in Eclogue Ten, but it is not only that. Gallus's torment represents one of the antitheses to pastoral experience, and one of the justifications for pastoral idealization. It is almost the final view of the pastoral in the volume, but it is not the last word; idealization may be necessary, but the pastoral is not necessarily ideal.

Mary Shelley, in *The Last Man*, shows how the pastoral world can be both disdained and envied. Her protagonist is torn between two ways of life, both dead to him: the pastoral (to which he was born and from which he feels himself separated) and the civilized (which he has come to love and which exists no longer). Lionel never sees the pastoral as ideal. Nonetheless, in his despairing last days its scorned simplicity tempts him. That which makes it unworthy of his higher faculties makes it compelling to his most basic emotional needs when they alone seem capable of fulfillment.

The last man's narrative records his alienation from his pastoral surroundings and separation from all those whom he had loved.

> I awoke in the morning, just as the higher windows of the lofty houses received the first beams of the rising sun. The birds were chirping, perched on the window sills and deserted thresholds of the doors. I awoke, and my first thought was, Adrian and Clara are dead. I no longer shall be hailed by their good-morrow—or pass the long day in their society. I shall never see them more. The ocean has robbed me of them. . . . I was an untaught shepherd boy, when Adrian deigned to confer on me his friendship. The best years of my life had been passed with him. All I had possessed of this world's goods, of happiness, knowledge, or virtue—I owed to him. He had, in his person, his intellect, and rare qualities, given a glory to my life, which without him it had never known. Beyond all other beings he had taught me, that goodness, pure and single, can be an attribute of men. [328][16]

This passage turns pastoral motifs inside out. In words like "untaught" and "deigned to confer" the narrator shows the attitude toward sophistication that has separated him forever from the pastoral world and its values. (He recalls with feeling, "All I had possessed of this world's goods.") Through this sophistication he has also learned about "goodness, pure and single," so that here one of the principal attributes of pastoral life is identified instead with the higher, educated standards of Adrian and his society.

As it happens, the narrator's origins actually associate him with both worlds. Lionel Verney is the son of a dissolute, fallen nobleman, whose financial ruin had led him to the countryside and eventually to marriage with "the daughter of a poor cottager." His father's life perfectly fits the picture of court society as it is represented in Renaissance pastoral satire. However, for Lionel, the rustic life he knows first hand cannot compete with the stories his mother tells of his late father's recollections of the court's elegance. For Lionel and his mother, the world of court society is the ideal that they can only imagine; for the father who had actually lived in it, it seems ideal in retrospect, a vision of a past filled with lost delights; the evils are forgotten, and the humble way of life that has given him a refuge pales.

Lionel's view of the herdsman's life accords rather with Fontenelle's and Pope's than with Vergil's or Spenser's.

> I cannot say much in praise of such a life; and its pains far exceeded its pleasures. There was freedom in it, a companionship with nature, and a reckless loneliness; but these, romantic as they were, did not accord with the love of action and desire of human sympathy. . . . I associated with others friendless like myself. . . . Thus untaught in refined philosophy, and pursued by a restless feeling of degradation from my true station in society, I wandered among the hills of civilized England as uncouth a savage as the wolf-bred founder of old Rome. [8–9]

So he sees Romulus, not Tityrus, as his ancestor. For him, the traditional pastoral friendship among equals becomes merely an association of the friendless, devoid of real "sympathy." This is necessarily so because he is not one of them, and because he senses that friendship should be Platonic, requiring spiritual elevation through a soul more highly developed. Sheltered from the temptations that had ruined his father, Lionel is also shut off from society's refinements and tutelage. He values pastoral freedom and closeness with nature but despises the lack of incitements to action and distance from human companionship. Indeed, did he not take himself quite so seriously, he might approve of Touchstone's paradoxical analysis of country and court.

Eventually, when human society becomes lost to him by the disasters that have stranded him as "the last man," Lionel has become so detached from rural pastoralism that he is no longer at home amid the natural environment in which he has grown up. He awakens to the sight of the sun and the sound of the birds but takes no comfort in them; his first thought is of his lost companions. Insofar as this passage begins the last man's equivalent of a pastoral elegy—his "Lycidas" for his friends indeed "sunk beneath the waves"—it is strikingly barren of any real affiliation with nature.

> Many nights, though autumnal mists were spread around, I passed under an ilex—many times I have supped on arbutus berries and chestnuts, making a fire, gypsy-like, on the ground—because wild natural scenery reminded me less acutely of my hopeless state of loneliness. [333]

The landscape is authentically Vergilian, but the speaker feels shut off from it, accepting it almost grudgingly as a partial anodyne. So he must face his separation from nature. He still has the shepherd's eye for natural detail, joined with the educated poet's verbal control; he has the makings of an authentic pastoral poet, and to some extent what he writes is, after all, pastoral. But it is pastoral with an important difference.

> A herd of cattle passed along in the dell below, untended, toward their watering place. . . . Why could I not forget myself like one of those animals, and no longer suffer the wild torment of misery that I endure? Yet, ah! what a deadly breach yawns between their state and mine! [334]

In this respect we are close here to the pastoral lament of the sufferer (usually love-wracked like Colin in *The Shepheardes Calender*) who strives to find in nature an emblem of his grief or a means to comprehend the measure and pattern of his sorrow. But Lionel finds no solace in nature, and his attempt at reconciliation shows how far this shepherd has come from being at home in what was once his natural world.

Following his resentment at the fellowship the cows have, he tries to reject the impulse to curse them, and this leads to his confrontation with a family of goats, those quintessential Theocritean pastoral animals.

> I will discipline my sorrowing heart to sympathy in your joys; I will be happy, because ye are so. Live on, ye innocents, nature's selected darlings; I am not much unlike to you. Nerves, pulse, brain, joint, and flesh, of such am I composed, and ye are organized by the same laws. I have something beyond this, but I will call it a defect, not an endowment, if it leads me to misery, while ye are happy. Just then, there emerged from a near copse two goats and a little kid. . . . I gathered a handful of fresh grass, and held it out. . . . The male stepped forward, fixing his eyes on me: I drew near, still holding out my lure, while he, depressing his head, rushed at me with his horns. I was a very fool; I knew it, yet I yielded to my rage. I snatched up a huge fragment of rock; it would have crushed my rash foe. I poised it—aimed it—then my heart failed me. I hurled it wide of the mark. My little visitants, all aghast, galloped back into the covert of the wood; while I, my very heart bleeding and torn, rushed down the hill, and by the violence of bodily exertion, sought to escape from my miserable self. [334]

Seen in the rich pastoral context of the setting and the speaker's origins, this scene comes close to black comedy. The erstwhile shepherd who ineptly maneuvers himself into a life-and-death confrontation with a billy goat is, through Mary Shelley's handling of pastoral motifs, a fitting image of natural man who has become too sophisticated to be at home in nature again and who can find no comfort in the natural world when human society is denied him. Seeking to make his peace with nature, he violates nature's patterns. Moved by feeling of kinship with creatures "composed" like himself and "organized by the same laws," he tries to disregard that which he has come to learn that he possesses "beyond this." Unfortunately, as Mary Shelley depicts his education, those higher qualities are not formed by human interaction within the pastoral world or by human perceptions formed through life in that world. As a shepherd boy, he was "untaught" not only in knowledge but also in "happiness" and "virtue." To him, the natural world was not pastoral, merely rustic; and when he must look to it for pastoral solace, it turns on him, in the appropriate form of a goat. He is a stranger now to this world and its ways. The little goats, naturally "aghast" at his unpastoral show of "rage," flee from him; he, aghast at his own uncivilized and unnatural response, tries to flee from himself. Mary Shelley's complex view of pastoral experience illuminates human reactions to nature and civilization.

In this chapter we have seen that the pastoral is used to satisfy a number of personal and artistic needs. In the pastoral an author embodies a statement about ideals and satisfactions, about ways of life and attitudes toward experience, about nature and human values. We have seen also that the pastoral is not a simple phenomenon but rather a group of images and attitudes which may appear in any combination. Even a pastoral lyric that is simple in construction and in its creation of an unambiguous pastoral environment may express several aspects of the pastoral. We have also seen that a major function of the pastoral is to express a distinction between experiences. Here, too, great variety is possible. We may be asked to judge the merits of the pastoral experience itself against human needs or the claims of empirical observation or some timeless ideal. The pastoral might be contrasted with cities or wild nature or the bustle of business or the turmoils of unrefined passion or the sophistications of high society. Pastoral attitudes might be rejected at last, or embraced. The pastoral ideal might be already lost, or waiting for us in the future. A view of the pastoral world might occasion a defense or a condemnation of the ordinary way of life or the generally accepted system of values. The complexity and familiarity of pastoral motifs make the pastoral a useful device for signaling attitudes, evoking certain emotions, and defining a way of life.

For these reasons it is not enough to label a work as pastoral or even indicate the appearance of pastoral elements in it. It is far more important to be able to say in what respects the material is pastoral, which of the possible pastoral elements it uses, and how it qualifies or characterizes them, what the structural use of the pastoral material is, how close to the surface are the evocations of pastoral traditions and feelings.

As it develops through history, and writers build on one or another aspect of the pastoral world described (or perhaps one should say created) by Theocritus and Vergil, the pastoral acquires a large set of attributes. Each pastoral work, each work that in some respect creates a pastoral moment, may draw on any number of these attributes. In so doing, it will create a pastoral situation with its own special characteristics. At times the pastoral element may be nothing more than an almost predictable, though evocative, gesture. For instance, when, in *The Great Gatsby*, Nick Carraway joins Tom Buchanan and Myrtle Wilson for their rendezvous in Manhattan, "We drove over to Fifth Avenue, so warm and soft, almost pastoral, on the summer Sunday afternoon that I wouldn't have been surprised to see a great flock of white sheep turn the corner."[18] At other times the reference may be less direct and less easy to limit. Evelyn Waugh's *Brideshead Revisited* does not seem clearly related to traditional pastoral literature; but Waugh's own title for part 1 of the novel is "Et in Arcadia Ego," a phrase full of pictorial and literary resonances. Here it must mean, "I too once lived in Arcadia." Alerted by the author to the controlling image that we might have missed otherwise, we can see in what ways that section is pastoral. It deals with the growth of friendship and homosexual affection; it is concerned predominantly with an artificial and playful society of almost carefree young men whose main interests are literature, entertainment, and comradeship; most of it is set in the sheltered environment of the university, which partially frees the characters from the constraints of their family backgrounds. Furthermore, this retrospective tale is retold in the contexts of the Second World War and the personal disasters that have touched the lives of all these characters, robbing them of their gaiety and culminating in the wretchedly unpastoral death of the "swain." In this setting, the first part of the novel becomes nostalgic, tinged like Vergil's First and Ninth Eclogues with a keen feeling of loss. Recognizing the generic background to this part of the novel means we are better able to understand its internal coherence, its structural function in the novel as a whole, and its dynamic expression of a way of life. These, after all, are the reasons for understanding a genre in the first place.

# 3

## The Pastoral as Genre and Mode

WHEN WE TALK ABOUT PASTORAL LITERATURE, WE ARE GENERALLY TALKING ABOUT works that fit comfortably into the pastoral genre, the general characteristics and history of which are evident enough to most of us. Even if Theocritus's *Idylls* and Guarini's *Il pastor fido* are themselves not widely read now, their titles are familiar and their genealogies have been traced so many times that the history of the pastoral genre from Theocritus to Arnold is well known in rough outline to professional students of literature. Pastoral elements in the work of some twentieth-century authors (Robert Frost, for example) have also been examined. This body of works comprises several familiar types of pastoral poems, characters, devices, and themes. Within the genre of the pastoral are many subgenres: for example, the mourning elegy, the singing contest (often amoebean, consisting of alternating variations for two "singers"), the lover's complaint, the wooing song, the lover's magical spell-weaving, the allegorical praise of a ruler, and rustic satire on contemporary affairs. All of these types have Theocritean or Vergilian precedents; to them one could add a small number of narrative forms stemming mostly from Longus. Some subgenres, like the spell-weaving, have relatively few pastoral descendents. Some come into fashion for a short time because they fit prevailing notions about art and culture and then recede when tastes change, perhaps leaving behind only a rare example of interest and vitality. So, in the Renaissance, extended pastoral allegories dominated religious and political encomia; a large number of poetic song contests were written to display verbal and intellectual wit; and the lover's complaint, which complemented other forms of introspective and self-absorbed art like the sonnet and the love elegy, was also popular. Some forms have long, rich histories. The pastoral mourning elegy, for example, begins with Theocritus's First Idyll and includes a remarkable number of other masterpieces through the centuries.

With such works we are in a familiar generic countryside. We know that they are pastorals because they use their tradition explicitly. Criticism, too, longs for pastoral simplicity, even if that simplicity is but a fictional construction. We are glad to think that the dimensions of pastoral literature can be circumscribed neatly, both in time and in form. With *As You Like It* or Arnold's "Thyrsis" we are still in comfortable generic territory. We may disagree about many points in analyzing these works, but we can be certain that referring to the pastoral tradition in discussing them is empirically justifiable. It will seem appropriate, and it will tell us something about the work in question, if only by giving us a standard by which to measure the work's variances from convention.

Góngora's poem "En los pinares de Júcar," for instance, keeps quite close to the conventional pastoral tradition. The poet clearly intends to show the truly pastoral delights that can be found in real-life rusticity. Góngora does not use the pastoral tradition simply or uncritically: he carefully distinguishes the country girls he writes about from mythological and literary nymphs. However, he is not rejecting or even questioning pastoral images or values, but merely revising their relation to the contemporary and natural landscape, insisting that the pastoral world is not only one created by poets and mythographers.

> En los pinares de Júcar
> vi bailar unas serranas,
> al son del agua en las piedras,
> y al son del viento en las ramas.
> No es blanco coro de ninfas
> de las que aposenta el agua,
> o las que venera el bosque,
> seguidoras de Diana:
> serranas eran de Cuenca,
> honor de aquella montaña,
> cuyo pie besan dos ríos
> por besar de ellas las plantas. [1–12][1]

[Amid the pines of Jucar I saw the girls of the hills dancing to the sound of water on the stones, and the sound of the wind in the boughs. It was no pale bevy of nymphs who make their home in the water, or those the forest worships, followers of Diana; they were country girls of Cuenca, the great honor of that mount, whose foot two rivers kiss to kiss the soles of their feet.]

This passage depicts the perfectly responsive harmony between the dancing girls and nature. It is nature itself that provides the music to which they dance; and just as they bestow honor on the hill on which they tread, so the rivers kiss their feet in tribute.

The following lines of the poem introduce the pastoral theme of friendships bound together by art and also hint at the shadow of change that so often flickers across the pastoral landscape, change that these pastoral maidens join together to shield themselves against, as if their joining hands were a form of mutual protection or a charm against the bad consequences of mutability that makes itself known as the dance of life goes on, as water passes incessantly over the rocks, and the wind blows and shifts, rises or falls.

> Alegres corros tejían,
> dándose las manos blancas
> de amistad, quizá temiendo
> no la truequen las mundanzas. [13–16]

[They wove sprightly dances, crossing their white hands in friendship, perhaps fearing the changes of the changing dance.]

The description of the girls pays tribute to their natural beauty by seeking words from the vocabulary of art and artifice that suggest visual brilliance. The dancing girls visually embody the world of nature but remain examples of purity. Their flower-and-ribbon-bedecked hair reflects the sunlight; their dresses are the color of the sky, "si no son de la esperanza" ("if not that of hope"); they have no desires that require hope, no ambitions to strive for, but exist in the delight of nature itself. Furthermore, they are

> Ellas, cuyo movimiento
> honestamente levanta
> el cristal de la columna
> sobre la pequeña basa. [31–34]

[Those girls who raise in their guileless movements a column of crystal on a tiny base.]

They are as pure as crystal and as lovely as blown glass, free to move with ease, yet modest enough to move "honestly," unlicentiously.

In their midst, like Colin in Book VI of *The Faerie Queene*, piping for the dancing Graces, an artist emerges from their ranks; and nature gives way to her song, which proves to be a celebration of these very girls and the lives that they lead. Clicking her black castanets and thereby making an instrument "que las musas le invidiaran" ("that the muses would envy"),

> las aves enmudeció,
> y enfrenó el curso del agua;
> no se movieron las hojas,
> por no impedir lo que canta. [41–44]

[The birds were silenced and the water stilled in its course; the leaves did not move, not to disturb what she sings.]

Though she silences nature, she does so through music-making appropriate to her pastoral environment, singing to the accompaniment of an instrument that is her nonshepherding equivalent of a reed pipe, her folk instrument made of two pieces of black slate. She sings,

> Serranas de Cuenca
> iban al pinar,
> unas por piñones,
> otras por bailar.                                          [45–48]

[The mountain girls of Cuenca went to the pines, some for pinenuts, some to dance.]

As the words of the song recall the opening of the poem, we recognize that the narrator has taken on the pastoral point of view. He has learned from these pastoral maidens the delights of innocence; he has also learned about the relation between art and nature. Granted, his poem is a more ambitious literary construction than the girl's, but it follows hers in its tone, imagery, and to some extent its literary form. If she is a natural pastoral artist, inspired and taught by her knowledge of nature and human arts, he is a cultured pastoral artist, bringing to the native pastoral art the tribute of sophistication.

As is appropriate to a pastoral lyric, the girl's song also alludes to the role of love in pastoral life and games. While they dance and collect their pinenuts, the maidens toy with tales of love; Cupid himself pleads to the sun to give him eyes so as to see them better. They, as if turning all love and yearning, all pain and desire into sport, prance about on "los ojos del Sol" ("the eyes of the sun"), the spots of sunlight shining on the forest floor. Love is around, but without barbs, without bitterness, without distress. The poem is not only a pastoral but, in the common usage, "idyllic." It finds delight and art in simplicity.

Some works, however, are more problematic in genre. In 1942 Conrad Aiken published a volume of poems entitled *Brownstone Eclogues*. In itself the notion of an urban pastoral is not unique. Not only do certain poems by Theocritus and Vergil have urban settings; in the eighteenth century both John Gay and Lady Mary Wortley Montagu published collections entitled "Town-Eclogues." In these earlier works, however, the characters' names, the imagery, and the diction place the poems explicitly within a pastoral literary context, even when (as in the works by Gay and Montagu) their relation to the tradition is ironic and satirical. Aiken, on the other hand, presents us with a more difficult situation. The snow falling on cars along Doctors' Row, the lady with platinum hair and pink pyjamas sitting outside the roominghouse on Pilgrim Place—such images seem far removed from the familiar, comfortable pastoralism to which Aiken alludes by calling his poems "eclogues."

The critic must assume that the author has used the allusion deliberately. It does little good to rest on the prescriptive understanding of the genre and insist that these are no eclogues. Instead, we should consider how the title helps our reading. Take, for instance, "The Lady in Pink Pyjamas." With her "pencilled eyebrows and masquelike face," she seems very unlike a shepherdess. Indeed, at the beginning of the third stanza Aiken sends us in a rather different direction by quoting Pater's famous sentence about the Mona Lisa: "She is older than the rocks on which she sits." The Mona Lisa is a fitting image for the impassive contemplation that marks the lady in pink pyjamas, and for a seemingly ancient association with the natural background.

> Outside her furnished room on the brownstone stoop,
> alone, yet one of the children, a changing group,
> (children who come to play, and stare, and stay)
> the lady in pink pyjamas waits all day.[2]

The phrase "brownstone stoop" signifies Aiken's urban equivalent to the cottage. His poem develops a description of this life of meager comforts and simple diversions, particularly those of playing, staring, staying, waiting. These may be mostly joyless equivalents of pastoral poetic entertainments; certainly a distance separates them from the leisurely play, meditative relaxation, and sensory gratification enjoyed by pastoral shepherds. Nonetheless, we can see an analogy in the languor and indolence of this private scene.

Another allusion draws us closer to the pastoral mode.

> The aged lioness dreams in the fly-loud zoo,
> the amber eyes look down, they sift you through;
> profound, contemptuous, a slow and amorous glare,
> and something that melts, and sweetens, in that stare.

Behind the first line of this stanza stands Yeats's "Lake Isle of Innisfree," in which the narrator plans to "live alone in the bee-loud glade." Yeats's poem, though devoid of sheep and shepherds, is well within the pastoral tradition. Aiken, evoking it so wryly, seems to remind us that his scene is and is not pastoral. There are important differences, appropriate to the difference between Innisfree and an urban brownstone, between the sweet voice and the hard, masklike eyes, between the Irish poet's poignant vision of his own future and the penetrating stare that sees through yours; yet in her own way the lady in pink pyjamas is like the Tityrus of Vergil's First Eclogue and the Silenus of his Sixth. Sitting in her place, quietly going about her work of dreaming, she is a seer who holds all knowledge frozen in the equipoise of her vision; she "knows them all." Even some of the visual imagery suggests that a pastoral context is appropriate. Sitting "in the sunlight" she stares with "a slow and amorous" look, "something that melts, and sweetens," so that "Deep is the welcome" in her eyes.

It is not a comforting look, to be sure. Nevertheless, though "alone," she is also "one of the children," talking to them with the same open candor with which they seem to take to her. As one of the children, she seems to hold on to some vestige of innocent abandon that persists in spite of her deep knowledge of life. The last stanza affirms this playfulness.

> And—strange!—she has a bicycle, and this too,
> somehow, in Pilgrim Place, looks old, though new.
> She and the children mount it to ride in turns
> as far as the Park, and the statue of Robert Burns.

The bicycle, at once old and new, seems to belong forever to this place, as if it too were part of the timeless scene. It is not a shiny piece of merchandise but already a familiar part of the landscape, comfortably integrated into the life of the community. The lady and the children, as equals, share it unselfishly. The poem concludes by stretching toward the real pastoral as they head for the park; and in their destination, the statue of Burns, we can recognize a tribute to the artistic commemoration of an artistic reworking of folk culture.

Finally, the poem as a whole affectionately depicts the daily life and emotional vitality of people who have no special significance beyond what the artist makes of them. In simple circumstances and with meager possessions, they live intensely, making art of their lives and finding both art and understanding of life from their acquaintance with their natural surroundings.

If one were to take this poem in isolation, without knowing the title of the work from which it comes, one probably would not analyze it within a pastoral context because pastoral motifs are not clearly part of the poem itself. However, recognizing the pastoral associations can help us to perceive its inner form: the emotional, thematic, and imagistic patterns that constitute its total expression.

Aiken's book presents one sort of problem: the text that claims to be pastoral, or claims an affiliation with the pastoral, but does not fit a conventional definition of the genre. There are other sorts of problems to deal with, however, when a work or element in a work seems suggestive of pastoral motifs but is not explicitly linked with the pastoral tradition. Here again the test for the reader ought to be whether or not a reference to the pastoral tradition helps to clarify the thematic or formal issues raised.

Let us consider two German plays written during a time when the idyll (usually set in the mountains) was a popular literary form and there was some interest in redefining the hierarchical relation of nature to society. Schiller's *Kabale und Liebe* takes place in the midst of court machinations and seductions. Luise Miller and her father, a proud and headstrong musician, try to maintain their middle-class integrity and righteousness against the connivances of the girl's aristocratic would-be seducers (even though maintaining their values will mean death). Miller splutters in rage to his wife that:

> Du wirst mir meinen roten plüschenen Rock
> ausbürsten, und ich werde mich bei Seiner
> Exzellenz anmelden lassen. Ich werde sprechen
> zu Seiner Exzellenz: Dero Herr Sohn haben ein
> Aug auf meine Tochter; meine Tochter ist zu
> schlecht zu Dero Herrn Sohnes Frau, aber zu
> Dero Herrn Sohnes Hure ist meine Tochter zu
> kostbar, und damit basta!—Ich heisse Miller."                     [I,i][3]

> [You will brush off my red plush cloak and I shall have myself announced to His Excellency. I shall say to His Excellency, "Your Excellency's son has an eye for my daughter. My daughter is too lowly to be Your Excellency's son's wife. But to be Your Excellency's son's whore, my daughter's too precious. And so much for that! My name's *Miller*."]

From this passage we can see the point of Schiller's subtitle, "Ein bürgerliches Trauerspiel," a bourgeois tragedy. The tension between the two classes, with their differing values—accentuated here by the clash of honorific titles against the climactic, plebian name of the speaker, proud that he is plain and honest—is the basic issue of the play. Luise is at once too lowly and too noble for the man who wants her; her father knows this and is proud of it. This is a version or mode of the tension generated in the pastoral between good country simplicity and haughty urban sophistication, such as we find in Vergil's Second Eclogue and Spenser's "January." For the writer who respects pastoral values, the things of the country might not be good enough to win the respect of refined urbanites, but they are too precious to be squandered on those who cannot or will not appreciate their special qualities.

The bourgeois Millers will not quite pass as "pastoral." However, when we recognize the connection between Schiller's plot and the corresponding pastoral motif, we understand the work a bit better. A complex set of social changes has turned the middle class into a pastoral class, at the same time making the pastoral class the middle class. At least in literature, the middle class now represents those virtues once ascribed to the lower, rural class; the former pastoral class, however, now seems impoverished, degraded, not satisfactorily pastoral. The author's audience, largely middle-class, can see itself as representing the traditional virtuous life and as the traditional victim of a rapacious, powerful, wealthy elite. At the same time, it does not have to locate those ideals in a class remote in geography and social standing, because it senses in its own situation the applicability of a familiar pastoral pattern of oppositions. Although this play records changes in the culture, it is built on a consistent dynamic relationship that places it in a long line of literary works. By recognizing the pastoral background of the conflict, we perceive more clearly the character and dimensions of the struggle within the play.

Lessing's *Emilia Galotti* takes us one step farther away from the pastoral's usual social level. The pastoral virtues are embodied not in a musician but in the army officer Galotti and his daughter, really representatives of the "county" establishment rather than the country. Even higher on the social scale than the Millers, the Galottis seem unlikely choices to be symbolically pastoral figures opposing a corrupt court or town. However, there can be no mistaking the alignment of sensibilities when Galotti remonstrates with his wife, who is unhappy that their daughter's impending marriage will mean that the girl will move to her husband's ancestral estate in a distant mountain valley. The prospect of that move delights the father, who sees it as an ideal life for her. Galotti warns his wife that her protest may cause him again to suspect that it was "mehr das Geräusch und die Zerstreuung der Welt, mehr die Nähe des Hofes" ("more the tumult and hurly-burly of the world, more the closeness to the court") than Emilia's need for a decent education that led his wife to move to the city. His worries about the licentiousness of these circles prove well founded; and Emilia, fearful for the destruction of her pure soul when she is subjected to the hedonistic court culture, commits suicide. Her fate helps us understand why her fiancé (since murdered) had intended to give up his diplomatic career, forsake the society of the leading families at court, and retire to his home in some distant valley with Emilia, who is, the villainous court chamberlain sneers, "Ein mädchen ohne Vermögen und ohne Rang" ("a girl with neither means nor station").[4] To a courtier, she and her family are simple countryfolk.

Such works constitute a mode of the pastoral. Not directly pastoral in their material, they nevertheless embody those attitudes and situations traditionally dealt with in the pastoral, and along lines familiar to the pastoral. One reason why the pastoral has so often been assumed to be a dead form is that its modal continuities may not be easily recognizable for what they are.

Any idyllic scene is at least a modal version of the pastoral. The two are linked throughout their generic histories, and in most societies idyllic moments bear traditionally pastoral qualities. Consider, for example, Walt Whitman's idyll of sunbathing in *Specimen Days*.

> Another day quite free from mark'd prostration and pain. It seems indeed as if peace and nutriment from heaven subtly filter into me as I slowly hobble down these country lanes and across fields, in the good air—as I sit here with Nature—open, voiceless, mystic, far removed, yet palpable, eloquent Nature.[5]

It is significant that this beneficent influence of nature relieves pain. The "good air" marks this spot as not only pleasant but healthful, an antidote to the ills of mortal and societal frailty. Whitman recognizes a sovereign cure in nature.

> Come, ye disconsolate, in whom any eligibility is left—come get the sure virtues of creek-shore, and wood and field. Two months (July and August, '77,) have I absorb'd them, and they begin to make a new man of me. Every day, seclusion—every day at least two or three hours of freedom, bathing, no talk, no bonds, no dress, no books, no *manners*.

Whitman's days are specimen: not merely journal entries, they are directed to a readership in need of enlightenment. What Whitman urges is a way of life less artful and sociable than literary pastoral life usually is, but nonetheless contrasted with the corrupting influences of society and science. "Shall I tell you, reader, to what I attribute my already much-restored health? That I have been almost two years, off and on, without drugs and medicines, and daily in the open air." Nature has not lost its power to heal; we need do nothing to be healed but let clean nature do its work.

This may mean setting art somewhat aside, though not wholly. One can still respond artistically to nature if one is given to respond to experience through art, but in small forms and casual ways appropriate to nature's variety and freedom. "By old habit, I pencill'd down from time to time, almost automatically, moods, sights, hours, tints and outlines, on the spot." In similar fashion one can respond to nature candidly and decently through the influence of the environment rather than social constraints: "no *manners*." Because nature wants no airs to take the place of its own air, there need be no artifice—or, in the terms of older pastoral literature, no courtly artifice.

In the dell, "which I and certain thrushes, catbirds, &c., had all to our-selves," Whitman takes "my Adamic air-bath and flesh-brushing." The adjective "Adamic" does not mean only *naked* here. It also suggests being single and whole, new, fresh in body and spirit, innocent in spirit but nocent of life, akin to all creation, respectful toward the specialness of each element in the world, and instinctively understanding creation's unity.

> Somehow I seem'd to get identity with each and every thing around me, in its condition. Nature was naked, and I was also. It was too lazy, soothing, and joyous-equable to speculate about. Yet I might have thought somehow in this vein: Perhaps the inner never lost rapport we hold with earth, light, air, trees, &c. is not to be realized through eyes and mind only. . . . Perhaps indeed he or she to whom the free exhilarating extasy of nakedness in Nature has never been eligible (and how many thousands there are!) has not really known what purity is—nor what faith or art or health really is.

Harmony with nature, purity, faith, art, health: all these, interpreted as they are by Whitman to coincide with simple directness of behavior and complete simplic-ity of needs and desires, are traditional elements of the pastoral experience. "Nature was naked, and I was also." We are not far from Sidney's "Come Shepheard's weedes, become your master's minde."[6]

Flannery O'Connor's story "A Circle in the Fire" is a more complex and less immediately recognizable modal version of the pastoral. Here the pastoral quali-ties are natural (as in Whitman) rather then societal (as in Schiller).

> "Every day I say a prayer of thanksgiving," Mrs. Cope said. "Think of all we have. Lord," she said and sighed, "we have everything," and she looked around her at her rich pastures and hills heavy with timber. . . . [217][7]

Mrs. Cope's pastoral enclave is, like John of Gaunt's England, an "other Eden, demi-paradise,/A fortress built by nature," but—Mrs. Cope seems to think—for her, rather than for Nature herself. The forest, "a solid gray-blue wall," a "fortress line of trees," is a barrier against an outside world that Mrs. Cope feels constantly threatening, a world of dangers posed by nature as well as by human enterprise. "Oh Lord, do pray there won't be any fires. . . . We might all be destroyed by a hurricane." If indeed "I can always find something to be thankful for," that is because the impending disaster continually holds back.

Mrs. Cope's attitude toward *haec otium*, however, is far from pastoral. She peers at those "hills heavy with timber and shook her head as if it might all be a burden she was trying to shake off her back." One could say that she is in truth a georgic character who pretends toward pastoral equanimity, as if that pretense were her protection against facing the intolerable burdens of her responsibilities for what she thinks of as her property.

> "I have the best kept place in the county and do you know why? Because I work. I've had to work to save this place and work to keep it." She emphasized each word with the trowel. "I don't let anything get ahead of me and I'm not always looking for trouble. I take it as it comes." [217–18]

These assertions, of course, are filled with ironies. Like Horace's Alfius, Mrs. Cope does not so much work as putter while directing the labors of her hired hands. On the other hand, while she might mind her own business and in that respect not look for trouble, she is constantly looking for the trouble that she fears—almost expects—is right around the corner: "I take it as it comes." So must we all; but she hardly feels as free from cares as this remark implies.

Trouble arrives in the form of three boys, one the son of a former employee. Exiled like Meliboeus to a place that will crush the spirit of anyone who has a feeling for nature (a housing project in Atlanta), the boy Powell has been obsessed by his recollections of the farm. Running away from home, he has lured two of his friends to accompany him on this journey back into the Golden Age or onward to the Fortunate Isles. Their journey will turn into a crusade when they find the land of their dreams in the hands of an infidel who, fearful of fires and lawsuits, wants them away from her horses and off her property. "'After all,' she said in a suddenly high voice, 'this is my place.'" Mrs. Cope may claim to believe that "deus nobis haec otia fecit" ("a god has given us this leisure," as Vergil's Tityrus explains in Eclogue I), but she very definitely believes that the land is hers. Against this notion of proprietorship the boys, angels unaware, take their stand; for they have already laid an imaginative claim to some share of the land, as if by divine permission.

> "Hollis said . . . that you didn't want no boys dropping cigarette butts in your woods and he said, 'She don't own them woods,' and Hollis said, 'She does too,' and that there little one he said, 'Man, Gawd owns them woods and her too.' . . . "                [225]

When they finally try to rid themselves of this Eden that they can neither enjoy nor bear to leave, one of the boys imagines his perfect vengeance: "I'd build a big parking lot on it, or something." Through this phrase we perceive urbanization as a form of violence against the pastoral world, executed out of jealous resentment. Powell, however, takes his stand with nature and against nature: he sets the woods on fire. As the smoke rises, Mrs. Cope's daughter, who has over-heard and seen it all, runs from the woods shouting something wholly pre-posterous and yet revealing, for what sticks in her mind is the country dweller's most awesome image of comprehensive violation: "Mama, Mama, they're going to build a parking lot here." In spite of ourselves we probably smile at the allegation, for all its naiveté and visible absurdity; yet we also shrink from the vision it conjures up, a vision we may recognize as too horribly close to the fate of these doomed woods.

Mrs. Cope, archly named, has believed that her protected enclave was something other than what it is: natural, mutable, vulnerable, answerable to forces beyond her control. While piously appreciating that all she looks upon is blessed, she thinks that it is in fact a fortress that she can labor to defend against all dangers. What she sees at the end is a vision of something more than destruction: "She stood taut, listening, and could just catch in the distance a few wild high shrieks of joy as if the prophets were dancing in the fiery furnace, in the circle the angel had cleared for them" (232). She has attempted to take possession of the pastoral world, to make it hers alone. Because of this she has paid a price, first by not being able to enjoy what she had when she had it, and second by being forced to give up the stewardship that she interprets as ownership.

Many more modal than generic examples of the pastoral occur in literature of the last two centuries. Previously the conventional pastoral genre was still accepted as artistically supportable, though not without some critical demurrals. However, the general feeling that the form had played itself out did not mean that the perceptions and feelings the form once embodied were similarly exhausted. These continued, and required artistic expression in some manner. What resulted was a body of pastoral literature in new artistic patterns, with slightly different images and nomenclature but similar relationships and values. For instance, Pippa in Robert Browning's play punctuates the work with a little pastoral interlude at each appearance; and her famous song touchingly asserts an innocent pastoral vision of natural and divine order.

> The year's at the spring,
> And day's at the morn;
> Morning's at seven;
> The hill-side's dew-pearl'd;
> The lark's on the wing;
> The snail's on the thorn;
> God's in His heaven—
> All's right with the world![8]

In the world of this play, everything is far from right. Pippa's assurance, however, usefully challenges the other characters' views of things. She is there because Browning needs her as a vital counterpoint to the main action. Although her song is not, narrowly defined, a pastoral lyric, devoid as it is of sheep and goats, it serves in this play the way a pastoral interlude would, introducing qualities similar to those traditionally represented by pastoral idylls.

Earlier literary works also contain modally pastoral moments. Again, the usefulness of seeing them as pastoral will depend primarily on the interests and discretion of the individual reader. For instance, in the *Iliad*, Book Fourteen, when an overwhelming desire for Hera distracts Zeus from the war, he withdraws from the arena of national events and human destinies in search of private pleasures, a tryst amid the flowers.

> . . . There
> underneath them the divine earth broke into young, fresh
> grass, and into dewy clover, crocus and hyacinth
> so thick and soft it held the hard ground deep away from them.
> There they lay down together and drew about them a golden
> wonderful cloud, and from it glimmering dew descended.
>
> [p. 303]

One might well argue that this is a pastoral interlude for Zeus but not for Hera, who knows that during their lovemaking and postcoital sleep Poseidon will intervene on behalf of the Greeks. Even she, nonetheless, seems to give in to the pleasure of the moment. Certainly for Zeus, and perhaps for the poem's audience as well, this lovely moment effectively brings the narrative action, the rush of events to a halt and slips us into the enjoyment of love and physical nature and even poetic lyricism. The scene and the text that embodies it are there to be enjoyed for their beauty, even as Hera is for Zeus. In this moment and this place, arranged by the two gods for themselves, the divinities find pleasure and peace with one another as woman and man. Their political bickering and tamperings with grand plans for nations and people are set aside temporarily for private delight. In some respects this passage is not at all pastoral; in others, it is the quintessence of pastoralism.

Shakespeare's *Tempest* is filled with modal examples of the pastoral, some of which we can briefly set forth. It is easy to understand why this play should be so closely related to pastoral literature. It is, to begin with, about the virtues and faults of the retired life. Prospero discovered both, as a ruler who tried to absent himself from the cares of state in order to devote himself to isolated study and the cultivation of magic—his "art," as he calls it. (Granted, his art is not the same as a pastoral singer's or eclogist's, but the analogy is not without point.) He develops this art to an extraordinary degree of refinement, but at the cost of isolating himself from the world of action, which is also a world vulnerable to evil. This evil, as it turns out, can destroy his idyll. But Prospero, seemingly favored by the gods and by one good man who respects him, undergoes a peculiar form of expulsion from his enclave. He is made yet more isolated, totally removed from the social setting. He suffers the consequences of his own preference for a way of life by being cast upon an island, where he can attempt to deal with his retirement.

There he confronts nature in the raw and primitivism in the form of Caliban, the far-from-noble savage whose undisciplined impulses, held in check only by force, mock pastoral naturalness. There too he encounters Ariel, the active force of the imagination that also requires human discipline in order to help create art. In pastoral terms, Ariel is that spirit in nature that inspires and helps one create, but only if one has the artistic ability to direct inspiration into art. Prospero also has Miranda, his daughter, a human being who will be raised and protected amid a luxurious natural setting filled with wondrous music but affording limited human contact. Her knowledge of what we would call the world is provided by the three creatures who constitute her isolated, rural, and apparently self-sufficient society. She is the pastoral queen of this enclave, living in what can be for her a sort of Golden Age, an Eden of leisure and integrity. Like many of her literary ancestors, including Shakespeare's own Perdita, this pastoral queen is a genuine princess by birth. It is no wonder that her first sight of that sorry batch of evildoers, dressed in Italian Renaissance splendor and generically classifiable as "noblemen," causes her to exclaim, with goodness of heart and narrowness of experience, "O brave new world" (V, i, 183), to which the most appropriate response is Prospero's, "'Tis new to thee.'" Having been raised in what is indeed a new world, she takes it for granted. Shakespeare's scenario thereby opens questions about some basic pastoral issues concerning contemplation and action, privacy and society, nature and nurture.

In Act II, scene 1, the shipwrecked nobles consider the brave new world on which they have landed. As Shakespeare suggests, it is what they make of it, given their varying natures. To those cynics whose imaginations are fully tainted, it is an abominable desert wilderness; to the rare good men whose souls come nearer in perfection to Prospero's, it is a verdant piece of perfection.

> *Adrian.* The air breathes upon us here most sweetly.
> *Sebastian.* As if it had lungs, and rotten ones.
> *Antonio.* Or as 'twere perfum'd by a fen.
> *Gonzalo.* Here is everything advantageous to life.

> *Antonio.* True; save means to live.
> *Sebastian.* Of that there's none, or little.
> *Gonzalo.* How lush and lusty the grass looks! how green!
> *Antonio.* The ground, indeed, is tawny.
> *Sebastian.* With an eye of green in 't. [45–53]

Sebastian's last line is admittedly problematic, but perhaps he means that the only green to be seen here is the brown earth's presumed green eye of envy for greener pastures, a fitting comment for this ruthless conspirator, who can see nothing green in this new world.

The good Gonzalo, on the other hand, imagines founding an ideal commonwealth on the island.

> . . . no kind of traffic
> Would I admit; no name of magistrate;
> Letters should not be known; riches, poverty,
> And use of service, none; contract, succession,
> Bourn, bound of land, tilth, vineyard, none;
> No use of metal, corn, or wine, or oil;
> No occupation; all men idle, all;
> And women too, but innocent and pure!
> . . . . . . . . . . . . . . . . . . . . . .
> All things in common Nature should produce
> Without sweat or endeavor. . . .
> . . . Nature should bring forth
> Of its own kind, all foison, all abundance,
> To feed my innocent people.
> . . . . . . . . . . . . . . . . .
> I would with such perfection govern, sir,
> T'excel the Golden Age. [II, i, 148–67]

Gonzalo's program is a bravura compendium of motifs from literary praises of the pastoral life, suggestive of the Golden Age fantasy in Vergil's Fourth Eclogue and similar in outlook to Whitman's "no talk, no bonds, no dress, no books, no *manners.*" Through its obvious excesses, and through the sardonic punctuating comments of Sebastian and Antonio, Shakespeare ridicules Gonzalo's notions while letting us appreciate their attractiveness. As Gonzalo ought to know, he is in the very presence of men who not only mock his fantasy but would make a mockery of his notion that good governance alone could create the Golden Age for what he imagines as "my innocent people" (160). Indeed, these are the very men who overthrew Prospero after he had created a dukedom that came very close, if not to the Golden Age, at least to civil perfection. There is a difference, this scene suggests, between idyllic fantasies and pragmatic realities. While it may be pleas-urable to imagine living where Nature brings forth all things, "all abundance," without human effort, it is necessary to take into account people like Antonio, whose commentary on this social vision is, "all idle; whores and knaves." On a less sophisticated level (but in terms more literally invoking pastoral literary motifs) Gonzalo articulates Prospero's earlier error.

Later Prospero creates a betrothal masque for Miranda and Ferdinand. In this masque the speaking parts belong to Iris, the celestial messenger; Juno, divinity of marriage; and Ceres, goddess of abundant harvest. Iris's opening speech described Ceres' realm as a very image of the world Gonzalo imagined:

> Ceres, most bounteous lady, thy rich leas
> Of wheat, rye, barley, vetches, oats, and pease;
> Thy turfy mountains, where live nibbling sheep
> And flat meads thatch'd with stover, them to keep;
> Thy banks with pioned and twilled brims,
> Which spongy April at thy hest betrims,
> To make cold nymphs chaste crowns. . . .          [IV, i, 60–66]

Ceres, in blessing the young couple, wishes this sort of life for them, perhaps not incidentally using the same unusual word (*foison*) that Gonzalo himself had used and defined (II, i, 159).

> Earth's increase, foison plenty,
> Barns and garners never empty;
> Vines with clust'ring bunches growing;
> Plants with goodly burthen bowing;
> Spring come to you at the farthest
> In the very end of harvest!
> Scarcity and want shall shun you;
> Ceres' blessing so is on you.          [IV, i, 110–17]

The performance properly concludes with a dance of Naiads and sicklemen, goddesses and harvesters, as the divine and natural worlds join in a rhythmic union.

About this masque we need to make two observations. The first is that it makes no claims to be anything other than what it is: a play put on by spirits that Prospero has conjured "by mine Art . . . to enact/My present fancies" (IV, i, 120). While Prospero's control over this well-circumscribed environment might make the island seem, as Ferdinand says, "Paradise" (124), Prospero understands that what the masque expresses is not immediate actuality but his desires for his daughter's future. Representing the orderly process of earthly fruition, Ceres wishes that the harvest time of the young couple will be succeeded not by the winter, which we all know must come, but by another spring; that their harvest season will carry on until the next season of new beginnings. The masque is inspired by love and created by art; it is neither more nor less real than that. Prospero himself has no illusions about the pragmatic, human limitations on this "most majestic vision" (118) of spirits that can dissolve into thin air.

Second, Ceres, goddess of the harvest, and the "sunburn'd sicklemen, of August weary" (134), belong not narrowly to the pastoral world but to the georgic. The universe depicted in the masque is idyllic; but impinging on it is its creator's consciousness of change, of reaping at the end of time, and of the effort required to make natural goodness available for human society. All of these he himself has learned through the practical experiences of his own life.

*The Tempest* is certainly not pastoral in the way that *As You Like It*, Fletcher's *Faithful Shepherdess*, Tasso's *Aminta*, or even Milton's *Comus* are. Its setting and characters are alien to the pastoral world that we have come to know through more traditional pastoral works. Although it has a number of characteristics in common with Renaissance pastoral tragicomedy, its differences from them are so striking that it can hardly be described as a typical example of this genre. But the play as a whole is certainly a version or mode of pastoral literature, and many of its elements are modal versions of pastoral motifs. The variations that Shakespeare works on pastoral material suggest his reservations about pastoral ideas and, for that matter, pastoral literary devices. Still, he perceives the essential value of the pastoral for expressing ideals, and for allowing a confrontation of basic opposing ideas about human nature, our relations with the natural world, and our social relations with one another.

To study a genre is to make definitions and distinctions, to draw similarities and differences that will enhance our comprehension of a text and deepen our understanding of the ways and functions of literature. Though nymphs and shepherds now dance less frequently than they previously did, the pastoral remains a major component in literature because the needs and desires that once found shape in the poetic images of Theocritus, Longus, and Vergil still exist. The literary genre of the pastoral is not dead; it continues in individual works by writers who value and make use of the allusive power of the form. But the pastoral continues, perhaps as widely as ever but disguised, in modal forms, in films and literature that deal with life and structure life in the ways that the pastoral has done for centuries. We may not choose to call these pastoral; the label itself is unimportant. But we will impoverish our understanding and our imaginations if we fail to perceive the connection between these modes of perception and expression and those of pastoral art.

# 4

## *Pastoral Insets*

IN MANY PASTORAL WORKS (INCLUDING MOST ECLOGUES), THE ENVIRONMENT, THE characters, and indeed the entire scope of reference are entirely pastoral; any conflicts or complexities arise from tensions within the pastoral setting, not between it and some external way of life. Frequently, however, the pastoral is shown to exist within a nonpastoral universe, as an inset within a larger frame of reference. Some of the most interesting pastoral texts fall into this broad category.

There are two general types of insets. One is explicit, where a pastoral place or experience is set within and distinguished from an extensively portrayed unpastoral context. This type includes the pastoral scenes within epics, romances, novels, and plays. The second type is the implicit inset, which merely suggests the existence of an unpastoral context. This type includes works using a sophisticated narrator whose knowledge and range of reference indicate existence outside the pastoral world, as well as works in which obviously nonpastoral personages (like religious figures, rulers, or usurers) are treated in pastoral terms.

To see first how the explicit inset works, let us begin with the pastoral interlude in the first act of Wagner's opera *Tannhäuser*. At the quiet beginning of the third scene, following the great passion and musical intensity of the Venusberg sequence, a shepherd appears. His arrival is signaled by sheepbells and an orchestral passage lightly scored for strings, clarinet, and offstage English horn representing the shepherd's pipe. The role of the shepherd is given to a lyric soprano, whose vocal timbre should suggest youth and purity, in contrast to the sensual and dynamic qualities of Venus, a dramatic soprano or high mezzo. The shepherd sings joyfully about "Frau Hold," whose name, from the German *hold*, implies beauty of appearance and temperament; it is Holda whose gracious descent from the mountains, bringing on springtime, gladdens his heart and inspires his song.[1] Next, pilgrims enter on their way to Rome, singing of Christ and the Virgin as they look ahead to redemption; the cheerful shepherd wishes them luck and asks them to pray for his soul. Tannhäuser, having rejected the carnal, cloying splendors of the Venusberg grotto, stands in this beautiful valley, penitent and prayerful, sensing the twofold contrast: between the goddess Venus and the Blessed Virgin, as well as between Venus and the shepherd's loving spring goddess, Holda. Significantly, the shepherd, despite his love for nature, recognizes a superior spiritual meaning in the pilgrims' journey. By asking for their prayers, he tacitly acknowledges that he lives in a double world of nature and grace but understands these worlds as hierarchical, not dualistic. The shepherd's joyful song and earnest entreaty to the pilgrims, expressing natural and spiritual innocence, contrasts with Tannhäuser's feelings of corruption and guilt following his erotic indulgences. As Tannhäuser finally prays, he responds directly to the pilgrims' devotion; but the shepherd's pleasant song has been a vital catalyst, expressing the simple pleasure that Tannhäuser has lost, a contentment with nature that seems accessible only to one whose life is clean and who clearly understands nature's place within a divinely ordered universe.

An explicit inset perforce interrupts the flow of a work. Such an interruption may constitute a diversion from the main direction of the work or a counterforce to the main movement; so it can represent an obstacle or even a direct challenge to the course of the main action. A further example is the sojourn of Calidore among the shepherds in *The Faerie Queene* (VI, ix, and x). During this interlude the knight of courtesy, smitten by the easy life the shepherds lead in the woods and by the quintessential beauty of Pastorella, listens with "greedy eare" to the aged Meliboee's praise of the country life's advantages over the courtly and then decides that he can and will join them, because "in each mans self . . . It is, to fashion his owne lyfes estate" (VI, ix, 31). Calidore thereby declares himself a private man, free of public responsibilities and devoid of commitments to anyone but himself. He initially claims that he wants only to "rest my barcke," but shortly afterward the narrator implies that this is merely a deception, either of himself or his host: "from henceforth he meanes no more to sew / His former quest, so full of toils and paine" (VI, x, 2). In becoming a private person, he turns his back on the life of romance and epic heroism.

Calidore, however, is not at home in the pastoral world and does not fully understand it. He stoops to conquer, trying to play the part of a herdsman, but clearly is out of place. Pastorella graciously does what she can to make his unaccustomed bucolic chores easy for him; but still he is a stranger, and as such he cannot even properly display the virtue he tries to exemplify—courtesy—because he does not know the rules here. So when he comes upon the chief musician of the pastoral world, the shepherd Colin, who is playing for a bevy of dancing deities, Calidore clumsily intrudes upon the scene, whereupon all the goddesses vanish from his profane sight, leaving Colin forlorn. Calidore does not understand, though Meliboee does without fully appreciating, that this pastoral world is specially privileged; it is not a club that one can join, but a society that one either is or is not part of.

Because he remains a stranger in this world, he is able to fight for it as it cannot fight for itself. These private people to whom all comes, who prosper while "The little that I haue, growes dayly more / Withouten my care" (VI, ix, 21), as

Meliboee expresses it, lack the means to protect themselves, just as they lack the means significantly to affect their own circumstances. God, Meliboee says, provides for them, so they are without any particular public means of support. Unfortunately, they become the victims of lawless people who live without a sense of public responsibility. Calidore must take up his sword again.

If the pastoral world is attractive, and it is, it is also a world set apart and not accessible to those who merely come to reside in the country. What is attractive about it comes from within. Further, the pastoral world, and the characters within it, are not devoid of faults, "cowherd" fear among them; and those faults can be ignored only so long as the pastoral world is permitted to constitute a fictive universe not violated by either higher or lower forces that will reveal the shortcomings or the points of vulnerability.

Finally, despite the real pleasures of participating in pastoral life, that participation is not necessarily beneficial. Calidore does find virtue there, but his stay amongst the shepherds does not directly promote virtue in him. He is forced to resume his quest and regain his previously cultivated virtue only when the pastoral world that he has enjoyed is destroyed, so he must attempt to rescue the remnants from dishonor and death. Thus, only by its failure does the pastoral world improve Calidore. In itself, it blocks his development without giving him the gratifications he sought, since he remains an outsider in spirit, a stranger in their midst.

As a moment set apart, an interlude can also crystallize the main experience, perhaps showing what is most perfect or pleasurable about it or schematizing its complexities. Camões, for instance, uses a pastoral scene to express the rewards of his heroes in *The Lusiads*. On an island prepared by Venus and Cupid, in a lovely valley luxuriant with fruit trees, gorgeous flowers, singing birds, and romping animals, flirtatious Nereids wait to be ravished by the explorers, who are to be their mates. So that we shall not mistake this for a victorious orgy of wild self-indulgence and unrestrained rape, the narrator explains that this is an allegory. (Readers familiar with the actualities of colonialism will need to suspend disbelief.)

> For Tethys, the so lovely ocean-nymphs, the magic island with its rich colorings, all are but symbols of the honors, delightful in themselves, that can make life sublime. The thrilling exaltation to the heights, the triumphs, the brow garlanded with palm and laurel, the glory and the wonder of it all, these are the island's joys.[2]

Those joys, therefore, are what the epic is about. If they look suspiciously material and sensual to us, they are nonetheless scaled to the values represented in the voyages the poem celebrates. Camões understands how easy it is for the mistake to be made. When the old man of Lisbon denounces ambition as he watches the Portuguese fleet set sail from the harbor at the end of canto 4, and when the narrator at the end of canto 6 praises as true heroism and nobility the willingness to endure hardship, to suffer and to sacrifice oneself for the common good, the poet knows that there is a thin line between grasping for rewards and accepting rewards for merit. He also knows that if the price of glory is physical deprivation, then the reward of glory must be portrayed in physical terms, even if in some mystical sense they are not supposed to be physical at all, or at least not merely physical. The pastoral island setting does what it is supposed to do by means of its bountiful flora and obliging nymphs: justifies what the heroes have endured.

These two uses of the pastoral inset—as counterforce and as quintessence— coalesce when Milton, in Book IV of *Paradise Lost*, portrays Adam and Eve before the Fall in the original paradisial landscape. That description is doubly tinted. First, we see it as Satan sees it; that is, our first sustained view of earthly paradise comes as a description of what Satan sees as he explores the newly created world. All that is described is already overshadowed by his presence, known to us but not to Adam and Eve. Milton's language, ever-subtle, works through the implications of this situation by wordplay. "So pass'd they naked on, nor shunn'd the sight / Of God or Angel, for they thought no ill" (IV, 319–20). They do not know, though we do, that they are in fact within the sight of an angel, albeit a fallen one, to whom their nakedness is a sign of their grandeur, innocence, tempting physical loveliness, and (at least to Satan's thought) vulnerability. The phrase "they thought no ill" comments on both their pure thoughts and their ignorance of their dramatic situation; they think no evil, and they think there is no evil around them.

Second, the entire poem is being narrated, we are continually reminded, by an inheritor of the consequences of the Fall, who perceives around him the effects of the Fall not only in his own life but in the world at large. So the narrator describing the scene is aware of the contrast between then and now.

> Then was not guilty shame: dishonest shame
> Of Nature's works, honor dishonorable
> Sin-bred, how have ye troubled all mankind
> With shows instead, mere shows of seeming pure,
> And banish't from man's life his happiest life,
> Simplicity and spotless innocence. [IV, 313–18]

The ensuing depiction of paradise shows not only what is there but what we can see.

The picture of Eden in its primal purity reminds us in both general and specific ways of what we have lost. When Milton writes, "Sporting the Lion ramp'd, and in his paw / Dandl'd the kid" (344), he invites our experiential understanding of this as an image of "spotless innocence" but also evokes our recognition of the messianic prophesy in Isaiah 11 : 6, itself a reminder of our present state of woe and therefore also a reminder of the course of events that brought it upon us. Further,

> . . . th'unwieldy elephant
> To make them mirth us'd all his might, and
> wreath'd
> His lithe proboscis; close the serpent sly
> Insinuating, wove with Gordian twine
> His braided train, and of his fatal guile
> Gave proof unheeded.                    [IV, 345–50]

The innocent elephant, all of whose might is used to make joy, and the still innocent but untrustworthy snake are bound together visually by the sinuous motion they have in common; that motion, expressed by the elephant's trunk, arouses by association the image of the serpent and its deviousness, for the narrator and we are now separated from "simplicity." This separation has occurred through the train of events explored in the poem. Those events reach a critical stage as Satan literally appears in Eden and sin's effects appear figuratively in the poem's images and sinuous verse.

We recognize that the moment *was* idyllic for the two people and the animals, who "now fill'd with pasture gazing sat, / Or bedward ruminating" (351–52). At the same time we recognize that the structure of the poem, and of the experience as well, disrupts the idyll for everyone else: Satan, God, the narrator, the reader. This scene presents an idealized pastoral enclave within the complexly tense ironic pastoral setting. Adam and Eve's first appearance disrupts the rush of major action for Satan, the ironic epic protagonist, who pauses to admire and study them; their calm of mind contrasts strikingly with what we have seen and what has been foreshadowed during the first three books. In this scene idealization and counteraction coexist.

In the sheepshearing festival of *The Winter's Tale* Shakespeare even more complexly works with the structural possibilities of the pastoral inset. To begin with, the situation is complicated dramaturgically. Perdita, raised as a shepherdess but by birth a princess, is embarrassed because she believes that it is foolish presumption to so bedeck the mere shepherdess she takes herself to be. She protests that she is a "poor lowly maid, / Most goddess-like prank'd up" (IV, iv, 9–10). With a royal sense of propriety, therefore, she expresses an appropriately pastoral notion of modest decorum. Florizel, on the other hand, is a prince who knows he is a prince but has, as Perdita says, "Your high self . . . obscur'd / With a swain's wearing" (7–9) in order to court the mere shepherdess, whom he sees as "no shepherdess, but Flora / Peering in April's front" (2–3). The pastoral and courtly merge into one another from both directions, each contributing virtues to the other. Further, in this inset Perdita's ease with the natural order of life contrasts strikingly with the suspicion and jealousy previously depicted in the royal palaces.

To Perdita, the pastoral world that she knows is lowly, though superficially pleasant; and though she adds luster to it, she herself believes firmly in the proper order of nature and society, seeing fitness in all, and therefore is troubled by the prince's love for her. To Florizel, Perdita is a queen crowned by nature, if not yet by society. (Perdita's pastoral naiveté keeps her not only innocent but modest, so that she cannot perceive the royalty in herself that is so clear to Florizel.) Her apparently natural grace, freshness, candor, and delicate judgment are special to the pastoral world and rightly warrant his devotion.

This inset, however, it not isolated neatly from the outside world. The festival itself is penetrated by King Polixenes and Lord Camillo, who, like Milton's Satan in the garden, will overshadow and at last destroy the mood of pastoral bliss. To Polixenes and Camillo, who see pastoralism as ignoble and therefore corrupt, Perdita is a "fresh piece / Of excellent witchcraft" (423–24)— like the spellweavers of Theocritus's Second Idyll and Vergil's Eighth Eclogue, presumably—and Florizel, "base." For the audience, this inset confirms our impression of courtly viciousness and insensitivity but affirms that natural goodness exists and can survive hostility. The pastoral scene promises a fresh start. The fusion of natural and social values that takes place within it points toward the reconciliation that is still possible in the play's outer structure. In this dramatic enclave, where a loving prince can become a mere shepherd and a shepherd-princess a festival queen, we find a world of guileless generosity that represents that Golden Age the feuding kings once knew and lost, and which they must strive to recover for their own peace of mind.

The implicit inset is distinguished from the explicit by degree and by structural technique. (The distinction may be difficult to make at times and should not be insisted on so rigorously that the critical usefulness of the concept is lost.) The explicit inset clearly sets apart the two spheres of pastoral and nonpastoral, and treats each fully enough to be knowable in its own terms; the implicit inset, rather, suggests knowledge of another way of life which the pastoral has surpassed or prevailed against.

For instance, Wordsworth's "Lines Composed a Few Miles above Tintern Abbey" clearly implies differences between the countryside the poet is revisiting and the city he has left, but we do not know that urban world in the same immediate way that we know Wagner's Venusberg. Wordsworth remembers the "lonely rooms," the "din / Of towns and cities," "evil tongues / Rash judgments, . . . the sneers of selfish men," and "greetings where no kindness is," as well as "the dreary intercourse of daily life," but these occur as passing moments of sad awareness in the midst of "this green pastoral landscape."[3] Of course, they are important remembrances; they give energy and significance to the entire experience and constitute the unspoken moving force behind the opening exclamation, "Five years have past; five summers, with the length / Of five long winters!" Through them, the pastoral world is implicitly set within a wider world that differs from it and contributes to its significance.

Explicit pastoral insets place a small pastoral moment or scene within a larger, nonpastoral context. "Tintern Abbey," on the other hand, does just the reverse. This is only in part a function of the poem's occasion, though surely that is an important aspect: the poet is concerned more with the immediately and imaginatively real pastoral scene before his eyes than with the busy world he has left. Even more is it a structural function of the way that all experience impresses itself on the speaker's mind. While there is a clear contrast between the poet's two worlds, they cannot easily by separated from one another. Much as the daffodils of his famous lyric appear to his mind's eye long after he has left the valley in which he saw them, so too the views from the banks of the Wye have remained: not

> As is a landscape to a blind man's eye;
> But oft, in lonely rooms, and 'mid the din
> Of towns and cities, I have owed to them,
> In hours of weariness, sensations sweet,
> Felt in the blood, and felt along the heart;
> And passing even into my purer mind,
> With tranquil restoration. . . .           [24–30]

The pastoral world remains somewhere within, once one has experienced it; it is present within, even when not visible without. Therefore, for Wordsworth in this poem there can be no real structural dichotomy between the two worlds. Wordsworth has felt the pastoral spirit within a setting that seems to exclude it by its contrary nature. The recollections of the busy and unfriendly world in Wordsworth's poem do not develop into a full-scale portrait of urban life partly because for him there can be no real separation between himself and the pastoral world. For all its assertive reality, for all "the heavy and the weary weight" (39), the outside remains an "unintelligible world" (40), offering no firm meaning to the "purer mind."

Even in the most idyllic landscape we are likely to catch a recollection of the world excluded by the pastoral, and thereby to see the pastoral as an implicit inset. Indeed, as we have noted, one of the central paradoxes of the pastoral is that those best able to appreciate it and those best able to express their appreciation are not themselves *of* the pastoral world. Even if they once were, they likely are no longer; so the pastoral is almost inevitably defined partly by what it is not, in addition to what it is. This passage from Gabrielle de Coignard illustrates how consciousness of the nonpastoral environment lingers even amidst idealization.

> Mon Dieu, le grand plaisir de voir sur l'herbe
>     paître
> La frisée brebis portant son agnelet,
> Et le cornu bélier, qui marche tout seulet
> Au devant du troupeau, comme patron en maître.
> L'air est délicieux, sans pluies ni chaleurs,
> Un petit vent mollet fait ondoyer les fleurs,
> Les bois portent encor leur superbe couronne;
> L'on n'oit point la rumeur d'un vulgaire babil,
> Sinon des oiselets le ramage gentil:
> Loué soit l'Éternel qui tous ces beins nous donne.[4]

> [My God, such a pleasure it is to see grazing in the meadow the fleecy ewe pregnant with her lamb, and the horned ram, who strides in solitary grandeur at the front of the flock, as its head and master. The air is delicious, without rain or heat; a soft little breeze makes the flowers nod; the woods again bear their glorious crown; there is no chatter of vulgar babble, only the gentle warbling of birds: Praise be to the Eternal, who has given us so much good.]

Although the poem is not structured as a series of contrasts, the first stanza quoted suggests that contrasts seem unavoidable. References to the climate indicate that this is more idyll than objective description of rural actualities; but the phrase "vulgar babble" clearly marks this as an aristocrat's interpretation of natural "eloquence." It is not enough to notice the delights themselves; one also records, perforce, how they differ from more common experience. Further, Coignard does not merely see the countryside: she sees a *pastoral* countryside, not to be confused with the clownish countryside scorned by Voltaire and laughed at by Shakespeare through the characters of Audrey and William in *As You Like It*. Wordsworth, in "Tintern Abbey," knows precisely what he means when he refers without redundancy or contradiction to "these pastoral farms." Wordsworth, though, would not countenance the possibility that the pastoral farms might be inhabited by mere rubes; Coignard does, and in a deft phrase removes her pastoral world from both base "civilization" and base rusticity.

"*Walde-Idylle*" by Eduard Mörike uses several instances of implicit insets to praise and place the pastoral world.

> Unter die Eiche gestreckt, im jung belaubten Gehölze
> Lag ich, ein Büchlein vor mir, das mir das lieblichste bleibt.    [1–2][5]

> [Stretched out beneath the oak, in the fresh new-leafed woods, I lie with a little book that still remains my favorite.]

Like Tityrus, he is *recubans sub tegmine*, but the book he is reading sets him apart from the piping shepherd who is truly a pastoral character and marks him as someone enjoying pastoral pleasures as a diversion. The book is nonetheless appropriate to the moment. Unlike Petrarch scaling Mount Ventoux with a copy of Augustine or Thoreau settling in at Walden Pond with the *Iliad*,

> Alle die Märchen erzählt's, von der Gänsemagd und vom Machandel—
> Baum und des Fischers Frau; warhlich man wird sie nicht satt.
> Grünlicher Maienschein warf mir die geringelten Lichter
> Auf das beschattete Buch, neckische Bilder zum Text.    [3–6]

> [It tells all the stories, about the Goose Girl and the Juniper Tree and the Fisherman's Wife—truly one could never exhaust its pleasures. May's greenness cast itself in rings of light onto the shadowed book, playful illustrations of the text.]

Not Theocritus (whom Mörike had translated) or Homer, but Grimm: much could be written about the cultural attitudes that would make this the appropriate bucolic text for Mörike's idyll; but here it is sufficient to say that in the midst of the real wooded landscape the poet immerses himself in what he takes to be real folk art. This is different from what he creates in his idyllic but not "pastoral" poem. He is in the country but not of it, and makes no pretense now to be of it. Yet he sees the light of the woodland itself as the appropriate illumination of the folktales, which also derive from the life and lore of the country, and the proper substance of his more polished art.

Into the scene first comes a neighbor's younger daughter, who innocently joins the poet while he begins one of the more dramatic tales, "Snow White," with its artful contrast of the dwarfs' untutored goodness toward the innocent princess with the jealous queen's villainous court intrigue. This story further suggests why the woodland holds us in its easy grasp. The woods' natural beauty and receptivity are recorded in the poem's opening lines; its clear, evergreen mythic tales grip the imagination and refresh us in art, even as the forest itself refreshes us in life. Its healthy innocence is an antidote to the mean-spiritedness of more cultured society. As for the little girl, "Müssig lief es in Wald, weil es den Vater dort weiss" ("She runs idly into the woods, for she knows her father is there").

Suddenly a nightingale sings.

Wie wenn die Göttinnen eine, vorüberfliehend, dem Dichter
Durch ambrosischen Duft ihre Begegnung verrät.          [39–40]

[As if one of the goddesses, flying above, had revealed her presence to the poet through an ambrosial scent.]

"The gods themselves with us do dwell." Here again the natural surroundings merge with the story to suggest, now on an even more exalted plane, the moving piety within the woods. And though here the poet must let the goddess pass (involved as he is with a secondary engagement with art, not through creation but through his enjoyment of someone else's story, and with life), the knowledge that she is there remains. At last the older sister appears, "Rüstig . . . bräunliche Dirne" ("the ruddy, tanned wench"), bringing her father a simple repast. The younger girl and the poet follow, though "Statt des Kindes wie gern Hätt' ich die Schwester geführt!" ("Instead of the child I would much rather have led the sister!") This healthy, earthy sensuality seems Theocritean and appropriately recalls that, when pastoral deals with love's frustrations, those frustrations are as often sexual as they are romantic.

In an address to the friend to whom the poem is dedicated, Mörike pays tribute to the creative power of the muse who, ages ago, inspired the folktales they both love.

Ihr Feld ist das Unmögliche: keck, leichtfertig verknüpft sie
Jedes Entfernteste, reicht lustig dem Blöden den Preis.          [57–58]

[Her territory is the impossible: impetuous, reckless, she ties together everything remote, heartily bestows the prize on a simpleton.]

He, too, feels attracted to a life that is opposite to his normal one, and to this girl who is so appealing and improbable, wholesomely and artlessly chatty, healthy and ingenuous. He confesses to his friend that he imagined:

> Wär' ich ein Jäger, ein Hirt, wär' ich ein Bauer geboren,
> Trüg' ich Knüttel und Beil, wärst, Margarete, mein Weib!
> Nie da beklagt' ich die Hitze des Tags, ich wollte mich herzlich
> Auch der rauheren Kost, wenn du sie brächtest, erfreun.
> O wie herrlich begegnete jeglichen Morgen die Sonne
> Mir, und das Abendrot über dem reifenden Feld!
> Balsam würde mein Blut im frischen Kusse des Weibes,
> Kraftvoll blühte mein Haus, doppelt, in Kindern, empor.
> Aber im Winter, zu Nacht, wenn es schneit und stöbert, am Ofen,
> Rief' ich, o Muse, dich auch, märchenerfindende, an.                    [63–72]

[Were I a hunter, a shepherd, were I born a farmer, if I lugged a stick and axe, Margarete, you would be my mate. Never would I gripe about the heat of the day. I would heartily enjoy even the coarse fare if you were the one who brought it. O how delightfully each morning's sun would greet me, and the sunset over the ripening field! My blood would be like balsam in my woman's fresh kiss, my house would bloom, full of vigor, doubled, with children, flourishing. But in winter nights, when it snows and howls, by the chimney I would call, inventive muse of the fairy-tales, on you.]

Here is the last stage of the idyll, indeed, an idyllic moment within the idyll. For in this vision we see the enjoyment of nature, the pleasures of domesticity and healthy sex, the gratifications of family life, the comfort of the home, and the delights of bucolic art, all set forth as a fantasy of the future and of the might-have-been. This inset contains the poem's vision of pastoral life in quintessence.

Included in that view of the pastoral is, of course, the real distance between the speaker of the poem and the two girls. He is not a hunter or shepherd or farmer, though he enjoys being with them and pretending that he is one of them. The pretense extends to imagining that lusty country girl (still to be found in popular television comedies, left over from the Daisy Mae of Al Capp's Dogpatch) as his Weib (not, of course, Frau—too bourgeois a title) and to becoming a fireside reader in the winter, though only when he cannot go outside to enjoy the fresh air. As he observes (59) about the perverse bucolic muse of the fairy-tales, "Sind drei Wünsche erlaubt, ihr Held wird das Albernste wählen" ("If three wishes are permitted, her hero will make the silliest"). His own wish may be as foolish as it is attractive. Indeed, his observation that he would make it come true if he were really of the pastoral world registers his unavoidable separation from that world. Whereas Marvell's mower concludes his poem by taking us to the meadows and truth, Mörike's literate visitor concludes his by turning an experience of the woods into a fantasy of the woods. Mörike's poem implies that the fantasy is artificial and inescapable. Even with the real experience of pastoral life before us, we want it heightened through art; and art and experience both feed the daydreams that we know are artificial, idealized, impossible because of who and what we are, yet nonetheless unavoidable. They are, after all, what the poem leaves us with: the desire to say, *I too live in Arcady.*

The "April" eclogue of Spenser's *Shepheardes Calender*, a fictive pastoral universe within which is a pastoral inset, shows the rich range of expressive possibilities available to the writer who sees the pastoral's complex meanings and knows what they show about life.[6] Thenot begins by asking why Hobbinol is unhappy, and in so doing runs through the list of likely pastoral woes.

> What? hath some Wolfe the tender Lambes ytorne?
> Or is thy Bagpype broke, that sounds so sweete?
> Or art thou of thy loued lasse forlorne?
> Or bene thine eyes attempred to the yeare,
> Quenching the gasping furrowes thirst with rayne? [2–6]

Hobbinol's sorrow proves to be a version of the third possibility: he weeps "for the ladde, whome long I lovd so deare," Colin Clout. In the "January" eclogue Colin has referred to Hobbinol's devotion to him, but "His clownish gifts and curtsies I disdaine" (57). Eros, however, has his revenge against those who disdain another's love, particularly in the pastoral world when that disdain is prompted by elitism. Colin himself is pining for the love of Rosalind, whom Hobbinol identifies as the daughter of the widow in the glen—not precisely gentry, but rather above a shepherd, it would seem. As Colin himself says in "January," she scorns "my rurall musick" and "Shepherds deuise she hateth as the snake" (65). Hobbinol may be a rustic primitive so far as Colin is concerned, but to the disdainful Rosalind even the best of shepherd-poets is no better.

Embittered, Hobbinol complains at the end of "April" that a man is a fool if he "loues the thing, he cannot purchase" (159). In his words we hear a simple pastoral injunction, "be satisfied with what lies within your grasp; do not strive for something higher." However, the coarseness of his economic theory of human affection seems to justify Colin's opinion of him, suggesting that his crude sensibilities are not the last word on pastoral emotions. Indeed, when Hobbinol speaks of having avidly wooed Colin, "Forcing with gyfts to winne his wanton heart" (24), he reveals that he is not even the aesthetic equal of Theocritus's Polyphemus (Idyll XI) or Vergil's Corydon (Eclogue II), though their courtship techniques seem roughly the same. Furthermore, his passion seems more explicitly sexual than romantic.

Thenot's depiction of the sorrowing Hobbinol is remarkably similar to Hobbinol's description of the sorrowing Colin. This portion of the poem therefore gives us two images of the disorders caused by love. Thenot's naive reaction ("Ys loue such pinching payne . . . ?") resonates ironically against the long tradition of pastoral love laments but also indicates that it is at least humanly possible to imagine love as something else. He also addresses a central issue of this poem and of the entire volume when he inquires about love's effect on Colin. "And hath he skill to make so excellent, / Yet hath so little skill to brydle loue?" His questions go unanswered here. They stand as rhetorical. To a considerable extent the entire volume is directed toward responding to these questions.

A partial answer to at least the first, and perhaps the second, is provided in the inset portion of this poem. For now Thenot's aroused curiosity about Colin's artistic skill demands a sample, which Hobbinol will provide by proxy. Though the excuse to begin a set piece looks transparent, it leads to a close view of Colin's talents before the love-pains afflicted him. Here, then, we have an opportunity to contrast Colin's earlier celebratory verse with his later lovelorn laments.

Colin's song fits into the framelike structure of the entire eclogue, indirectly reflecting on the emotions and values expressed within the frame. It is also isolated in time, a work of the vibrant past now transposed for a special moment into the needful present and isolated within it, out of time's flow. Further still, the spacial settings associated with the song suggest isolated and protected enclosure: Thenot observes that they now have the leisure to listen, while their sheep "graze about in sight" (31) and they themselves are "close shrowded in thys shade along" (32). Hobbinol also recalls that Colin devised the song in consort with nature, "as by spring he laye, / And tuned it vnto the Waters fall" (35–36), making it answerable to natural laws rather than to literary artifices. Finally, the song celebrates a pastoral epiphany, a moment in which the pastoral and the divine blend in a special moment of affection and devotion.

The song is about "fayre *Elisa*, Queene of shepheardes all" (34), identified by the scholiast E. K. (as if anyone might be in doubt) as Queen Elizabeth. In his gloss, E. K. (ever a troublesome commentator) insists that Colin's abbreviation of the royal name is pastoral decorum, "it being very vnfit, that a shepheardes boy brought vp in the shepefold, should know. or euer seme to haue heard of a Queens roialty." If E. K. gives us any insight into his contemporaries' reasoning, then Elizabeth is recognized by Colin as particularly and sufficiently the queen of *their* world, regardless of what her standing might be in some greater sphere (distantly evoked on the horizon of the poem's accompanying woodcut), about which they are necessarily and appropriately ignorant. Unlike Rosalind, Elisa is not too proud to be in and of the pastoral world. Granted, she has the satisfaction of being its queen, not merely the sweetheart of a poor herdsman, but she also shows the easy grace that combines the regal and pastoral, and that figures frequently in pastoral allegories of royalty.

Perhaps it is not a mere coincidence that this encomium is in the fourth poem of the volume. As a vision of a human deity and of the special contentment (human and natural) created by that deity, it is analogous to the fourth eclogues of Vergil and Clement Marot; and as a poem about the Virgin Queen it is related ironically to Mantuan's fourth eclogue, a famous satire against women. Elisa is "*Syrinx* daughter without spotte, / Which *Pan* the shepheardes God of her begot" (50–51). E. K. observes that the pastoral analogue implied by the allegory is inherently complex.

> But here by Pan and Syrinx is not to be thoughte, that the shephearde simplye meante those Poetical Gods: but rather supposing (as seemeth) her grace progenie to be diuine and immortall . . . could deuise no parents in his iudgement so worthy for her, as Pan the shepeheardes God, and his best beloued Syrinx. So that by Pan is here meant . . . K. Henry the eyght. And by that name, oftymes . . . be noted kings and mighty Potentates: And in some place Christ himselfe, who is the verye Pan and god of Shepheardes.

Needless to say, there is no elaboration of the sardonically appropriate choice of Syrinx, turned into a reed as she desperately fled Pan's lust, to stand for Anne Boleyn. Rather, this genealogy contains several other implications. The most immediate meaning is that Elisa is the daughter of the late king, whose reign is seen here poetically as a deific rule of pastoral harmony with nature. Biographically, the passage also rejects the taunts against herself and her mother that Elizabeth had to endure from the Catholics, as well as from her own father. Also, as the unspotted daughter of a virtuous maiden and the deity himself, her virtue is analogous to the Virgin Mary's. Further, being Pan's (Christ's and Henry's) daughter, she in some sense represents the true and English church. Finally, as the offspring of Pan and Syrinx, she embodies pastoral bounty, pastoral freedom, and pastoral lyricism. Through these knotted equivalences, the pastoral and royal and religious realms are fused, joining their beauties and dignities in a way that heightens the value of all three realms.

Colin first perceives Elisa as a vision of a goddess that he can barely mention, much less approach. In his song itself, therefore, these multiple meanings evolve through his gradual understanding of Elisa. An opening invocation to the local proprietary nymphs and the muses—that is, to the deities of song and of this particular place, to art and nature—attests to the singer's need for divine help to celebrate his subject, whose identity he at first can only imply, one who "her sexe doth all excell" (45). Through the second stanza Elisa remains a rather distant "she."

> So sprong her grace
> Of heauenly race,
> No mortall blemishe may her blotte. [52–54]

The physicality of the metaphors at the last line prepare for Colin's "discovery" of Elisa, who is actually present: "See where she sits vpon the grassie greene, / (O seemely sight)" (55–56). Having approached Elisa from a distance, and obliquely, the speaker has now progressed far enough to look at her. He is struck first by admiration and describes an obviously emblematic vision of the queen. She is verbally portrayed in this passage, even as she is so often pictorially portrayed, decked out with *English* flowers: the coronet Colin describes contains primroses, daffodils, and violets. The image remains fundamentally heraldic, even when Colin treats the heraldic colors as personal charms; she is, for instance,

> Yclad in Scarlot like a mayden Queene,
> And Ermines white. [57–58]

> The Redde rose medled with the White yfere,
> In either cheeke depeincten liuely chere. [68–69]

The portrait eloquently persuades us of her beauty and majesty, justifying Colin's exclamation that attempts to express the various significant elements evoked by his description:

> Tell me, haue ye seene her angelick face,
> Like *Phoebe* fayre?
> Her heauenly haueour, her princely grace
> can you well compare? [64–67]

Angelic, heavenly, princely—these qualities are all embodied in Colin's lines. But because the depiction is thus far iconic, like Elizabeth's commissioned portraits, it is an unanimated (though lovely) figure who "sits" in the midst of this pleasance, expressing appropriate cheer because in her person she unites the York and Lancaster roses to maintain the realm's pastoral, tranquil efflorescence.

The question Colin asks at the end of his fourth stanza, "Where haue you seene the like, but there?", initiates a new movement in the poem, as Colin, in search of comparisons, summons two mythological deities to witness her perfection. Again in this segment, words relating to visual observation play the most important part and remind us of the narrator's distance from what he speaks about. Colin "sawe" Apollo, whom he refers to here by the name Phoebus (meaning "the bright one"), thrust out his head to "gaze" at Elisa, the brightness of whose beams "amaze" him when he sees them. Colin also invites Cynthia to "Shewe" herself, warning that she too will be unequal to the "beams" of Elisa's beauty.

This mythological excursus then takes a surprising turn as Colin recants the comparisons he has just made, a passage highly significant to the development of his song:

> But I will not match her with *Latonaes* seede,
> Such follie great sorow to *Niobe* did breede:
> Now she is a stone,
> And makes dayly mone,
> Warning all other to take heede. [86–90]

As if suddenly conscious of the lurking danger of impiety, and conscious therefore that one development of his mythological allusions poses a possible threat to the character whose mythic dimension he has been insisting upon, Colin alters the flight of his imagination. In his abstract adulation of Elisa rests some seed of tragedy, because his elaborate deification of her makes her vulnerable through dehumanization.

Through the early stanzas of his tribute, the poet seems constrained to an observer's role; but then so are the deities. He can depict Elisa; he and they can admire her; but she remains isolated, unreachable not only by the humble shepherd-poet but even by the other gods and goddesses, as well as by the audience for whom the poet is mediator. During the first six stanzas the poet is an observer who tries to exert some imaginative, artistic direction over powers beyond his control. The prevalence of visual terms marks Elisa's distance from him and the mythological figures; they also mark the poet's distance from the figures with which he deals. He is clearly a pastoral spectator looking at greater forces. His adoration for Elisa makes her a devotional figure who can give him some reflected power over those deities greater than he but less than she—thus his gleefully brazen challenge, "Shew thy selfe *Cynthia*" (82).

Yet even though Elizabeth may surpass the pagan deities by her greater, purer, more devout glory, in this poem she is still a creature of the singer (a literary child of the poet who remembers Niobe) and in the larger world a human being still vulnerable to greater, more absolutely divine, powers. Recognizing this, Colin shies away from tempting fate, having realized through the process of deification that Elisa is vulnerable; in recognizing this fact he becomes sensibly aware of her individual meaning for him. That acknowledgment of her vulnerability, and the consequent withdrawal from poetic heroicizing, contain the poem within pastoral dimensions as the pastoral singer ventures to his limits.

When Colin again mentions Elisa's ancestry in the seventh stanza, the reference is more personal than genealogical. Rather than wanting only to assure us that the child was "without mortall blemishe" (54), Colin now leads us to think of Pan and Syrinx as happy parents. During this passage appears the first verbal rusticism of the song, and the first suggestion of Colin's personal feeling toward Elisa.

> *Pan* may be proud, that euer he begot
>     such a Bellibone,
> And *Syrinx* reioyse, that euer was her lot
>     to beare such an one.                    [91–94]

We now find ourselves in what anyone would recognize as a conventional pastoral setting.

> Soone as my younglings cryen for the
>     dam,
> To her will I offer a milkwhite Lamb.                    [95–96]

While the earlier stanzas of the poem can certainly be accomodated by the range of pastoral poetry—they do not exceed the reach of Vergil's Fourth Eclogue, or of the elegy to Daphnis in Vergil's Fifth—the overt resumption of pastoral language and imagery in this stanza signifies that Colin now more personally regards Elisa as someone about whom he can and does care emotionally. Having too far challenged, for her sake, the prerogatives of the divine, he now retreats to the safety of the pastoral world, where he can still worship her, but with a greater depth of feeling because they can *meet* in the pastoral world.

Elisa is now more than an idol, a portrait icon to be wondered at and admired. Colin's present feeling for her, a different kind of devotion, allows him to think of her as more immediately relevant to him, and therefore more strikingly alive. He now senses metaphor as fact: she is not only "sprong . . . / Of heauenly race" (52–53) but,

> She is my goddesse plaine,
> And I her shepheards swayne,
> Albee forswonck and forswatt I am.                    [97–99]

In awakening his own emotional attitude toward Elisa, he more perfectly comprehends her divinity. While moving closer to her, becoming her devoted swain, he still recognizes the distance between them, a distance of class and degree of perfection but not of emotion. He realizes that he can love and pay tribute to her, approach her as a devoted admirer, confident that this "Bellibone" is also human, also a pastoral inhabitant, and will be kind to a follower of Pan, although he knows himself but a herdsman "ouer-laboured and sunneburnt" (E. K.'s translation of "forswonck and forswatt").

The psychological relationship between the singer and his subject has been redefined during the course of the song. He now has a proprietary interest in her. Except for his initial mention of Elisa's name, in the first line of his second stanza, Colin has referred to her heretofore solely by means of the third-person pronouns; but in the subsequent stanzas, he also calls her "my Goddesse" (101), "my Lady" (114), and "Elisa" three times (105, 145, 150), the second instance in direct familiar address ("thou"). The poet, while apparently evincing his rusticity, has been elevated; his new relationship with Elisa, developing purely from a deeper understanding of her nature, allows him a degree of intimacy that earlier seemed impossible; as *her* shepherd-swain, he is far more powerful, and happy, than he was as the objective and omniscient poet of the earlier stanzas. He discovers the limiting mortality of the "goddess," discovers in his fears for her his love for her, and feels instinctively that such sentiments find their fullest and most gratifying expression in the terms of the pastoral world. For there Elisa can be "his" goddess and still protected; there he can praise her without threatening the envy of heaven. In the complicated laws set by the pastoral tradition, a queen can be called a queen of shepherds without fear of offending her; and a queen of shepherds can be called a goddess without fear of offending the real divinities; for everyone knows that simple shepherds cannot understand the magnitude of the world beyond their pastures and therefore reduce things to their own terms, just as everyone knows that simple shepherds are easily impressed and inflate everything strange to tremendous magnitudes. The pastoral permits Colin to express the totality of his devotion to Elisa. In fact, it is for that reason that he returns to the pastoral frame of reference.

In the pastoral world, which is shared by the queen-goddess and the poet, the poem and its characters come alive.

> I see *Calliope* speede her to the place,
>     where my Goddesse shines:
> And after her the other Muses trace,
>     with their Violines.                                          [100–04]
>
> Lo how finely the graces can it foote
>     to the Instrument;
> They dauncen deffly, and singen soote,
>     in their meriment.

Wants not a fourth grace, to make the daunce euen?
Let that rowme to my Lady be yeuen:
  She shalbe a grace,
  To fyll the fourth place,
And reigne with the rest in heauen.      [109–17]

All the worlds merge; even the poet-shepherd has the right to give instructions here, as a gentleman-usher or perhaps as a master of revels. All of the deities whom Colin, as an artist, worships, come to celebrate for and with Elisa. And Elisa, now in her natural milieu—which is to say, among the goddesses of art who accept her as one of them and in the fields with a devoted shepherd near—can rise and dance, signaling at once her eventual deification among the other graces and her satisfaction in what Hobbinol earlier called "shepheards delights." The excitement of the scene affects Colin himself, who enthusiastically begins summoning the shepherdesses to bedeck Elisa with flowers, at his bidding virtually transforming her into a work of pastoral art. These figures are all spontaneously generated at the borders of the pastoral poem, arriving (like those in "Lycidas") when the aesthetic moment is propitious, intensifying the poem as they crowd its space, and disappearing when their work is done. In this final segment of Colin's song, Elisa becomes the central figure in a pastoral dance of harmony and fruition, joined first by the muse of epic poetry, then by the others, the graces, a bevy of nymphs (the most prominent bearing the olive branches of peace), and finally by the maidens who clothe her with the riches of the pastoral world. The poem does not really expand its perspective to embrace them; rather, they are invited into its existing area, making it appear more vibrant.

Colin's song began with a depiction of Elisa suitable to an epic. For all the majesty, it makes her seem aloof and solitary. When the poet less pretentiously withdraws his gaze from celestial reaches to the pastoral world, the deities come of their own accord. As a result, the finished portrait of Elisa seems rich, exciting, and both socially and personally meaningful. She has a central place in the divine and human societies that pay tribute to her. And we understand that Colin's song attests to the humane sense of pastoral: it can express the vulnerability and therefore the kinship of all people (including people like Elisa), along with the sense of deification that can come from control over some segment of the world.

Queen Elizabeth, when portrayed as a pastoral goddess, seems both cosmically essential and romantically engaging. Both of these facets are vital to a full understanding of her specially cultivated role in her kingdom. Both figure in Colin's emotional and intellectual experience of what she means to him. These qualities crucially modify our understanding of Elisa's complex embodiment of beauty and majesty, and the poem thereby becomes a significant revelation of a political myth. The concluding "emblems" or mottoes of Thenot and Hobbinol both use Aeneas's words (*Aeneid* I, 337–38) when he perceives the presence of a goddess (actually his mother, Venus) in the likeness of a mortal huntress: "O quam te memorem virgo . . . O dea certe" ("O what shall I call you? . . . O goddess, surely"). Through the song, we see Elisa simultaneously as goddess and as a beloved lady.

> And was thilk same song of *Colins* owne making?
> Ah foolish boy, that is with loue yblent:
> Great pittie is, he be in such taking,
> For naught caren, that bene so lewdly bent.                   [154–57]

Thenot's reaction to the song embodies his present knowledge of Colin: the poet who could compose so excellent a work, celebrating so divine a figure, is indeed foolish to let love blind him, making him forget both poetry and Elisa. This judgment constitutes a criticism of one aspect of the pastoral world from the perspective of another aspect of that world. Hobbinol's pragmatic dismissal of idealistic devotion to someone beyond one's class is yet another perspective on the pastoral situation. They jostle briefly, but are resolved in common appreciation of the vision that Colin has described.

Colin's song expresses the vital power of the pastoral vision. It suggests that love, if properly directed, need not be painful. Of course, Colin can handle art but not his own emotions. To the extent that this is a particularly pastoral trait, we can see in what way we all live in Arcadia. However, his devotion to Elisa, being devotion rather than passion, is requited in a special way. Willingly accepting a qualitative difference between himself and her, Colin is still able to feel her emotional equal because they respond mutually to pastoral pleasures. His love for her brings him only joy.

His song, set off from the flow of the poem because it is a recollection from the past, is a lyric moment in a prosaic conversation. Brought forth as a work of art unrelated in its subject to the ostensible topic of the framing conversation, it stops the show. It becomes the justification for the pastoral world. Within the fictive universe, this inset gives a transcendent vision of life in pastoral terms. The whole poem moves through complex perceptions and stages of idealization while keeping within pastoral boundaries. "April" teaches us about the pastoral, while our awareness of pastoral's variety teaches us about the poem. The eclogue treats the pastoral world as a scaled version of life. Colin's song expresses within the context of life's complexity the exemplary modes of love, governance, religion, and art. It is appropriate that perfection should be expressed at the end of Colin's song by a musical image uniting dancing, instrumental music, and song. Making music, after all, is the quintessential pastoral activity in literature from Theocritus onward, and indeed it is contained in the nature of the pastoral god, Elisa's father, Pan. In pastoral art and pastoral life, harmony is all.

# 5

## Pastoral Irony

The pastoral thrives on implications; it dwells amid nuances and flourishes in the shade.

You'll sing the sweeter if you'll sit over here,
under the wild olive and those taller trees.
[Theocritus, Idyll V, 310–32]

tu, Tityre, lentus in umbra
formosam resonare doces Amaryllida siluas.
[Vergil, Eclogue I, 4–5]

[You, Tityrus, at ease in the shade,
teach the woods to resound with the name of Amaryllis.]

Pastoral shade is more than a natural setting, and may be more than an image of poised detachment.

Tityre, tu patulae recubans sub tegmine fagi.
[Vergil, Eclogue I, 1]

[Tityrus, you can lie sheltered by the spreading beech.]

This is the opening line of a work that for many centuries exemplified pastoral poetry and the pastoral life.[1] The earliest extant commentary claims it is auto-biographical. Vergil, as Tityrus, writes to thank Octavian for saving his home from the rural land confiscations that followed the republican defeat at Philippi; Meliboeus, grief-stricken as he faces exile, shows the plight from which Vergil has been saved. This biographical allegorizing, though too simple, is useful. A *tegmen* is a protective garment, like a cloak; and to the extent that any poem embodies its author, the pastoral fiction, here represented metonymically by the beech tree, is a cloak for the author. If we can see them as protective, the leaves of the beech tree give only flimsy protection. Consequently, they offer an imaginary cloak that the author can use only because we respect its fictional usage. No thunderhead will come suddenly over the mountains to drench Tityrus through the leaves; no politically aggressive reader will drench the poem with "meanings" made for the moment.

Therefore, the very first line of the text insists upon its privileged situation. And it does so while frankly confessing the artificiality of the literary construction: Tityrus is comfortably shaded, protected by a cloak of leaves. Meliboeus, however, is both unprotected and uncomfortable. He is also unprivileged because he has been dispossessed of his place; but by standing outside of the shade he is rhetorically privileged to speak lines that the protected Tityrus need not, will not, cannot say.

Pastoral shade is not the dense cover of blackest night. We seem to see the pastoral world plainly, and yet we remain at a slight remove from the clear light of fact. Pastoral shade protects covert meanings. What happens when the cloak is removed can be demonstrated through Sidney's defense of the pastoral. Sensitive poet though he is—and indeed, an important poet of the pastoral, "borne in Arcady"—Sidney the critic here pierces the shade with a glaring light.

Is the poor pipe disdained, which sometime out
of Meliboeus' mouth can show the misery of
people under hard lords or ravening soldiers?
And again, by Tityrus, what blessedness is
derived to them that lie lowest from the
goodness of them that sit highest. [2]

In a way, he is right. The poem, through its sympathetic treatment of the way sorrows and joys come to the lowest classes, does express the pastoral's moral capacity for addressing the social and political problems in a hierarchical society. But Sidney has lifted the scrim on which much of the work's meaning is shown forth. He has done so because he is deliberately making a case for the moral necessity of art; and he makes that case by taking "the motive for metaphor" (in Wallace Stevens's phrase) to be strictly diplomatic. This it is not. The poem's artifice is not just the poet's protection against the sword's steel. It is also the poem's protection against the mind's steel.

Furthermore (as Sidney the poet knew) the pastoral shade can be a shelter from many kinds of turmoil.

So in Vergil, the herdsmen are outside in more ways than one. In the midst of Tityrus's piping, Meliboeus appears with his herd of woes ("undique totis / usque adeo turbatur agris" [11–12], "There is such trouble all around in the country"). Any mastery of the elements takes place in a tight space: for Tityrus, on his little parcel of land.

Fortunate senex, ergo tua rura manebunt
et tibi magna satis, quamuis lapis omnia nudus
limosoque palus obducat pascua iunco:
non insueta grauis temptabunt pabula fetas,
nec mala uicini pecoris contagia laedent.
fortunate senex, hic inter flumina nota
et fontis sacros frigus captabis opacum;
hinc tibi, quae semper, uicino ab limite saepes
Hyblaeis apibus florem depasta salicti
saepe leui somnum suadebit inire susurro;                    [46–55]

[Lucky old man, so your fields will remain yours, and grand enough for you,
though barren stone and marshland reeds may keep smothering the pastures. No foreign foods are going to upset your breeding ewes, no dangerous
infections from a neighboring flock. Lucky old man, here by familiar streams
and sacred fountains, you will enjoy the cooling shade. Here, as always in
the past, the hedgerow that leads from your neighbor's land will offer its
willow-blossoms to Hyblaean bees and lull you to sleep with its gentle
murmurs.]

Life here can be very nice. Amid the blooming and the ordered continuity of
breeding lambs and the pruner going about his tasks, one still has time for a nap in
the shade of a bee-loud shrub. The pleasures, however, are to be measured
relatively. As delightful as it is, this is no lavish estate. There are, for example,
rocks and marshland. In Latin the passage about them is under pressure from the
subjective *obducat*, implying that this is a continuing problem. Nor is the farm very
big. It will, of course, suffice; and though it does not have choice farming or grazing
land, out there—just beyond the property line—the soil is barren. Out there also
are plants and diseases to endanger the livestock. One is reminded of the closeness
of the borders by the enroaching scrubland and the hedge that runs in from the
neighbor's place. The pastoral realm takes its meaning from its vulnerable borders.

In the first two lines, Vergil permits his reader a brief moment of tranquillity. The mellifluous and delicate antique names (*Meliboeus, Tityrus*) immediately
suggest time-honored rustic placidity. So, too, does the description of the "activity"
going on while we watch: Tityrus lies against a tree and plays his tune. But
Melibeous continues:

nos patriae finis et dulcia linquimus arua.
nos patriam fugimus; tu, Tityre, lentus in umbra
formosam resonare doces Amaryllida siluas.                    [3–5]

[We must give up our country's sweet fields, and put the border behind us. We flee from our country; you, Tityrus, at ease in the shade, teach the woods to resound with the name of Amaryllis.]

The announcements of departure that begin lines 3 and 4, underscored by the insistent alliteration, jar the mood, making us feel the urgency of Meliboeus's flight. So the first speech in the poem reveals the antithesis that will prove to be an ever-deepening dialectic opposition.

The verbs immediately call our attention to Tityrus's peace of mind. The first, *meditor*, can mean "meditate," "practice," or "rehearse." Through it Vergil evokes Tityrus's reflectiveness, and Milton's evocation of this line, in "Lycidas," rightly insists on the complex Vergilian verb: "And strictly meditate the thankless muse" (66). The second, *docere*, means "teach" and extends the idea of *meditor* to another form of activity connected with cogitation and action. So Tityrus's indolent music-making links his own presence with the world around him. He is associated with the tree and its shade by his presence, with the woodlands through his song, with the rustic muses through his oaten flute. In these evocative and junctive images, Vergil's Meliboeus depicts Tityrus as a figure of continuity, union, and stasis.

The syntax of the initial speech is important. The chiasmus ("Tityre, tu . . . tu, Tityre") rhetorically links the two references to the fortunate shepherd. These surround the anaphora by which Meliboeus refers to his own plight ("nos patriae finis . . . nos patriam fugimus"). As the image of Tityrus syntactically envelops these declarations of loss, so it seems metaphorically to overleap it as well. Meliboeus feels that he himself (and whoever else is included in his "we") is the isolated one, even though it is Tityrus who seems to be alone physically and psychologically. But Tityrus is "alone" in enjoying his union with the country around him, with music, and with the past. As much an image as a man, the piping shepherd implicitly defines the meaning of Meliboeus's loss.

Meliboeus, however, does some explicit defining in the barrenness of six words arranged to convey the stark conclusiveness of his future. His imagination is engrossed by Tityrus's comforts and the country Tityrus still enjoys; he thinks of them in the midst of his own lament; and as he goes, he stops to look behind him at the fields and the life he must leave. He notes the rugged borders (the rock, the hedge, the marsh, the stony place) and knows that what lies beyond is the worst of what he has found here. As Meliboeus longingly describes this pastoral scene— perhaps more pleasant in his sad eyes than it has ever seemed before—he, the exiled one, takes note of its limits.

Arcadian life is frail and precious, at least in part, because of its frailty. Here we see the bucolic world through the eyes of someone who, aware of its shortcomings, is being deprived of its pleasures, and whose four negatives signal his oppressed awareness of that deprivation ("non," "nec"). Those who appreciate Vergil like to praise his "elegiac" quality, "that vespertinal mixture of sadness and tranquility" that seems to mark the *Eclogues*.[3] More than a cast of temperament, it is also a medium of perception. Furthermore, although Vergil seemingly places his poems in a timelessly ancient world, he intertwines them with contemporary events. They are in the present tense. They unfold before us and are about a world in flux. Though they may feel aesthetically "right," they are marked by the signs of uncertainty.

These come forth—for example—in Tityrus's unsettlingly oblique replies to Meliboeus's questions and comments. In the midst of recounting his woes, Meliboeus stops suddenly to ask, "sed tamen iste deus qui sit, da, Tityre, nobis: (18); "But yet, who Tityrus—tell us—may this god be," for Tityrus has said that he owes his comfort to one whom he will always consider "deus." The answer seems not quite to the point of the question.

> Urbem quam dicunt Roman, Meliboee, putaui
> stultus ego huic nostrae similem, quo saepe
> solemus
> pastores ouium teneros depellere fetus.                    [19–21]

[The city they call Rome, Meliboeus, I foolishly thought was like the one of ours where we shepherds always take our just-weaned lambs.]

One really expects Meliboeus to repeat his question, but instead he follows Tityrus on this new tack and asks why he went to Rome. In fact, the first question is never answered specifically, for the poem develops a complex *mythos* about power and protection rather than about one person's generosity.

At the conclusion of Meliboeus's "Fortunate senex" speech, following the lines about the birds that will never cease cooing, Tityrus seems to pick up his friend's thoughts.

> Ante leues ergo pascentur in aethere cerui
> et freta destituent nudos in litore piscis,
> ante pererratis amborum finibus exsul
> aut Ararim Parthus bibet aut Germania Tigrim,
> quam nostro illius labatur pectore uultus.                 [59–63]

[And so, sooner will stags graze in the air and seas leave their fish stranded on the shore, sooner will people wander without borders, the Parthian in exile drinking from the Saône and Germany from the Tigris, than our heart will lose the image of his face.]

Surely in this context the beginning of his speech leads us to expect that the end will be something like ". . . than I will leave my home."

Tityrus is immersed in his own world. He hears his companion talking, but instead of carrying on a conversation with Meliboeus he uses the other man's words as recitatives on which to build his own arias. Tityrus's single-minded felicity leaves him provocatively oblivious to the other man's plight. (Given the situation, his hyperbolic reference to the nations wandering in exile seems particularly obtuse.) The lack of a common meeting-ground is represented by the abrasion of pronouns. Meliboeus sharply differentiates between "you" (Tityrus) and "we"; but Tityrus constantly uses "we." He responds to Meliboeus's first speech with the words, "O Meliboee, deus nobis haec otia fecit" (6), "Oh, Meliboeus, a god has granted us this leisure." We later learn that he is not the only privileged one; but at the moment he is clearly, splendidly alone. Tityrus is less interested in what he sees around him than in what he sees in his mind's eye ("siluestrem . . . musam meditaris," "meditating the woodland muse").

Each speaker, by referring to his version as "our" experience, invites us to recognize in his tribulations or joy those of Vergil's contemporary reader. For indeed, in the leisure that makes the enjoyment of art possible, one shares Tityrus's leisure. Yet the world remains disordered, so we (like Meliboeus) are also threatened with exile from the place of seeming peace, spiritual exiles in our own land.

Through the two speakers we come to know the disparate effects of these antithetical views of experience. Meliboeus is a "prisoner of an unstable and fleeting reality."[4] His exclusionary discrimination between "you" and "we" tells us the literal truth, and hard reality drives him to talk to Tityrus as to a man set apart, a man whose situation becomes the substance for Meliboeus's daydreams. Tityrus, on the other hand, is immersed in his sudden spiritual affluence.

In the First Eclogue, Vergil creates a tension between the pastoral and its antithesis, generating from that tension a truly dynamic idyll, expressed in political terms and geographic metaphors. And the dialectic is unresolved, merely held together by the dramatic situation. In fact, even the ending of the poem is equivocal. All we can be sure of is that it opposes the driving, pathetic perturbation of Meliboeus with the reflective, cozy domesticity of Tityrus.

*Meliboeus.*
At nos hinc alii sitientis ibimus Afros,
pars Scythiam et rapidum Cretae ueniemus Oaxen
et penitus toto diuisos orbe Britannos.

. . . . . . . . . . . . . . . . . . . . . . . .

ite meae, felix quondam pecus, ite capellae.
non ego uos posthac uiridi proiectus in antro
dumosa pendere procul de rupe uidebo;
carmina nulla canam; non me pascente, capellae,
florentem cytisum et salices carpetis amaras.

*Tityrus.*
Hic tamen hanc mecum poteras requiescere noctem
fronde super uiridi: sunt nobis mitia poma,
castaneae molles et pressi copia lactis,
et iam summa procul uillarum culmina fumant
maioresque cadunt altis de montibus umbrae.          [64–66, 74–83]

[*Meliboeus.* But we have to push on, some to the thirsty Africans, some to Scythia and Crete's swift Oaxes and to the Britons, totally cut off from the rest of the world. . . . Forward, my once-happy herd of goats, forward. I shall no longer stretch out in some mossy grotto, watching you, far off, as if hanging from the shrubby rocks. I shall sing no more songs, and it won't be me tending you while you crop the flowering cytisus and bitter willows.

*Tityrus.* But still, you could rest this night with me, here on the verdant leaves. We have ripe apples, tender chestnuts, and plenty of cheese. And the smoke is rising just now from the rooftops of the farms far off, and from the mountain-tops longer shadows fall.]

Tityrus's phrase "poteras requiescere" ("you could rest") is a troublesome one, an imperfect that has been called "curiously tentative."[5] He holds out the possibility but certainly does not urge. It seems a lame way to make the offer. But, after all, there is little that he can do now except extend, as one critic puts it, "an invitation that cannot be accepted."[6] The pastoral character can offer shelter and creature comforts only so long as his friend is graced with the right to stay in the pastoral world.

Those shadows that adumbrate the valley of the poem and reappear at the end of Eclogue X to cast gloom over the entire volume bespeak the imposition of the uncertainties of the outside world onto the enclosed space of the pastoral poem and onto the pastoral world. Tityrus, though immersed in his own good fortune that he finally thinks to share with his desolate compatriot, can hardly pretend that nothing is changed here. The small, brief comforts can get Meliboeus through the night only to face again the same sorrows and hardships against which he has bitterly steeled himself in his concluding speech, his valedictory to the pastoral life. Tityrus, scarcely able to descend from his summit of bliss to come to terms with Meliboeus's exploration of the abyss, has only weak solace to offer. He enjoys this leisure by a divinely granted privilege, and simply has no power to make life more than momentarily happier for everyone. He offers what little he can. In the silence at the end of the poem, we are left to meditate on the mysterious pastoral union of passive helplessness and carefree liberty. But what reverberates in that silence is the offer of compassion, the attempt to heal the violence done to Meliboeus's feelings, the gesture that wants to embrace Meliboeus once again in the meager comforts of the pastoral life that now seem so much more precious than they could have seemed before their vulnerability became clear.

Suppose that Meliboeus and Tityrus are two figures created by Vergil to give voice to his antithetical perceptions of Roman life, and therefore his antithetical notions about his role as a poet. Meliboeus is only a step away from moral satire; Tityrus is a half-step away from the encomium. Both these (as Sidney hints) will become familiar tones of the pastoral voice, particularly in the Renaissance. In Vergil's poem the unresolved tension of their attitudes and points of view is also an unresolved tension of poetic expression and responses, attesting to the poet's artistic dilemma in reacting to the complexity of his experience. Within the limits of the pastoral lyric he can permit each voice, each respondent, full expression. By so doing, he sets aside a moral choice in favor of an aesthetic one, creating a sophisticated morality that gives to each of the two positions an emotional force that we cannot gainsay. Tityrus, from his privileged position, celebrates his liberty but also reveals his limited ability to help or even respond to his friend's distress. Meliboeus, from his position, provides a context for understanding and judging Tityrus's joy but also shows his own lack of a focus: Meliboeus cannot give direction or meaning to his implicit criticism of contemporary politics or (even more immediately) to his disintegrating life. Between the solipsistic reflection (Tityrus contemplating his own happiness) and the external critique (Meliboeus expressing his own and a communal perplexity and outrage) no third voice is heard, giving the final word on these two approaches to fictional autobiography. Instead, the two speakers face one another in a profoundly ironic dialogue that is not an exchange but a fusion of contrarieties, held together by the outcast's unwillingness to envy his friend and the saved man's unwillingness to let his friend part without a gesture of generosity.

This poem is a revealing text because it holds within itself so much of pastoral's generic and modal complexity. It places the pastoral world ironically with reference to that which surrounds it: we can see the value of the pastoral enclosure while also seeing its vulnerability, its powerlessness to preserve its own integrity. The poem also presents an ironic look at the interior of the pastoral world; Tityrus has a god to thank for the mediocre land that becomes his in old age, after (we also discover) he has spent many years as a lovesick slave unable to save enough to buy his own freedom. Praise and censure are knitted together here; and though they will not always be inextricable in the pastoral, their combination in the First Eclogue sets a pattern that will become familiar. Moreover, the potential irony in the pastoral situation itself may become the central issue of the pastoral work.

In his "January" eclogue, for instance, Spenser leaves serious doubts about the powers of recovery left within the shepherd who is bound to the emotional life or the natural cycle, which are so obviously essential elements of the pastoral experience. Colin Clout, the main figure in this collection of eclogues, is alone with his sheep on a frozen hill. Colin feels very much a part of the landscape, and, in its barrenness, that landscape seems to reflect his sufferings for the love of Rosalind. He longs for and is spurned by someone who disdains country boys; but the fact that his problem originates within himself makes his helplessness before it particularly pointed. The "naked trees, whose shady leaves are lost . . . And now are clothd with mosse and hoary frost" ("January," 31, 33) only deepen his depression and assure him that his sorrows are in keeping with nature's plans, while spring is out of mind. Because of the simplicity and helplessness it betokens, Colin's rusticity compels our sympathy. He is beset by problems he cannot combat. Brute nature subsumes him; not even the god of nature, Pan, to whom he pleads, will free him.

> A thousand sithes I curse that careful hower,
> Wherein I longed the neighbour towne to see. [49–50]

The pun on *careful* suggests that we must take one sense of the word literally, because he has become full of cares, but we must recognize the calculated authorial irony of the other sense, for Colin has become careless with his affections and life.

His emotional recklessness links him with Corydon, and it lies at the apparent source of his problem, though beneath that we can see the true source: his kinship, as mortal creature, with the lower orders of nature that he significantly alludes to in finding natural comparisons for his woes. Colin pities the "feeble flock" and knows that they suffer through his "ill gouernement" (45); but just as the word *careful* passes his lips unheeded, welling up as an irrepressible but unrecognized intuitive perception, so he speaks but is unable to put to use these words that could serve as the basis for his own growth. He is powerless over himself and over the lower beasts in his care.

The powerlessness is a form of pastoral vulnerability, but it is not the only pastoral reaction. Another is indicated by the no less rustic poet who provides the verbal frame around Colin's lament, reminding us by his speaking presence that, although Colin's song is clearly an artistic success, Colin is unable to write this eclogue in which he figures. He cannot stand back from himself, nor can he take an interest in another's lament.

Through the course of Spenser's eclogues Colin's absorption with his own problem divorces him from other people and leaves him in meditative isolation; he can no longer participate in the usual patterns of conversation because his grief has become the world in which he lives. He cannot see youth and age as elements in an educative and reassuring dialectic between vigor and maturity (the subject of "February"). He has been young; he is now in agony; the winter of his discontent seems endless to him; can death be far behind? "January," therefore, is filled with the beauty and pathos of pastoral romantic experience, and with its reckless and self-pitying folly. As children of the earth we naturally respond, fully and instinctively, to the earth on which we live; but as children of the earth we are linked to the cycles of life and the pulls of passion, not only through joy but also through grief and pain.

Pastoral literature concerns itself with delicately poised simultaneities: the passing and the coming, the rare and the common, the simple and the complex, the fool and the philosopher. "In my humble opinion," and "I'm no expert but . . . ," familiar rhetorical figures of the modest pose, are pastoral in mode, even though not in genre. Lacking artifice compensates for allegedly lacking art; indeed, being artless clarifies one's understanding; further, because artlessness is a form of powerlessness, one's opinions should be treated compassionately. It is a defense that tries to disarm opposition. Finally, being without power allows one to understand better the strengths and defects of the powerful, and to appreciate how those are intertwined, even though one may naturally wish they were separable. [7]

So there is a doubleness, an irony, that is truly a creative element in the pastoral. Pastoral literature has flourished in times when intellectual sophistication and artistic experimentation have given rise to concerns over the functions of art. These have also been times of more general unsettlings of values: the Alexandrian Ptolemaic time of Theocritus, the Augustan era of Vergil, the Elizabethan period of Spenser, and so on. Pastoral literature expressively embodies the resulting cultural and moral tensions. Might lyric poetry seem to be a private indulgence? By putting on the shepherd's cloak, the pastoral lyricist confesses to taking on a limited, private role; but by picking up the shepherd's pipe, the poet says, I sing about the feelings we share, kings and shepherds alike. Therefore this "limitation" is a special privilege, even though it might be the privilege of articulating personal grief. Does the writer who touches on contemporary affairs or lofty topics meddle ignorantly as an outsider? The bearer of the shepherd's staff responds: Indeed I am powerless, but that is in the nature of things, so it is hardly my fault and not exactly just; but, thanks to my simplicity, I can see the ungilded truth just as anyone could; and though I may have to be excused for my bluntness, my candor and disinterested perceptiveness are valuable.

In Sir John Suckling's "Ballad upon a Wedding," the pastoral strategy allows the poet to turn some rather elaborate compliments while it also covers some piquant observations about sex and marriage. The poem probably celebrates the wedding of a titled couple, though we are not certain which because the narrator, who speaks as an enthusiastic country fellow, never has a name for them. He has simply come upon the magnificent wedding procession during a visit to the city, found himself incorporated without ceremony into the festivities, and tells his friend Dick about it in the monologue that comprises the poem. The underlying jokes are rich. Suckling came from an extremely wealthy family, was well traveled, held ceremonial posts at court, and was (apparently) reputed to be a notorious profligate. "Dick" may be his fellow poet and gallant, Richard Lovelace. And the location is outrageously set:

> At Charing Cross, hard by the way
> Where we (thou knowst) do sell our hay,
> There is a house with stairs. [6–8][8]

Line 8, of course, signals the rustic's impression of the Big City and its Tall Buildings. Through the pastoral role Suckling suggests that he felt like an amazed rube amid the fine folk, which is really to say that they were so grand that despite his sophistication and breeding he could think himself a mere country laborer come, by chance, into their midst. But furthermore, his easy familiarity in writing about the events and his automatic admittance into the full celebration imply that they all seemed so perfectly "natural" and gracious that anyone would have felt delightfully at home.

He himself feels particularly at home in talking about the bride, whom he describes minutely, enthusiastically, and familiarly.

> No grape that's kindly ripe could be
> So round, so plump, so soft as she,
> Nor half so full of Juice. [34–36]

She is, in brief, a tempting morsel. His pastoral guise lets him go past the traditional praise of the bride's grace, modesty, and celestial beauty to deal with her frankly as sexually desirable, indeed visibly sensuous.

The poem suggests that at times we all behave alike, regardless of class; and in the last stanza the idea is more than suggested.

> At length the candle's out, and now
> All that they had not done, they do:
>   What that is, who can tell?
> But I believe it was no more
> Than thou and I have done before
> With *Bridget*, and with *Nell*.                    [127–32]

Allusion to the "first-night rite" is as much a part of the formal epithalamium as it is a part of the coarsest stag party. But Suckling's phrasing ("no more / Than") takes us rather close to Herrick's notorious epigram,

> Night makes no difference 'twixt the Priest
>   and Clark;
> *Jone* as my Lady is as good i' the' dark.[9]

What saves Suckling's poem from offense is that the pattern of pastoral comparison allows us to take this for what it purports to be: an exit line delivered by someone who is not really fit for the woman he has so avidly described. This pattern also permits us to look past the covert message from one young man of the world to another that, although this was a particularly tempting plum that they missed, when you arrive at the act for which all this has been simply the necessary preliminary, it is nothing more than what they already know. This general pattern of pretended self-deprecation existing along with familiar graciousness toward higher powers often occurs later, in the elegant pastorals of the neoclassicists.

In *As You Like It* Shakespeare perceives the pastoral environment of Arden ironically; but he complicates our view of it by also placing it in ironic relationship to the unpastoral world from which it is a gratifying haven. The forest is most simply a refuge from the unnatural, discourteous meanness of the ducal court. However, in the forest the most gratifyingly "pastoral" characters are those born to courtly, rather than pastoral, life. Wit, sense, dignity, poise, and nobility are the products of good breeding. The pastoral environment, so limited in culture and spirit, cannot be a satisfactory permanent home for those turning to it out of absolute necessity or despair with their current lives. For them, it will always seem both shallow and artificial. Consequently, Duke Senior and his followers accept their "new-fallen dignity" and return to the court, bringing back with them such virtues as they took and preserved during their forest sojourn. A private, modest pastoral life is preferable to an ambitious, jealous court life; but if the larger society has room for virtue, or can be made virtuous, then the pastoral is inferior precisely because it is sequestered, lowly, powerless. The courtiers could have lived their entire lives without noticing, much less dwelling in, Arden. It is useful to them when they need it; it is deeply meaningful to some, like Oliver and Duke Frederic, who do not know how badly they need it; and yet, in the social and political lives of these people, it is inconsequential.

Here the internal pastoral irony shapes the external. The two pairs of pastoral lovers, Audrey and William, Phoebe and Silvius, represent (as their names imply) the rustic and the artful versions of the pastoral. On the one hand are the scruffy, unlettered, boorish hayseeds, well characterized by Audrey's boast, "I am no slut, though I thank the gods I am foul" (III, iii, 38). On the other are the artificial, coy, fickle shepherdess and the pining, lovesick, monomaniacal shepherd, doubly preposterous for being totally submerged in their roles and for not seeing what each is truly worth. As Rosalind tells Silvius,

> 'Tis not her glass, but you, that flatters her,
> And out of you she sees herself more proper
> Than any of her lineaments can show her.          [III, v, 54–56]

We thereby distinguish Silvius and Phoebe from the equally lovestruck Orlando and Rosalind, who sometimes resemble them in behavior. The former pair becomes ludicrous by their behavior and faulty judgments; the latter are sometimes ludicrous, but their estimates of one another's worth are accurate and show that good blood or breeding will make itself known even in lowly surroundings.

Because the pastoral world is devoid of significant social ranks, living in it means accepting equality with Audrey and William or enduring the false pride of Phoebe without asserting one's own social position. It means accepting all things and all people in common as equals, which is rather hard to do if you can judge some of them clearly enough to ridicule them. The pastoral scene does contain boors and poseurs; it can be base and artificial.

The first speech of Duke Senior particularly suggests the ways in which this pastoral environment requires some thoughtful adjustments. Arden is not quite a dreamland, though its discomforts may do some good.

> Here we feel but the penalty of Adam,
> The season's difference; as, the icy fang
> And churlish chiding of the winter's wind,
> Which, when it bites and blows upon my body

Even till I shrink with cold, I smile, and say,
"This is no flattery; these are counsellors
That feelingly persuade me what I am."     [II, i, 5–11]

It is one thing to praise the pastoral environment for its gentle breezes and cooling shade, and quite something else to praise it despite its chilling blasts. Duke Senior, goodly philosopher, may believe that "Sweet are the uses of adversity." Perhaps in his royal fashion he is at heart a pastoralist, content to be content, no matter what. Nonetheless, even he has no doubt that this life he now leads is a kind of adversity, which he somewhat amends by his good nature and by the courtly graces he brings to the forest: there is, if he and his followers can do anything about it, venison for the table (despite his gentle qualms and Jaques' maudlin chagrin) and a due preserving of decorum.

Their Golden Age is like that described by the Arcadian King Evander in *Aeneid*, Book VIII, when he contrasts the "hard primitivism" (to use the terms of Boas and Lovejoy) of earliest people, "quis neque mos neque cultus erat" (316) ("who had neither manners nor culture") with the "soft primitivism" of the Golden Age, when Saturn brought laws to the unruly; "sic placida populos in pace regebat" (325) ("thus in peace he ruled a quiet people").[10] However, Arden is golden only through being well ruled, or in this case not ruled at all. It is hypothetically presided over by a beneficent presence who seems uninterested in exercising any prerogatives of authority, and is protected by its own sanctity, seemingly guaranteed by a similarly passive divinity of silence and slow time. The country-folk, after all, carry on their affairs with virtually no notice of, or from, the exiled duke, and no show of religion even toward the traditional pastoral deities. (It is Rosalind who brings forth Hymen.) The only figure of authority who concerns Corin, the oldest and most responsible of the real pastoral characters, is the most immediate one.

But I am shepherd to another man
And do not sheer the fleeces that I graze.
My master is of a churlish disposition
And little recks to find the way to heaven
By doing deeds of hospitality.     [II, 78–83]

This little speech proves gratuitious: immediately following, Corin explains that his "churlish" master has put up for sale all of his property and moved out, so he would not be able to provide hospitality anyway; and Corin then offers in good pastoral fashion to do what he can for the strangers. Though the speech contributes nothing to the plot, it helps distinguish his authentic pastoral attitude from the exploitative oppression of the pastoral world by those to whom it is, like a sheep, passive before the shears.

The narrowness of pastoral contentment can be sensed in pragmatic as well as ethical matters. When Duke Frederick sets march against the growing ranks of discontented nobility who have found contentment with Duke Senior in Arden, where they "fleet the time carelessly as they did in the golden world" (I, i, 124–25), the dwellers in this pastoral world (unlike Meliboee and his compatriots in *The Faerie Queene*, VI, x) are protected from harm by the religious sanctity of the woods themselves. Only the sure functioning of cosmic love has kept them safe. Similarly, when Orlando is moved by the spirit of kinship to save his unnatural brother from the internal dangers of the forest, nature is nature's defense. Pastoral experience can beneficially affect the human soul, which retains some natural sympathies despite hardships and the overlying corruptions of social experience; the larger scope of love in the play goes beyond spiritual adolescence. However, the deftly manipulated happy endings mark off imaginative limits for playfulness. This pastoral region is not trouble-free, but its troubles are balanced by its capacity for human healing.

Arden is made for love because it permits the characters to immerse themselves in their private relationships, oblivious to war, cold, hunger, or work; there are no politics or parents. (Rosalind not only hides her identity from her father; she also keeps herself private from him until the denouement.) Regardless of the actual ages of these characters, their culture is adolescent. In this lies delight, pain, beauty, and comedy; in this, too, lies impermanence; happy love leads to marriage and the social responsibilities it implies.

Richly compounded of elements, Arden is at once better than and not as good as the court. Within itself it has virtues, as do its characters, who may be foul, as Audrey says, but never are mean or treacherous, like the corrupt nobles. The pastoral world occupies the middle ground between high virtue and low wickedness. Set apart from a court that threatens death, Arden offers comedy; set apart from a society filled with envy and hatred, Arden affords friendship and love; set apart from a fast-paced, close-confined royal environment of precipitous action, Arden offers world enough and time. Despite all this, Shakespeare makes Arden more a restorative place than a counterforce to the court. It offers much but leaves much to be desired. Duke Senior, Rosalind, and Orlando come to Arden and find it congenial; but they have brought virtues with them; and in the midst of what Rosalind calls "this desert place" they contribute the strengths and graces of their minds and tongues.

Pastoral withdrawals in epics also can express ironies and complex tensions. The place of pleasing retirement may be temporarily salutory, unworthy when measured against epic values, or even deceptively dangerous. These possibilities are well represented by two episodes of Tasso's *Gerusalemme liberata*. In the first the pagan noblewoman Erminia, still dressed in armor after an unsuccessful attempt to get into the Christian camp to attend the wounded Christian knight whom she loves, flees from the charging cavalry and wanders into the woods, where she intrudes upon a pastoral society. In the second, the hero Rinaldo languishes in Armida's pleasure-garden, a carefully manipulated false image of pastoral bliss. These two episodes are like complexly reflecting mirrors of each other and of the issues in the poem; each scene also contains its own ironic tensions.

The first interlude brings about ironic sudden reversals in Erminia's power. Fleeing for her life, she charges armed into the midst of the pastoral woods, becoming an authoritarian figure who, like the "god" of Tityrus, can say, "pascite, ut ante, boues, pueri; submittite tauros" (Eclogue I, 45), "pasture your cows, as before, lads; breed bulls."

> Vendendo quivi comparir repente
> l'insolite arme, sbigottir costoro;
> ma gli saluta Erminia, e dolcemente
> gli affida, e gli occhi scopre e i bei crin d'oro:
> —Seguite, dice, aventurosa gente
> al Ciel diletta, il ben vostro lavoro;
> ché non portano gia guerra quest'armi
> a l'opre vostre, a i vostri dolci carmi.                [VII,vii][11]

[Seeing one in unaccustomed arms suddenly appear, they were dismayed; but Erminia greeted and graciously comforted them, letting them see her eyes and golden hair. "Follow your good labors," she said, "carefree people—Heaven's delight. This armor portends no warfare against your work, or your sweet songs."]

At the same time she sees something else in this scene. Though to them she may be like a god, holding the power to destroy or bless, she herself feels like Meliboeus wondering at the good fortune of Tityrus.

> O padre, or che d'intorno
> d'alto incendio di guerre arde il paese,
> come qui state in placido soggiorno
> senza temer le militari offese?                [VII, viii, 1–4]

[O father, surrounded by the fires of war that scorch the countryside, how do you abide in peace, without fear of military threat?]

As Meliboeus puts it: "non equidem inuideo; miror magis" (11) ("It is not that I am jealous; I am just amazed.")

The jolly old shepherd's response to Erminia sets up complex reverberations. They are safe, he explains, because of "sia grazia del Ciel, che l'umilitade / d'innocente pastor salvi e sublime" (VII, ix, 1–2; "heavenly grace, which protects and dignifies the innocent shepherd's humility"). But there is another way of looking at it, as he also acknowledges: "né gli avidi soldati a preda alletta / la nostra povertà vile e negletta" (VII, ix, 7–8; "greedy soldiers are not inclined to prey on our base and scorned poverty"). To him and to Erminia, however, humble isolation has other meanings. This entire episode is set within the epic as a whole and Erminia's story in particular. Within it, furthermore, is yet another inset, the old shepherd's brief autobiography. Though he was raised in the country, he despised it and went away to the court, becoming merely a palace gardener but nonetheless familiar with the court's corruption. When he grew old and could stand it no longer, he fled back to the woods to live happily with his family. The insets show that the country is what it seems to be because the shepherd and Erminia are what they are: a native who once scorned it but has learned to appreciate it after a double flight, first from pastoralism and then from "civilization," and an outsider who has found it by accident while in flight from the heroic milieu and sees in it the perfect relief from external dangers and inner turmoil.

In the midst of her private sorrow, loving an enemy hero who does not know she exists, Erminia finds the retreat she needs and retires for a while into pastoral seclusion. However, having so retired, she senses herself cut off not only from the man she loves but from the world as well. Her seclusion becomes a kind of death that leads her to deliver a premature elegy for herself, imagining that Tancredi might one day discover in the woods her grave and the tokens of her love, so assuring her soul peace in death. By its very nature the place of healing becomes a place to die.

Armida's garden is viewed differently. Here nature is artificed and

Stimi (si misto il culto è co 'l negletto)
sol natura arte par, che per diletto
l'imitatrice sua scherzando imitri.
L'aura, non ch'altro, è de la maga effetto,
l'aura che rende gli alberi fioriti:
co' fiori eterni il frutto dura,
e mentre spunta l'un, l'altro matura.                    [XVI, x]

[It seemed (so mixed were cunning and casualness) that art were nature, which for delight would herself imitate her own imitator. The air, for it was nothing more, has a magical touch, the air which makes the trees bloom; eternal flowers sustain eternal fruit, and as the one blossoms, the other ripens.]

It is meant to persuade the eye that this place shows life's pattern. A canny bird sings the moral:

Cosí trapassa al trapassar d'un giorno
de la vita mortale il fiore e'l verde.                    [XVI, xv, 1–2]

[So passes in the passing of a day
the bud and flower of mortal life.]

"Gather ye rosebuds while ye may." Erminia's pastoral retreat suggested that the value of the pure pastoral setting is precisely its naive lack of artifice, its spontaneity which makes no claims beyond the statement of its own worth. Armida's garden, appropriately set in a labyrinth, has been *styled* to create a delusive semblance of ordered creation. Its easy concatenations of images and sounds ("fiori eterni eterno," "mortale il fiore e'l") induce mental sloth. The garden's success in holding Rinaldo demonstrates how easily the protected enclave can delude one into false moralizing and false valuations. His spell must be broken by the sudden appearance of armed men; the intrusion of epic values ends the idyll. For Tasso, as for so many other writers, the pastoral image takes shape in the subtle shadows of complex, haunting ironies.

We need to remember that irony takes many forms. It includes the moral and epistemological ambiguity that lies in unresolvable tensions, as well as the "stable irony" (as Wayne Booth calls it) found in clearly directed moral satire.[12] When it qualifies, restricts, denies, or satirizes in pastoral texts, it may direct its energy against some imagined antithesis of pastoralism, against pastoralism itself, and perhaps both at once. Internal ironies within pastoral literature extend as far back as Theocritus, who encompasses various emotions, events, and language from the most vulgar to the most lofty, often within the same poem, indeed, often immediately juxtaposed; and he does so without strain, without implying a judgment or hierarchy, without seeming to discriminate among them. All are fit into a broad field of images and metaphors. As Booth has observed, there may not always be a clear vision between metaphor and irony. To allude to a king as Pan is metaphoric; but the metaphor may well become ironic, given the traditional attributes of Pan and the traits of the particular monarch. The double voice of so much pastoral literature, carrying on two discourses simultaneously on different levels of significance, can easily turn into another sort of equivocation.

Consider, for example, the invitation from Marlowe's "Passionate Shepherd to His Love" to "Come live with me and be my love."

> And we will sit upon the rocks,
> Seeing the shepherds feed their flocks
> By shallow rivers, to whose falls
> Melodious birds sing madrigals.                    [5–8][13]

The poem seems to accept this idealized pastoral fantasy as its own ideal of life, in fact its own projected actuality. Metaphorically, it expresses the qualities of the poet's imagination and implies what he would be like as a companion and mate, "If these delights thy mind may move" (23). However, one may also find that the distance between the passionate supposed "shepherd" of the title and the real shepherds who busy themselves feeding "their" (not *our*) flocks in line 6 is an ironic distance, perhaps increased by our opinion of the author. This opinion would be affected not only by our views of Marlowe the man and Marlowe the writer in general; it could also be shaped by the irony in *Hero and Leander*, and by the scene in *Tamburlaine* where the Scythian shepherd removes his rustic garb to reveal that of a warrior. We may also sense irony in artful contrivances that indicate just how fictional the poetic scene is. For instance, the birds' "madrigals" may be not only a pleasant fancy but an ironically undercutting reminder of the distance between art and nature.

If we consider Marlowe's poem ironic, it does not seem to be ironic on the surface about the desirability of this sort of life. We may suspect that Marlowe regards this as a lyrical daydream, but it seems to be one he enjoys. Contrast Ralegh's "Nymph's Reply."

> But Time drives flocks from field to fold,
> When rivers rage and rocks grow cold,
> And Philomel becometh dumb;
> The rest complains of cares to come.                [5–8][14]

Here the irony is directed against the pastoral fiction's instability in the face of time's changes and the skepticism of the critical, pragmatic imagination. Ralegh is willing to grant the charm of the fantasy, but is less prepared to consider it even semiseriously, is certainly less prepared to accept it as an image of his own imagination.

At a further remove in the continuum of irony is "The Dispassionate Shepherdess" of Babette Deutsch: "Do not live with me, do not be my love."[15] Her tone implies an even greater distance from Marlowe.

> You'll give me once a thought that stings, and once
> A look to make my blood doubt that it runs,
> You'll give me rough and sharp perplexities,
> And never, never will you give me ease.       [13–16]

One cannot say that she rejects Marlowe's ideal as unworthy or even (like Ralegh) impractical. She sees life's patterns as so different that she can only recall the original imagery in distant verbal and imagistic reverberations, so that Marlowe's pleasant "shallow rivers" become the stream of blood congealed by a harsh look. Her irony simultaneously attacks both pastoral's presumptions about love and life's unromantic cruelties.

Not every pastoral text is ironic, though the ones we find interesting are. Not every ironic pastoral text makes pastoralism the target of its irony. However, ironies of various sorts are so vital to pastoral literature that one cannot ignore them; indeed, just as a full understanding of the pastoral necessitates understanding the pastoral metaphor, so it also necessitates understanding the ironies of pastoral statements.

# 6

## Death in Arcadia

FITTINGLY, IN THE MOST FAMOUS OF ALL FORMS OF PASTORAL POETRY, THE mourning elegy, we find some of the strongest tensions of irony. The purposes of the pastoral elegy can be seen in the very first poem of the earliest book of pastorals, Theocritus's *Idylls*. Here Theocritus brilliantly separates the celebration of art's glory and the song of mourning, so that we appreciate the separate powers of art and mourning while also responding to the powerful synthesis of the two.

In this poem the unnamed goatherd offers the shepherd Thyrsis two gifts in exchange for a performance of Thyrsis's lament for Daphnis, which has made the shepherd renowned for pastoral art. The one present comes strictly from nature: three milkings of a prize ewe. The other, a grandly carved cup of fragrant wood (described in a passage of some thirty lines) joins art with nature, transcending nature while paying tribute to it. For the cup, carved to mimic nature—"High up, round the rim, twines ivy with sprays / of gold helichryse, and all down the handles / brave with its burden, the tendril winds on" (29–31)—contains three elaborate scenes of life's three ages. In the scene of youth, a beautiful woman listens to two care-worn suitors who woo her alternately while she smilingly but unfeelingly turns from one to the other. In the scene of age, an elderly fisherman possessing youthful strength strains to lift a huge net that he will cast into the sea. And in the scene of childhood, a boy is preoccupied in making a cricket cage, while one fox is devastating the unwatched vineyard and another intently creeping up to the boy's lunch.

The carver has preserved fleeting moments of balanced energies in revealingly detailed vignettes, each of which contains its own delicate balances of effort and attention, and all of which taken together comprise a balanced composition. The two scenes with three participants flank the scene with one (the fisherman). Youth and childhood flank youth-in-age, suggesting that art recognizes but is not bound by the unrelenting sequence of nature but envisions its own order and makes that order into an aesthetically harmonized whole. Furthermore, the cup has been "created" through poetry. It shows the ages of life and expresses life's emotions by holding images and emotions in an artistically unified and balanced object of beauty, whose appeal is to the eye but whose mode of existence is verbal. The goatherd's speech, which is both narrative and descriptive, celebrates art's power to tell, describe, create, and give order.

The song Thyrsis sings to earn this cup recalls how Daphnis was made to waste away by jealous love. Daphnis's lament suggests (as did the cup) art's visionary power to rearrange nature.

> Now briars bear violets! Violets spring on thorns!
> Junipers blossom with narcissus flowers,
> and all things be confounded: pines grow pears!
> Since Daphnis is dying, the hart may harry the hounds,
> and mountain owls find tongue of nightingale! [140–44]

As the following stanza makes clear, these lines do not describe some Ovidian transformation of the landscape; they attest instead to the power of emotion-driven rhetoric, a fusion of nature and art that expresses something important *against* the processes of nature, even though (perhaps especially when) those processes are beyond control. "So much he spoke, and ceased. Then Aphrodite wished / to raise him up, but the thread of the Fates was all / spun out; so Daphnis came to the river; the flood hid / the man loved by the Muses, nor to the nymphs unpleasing" (146–49). Thrysis's final refrain and concluding comment put his telling of the poem, the *legend* of Daphnis, into two different contexts, the immediate reality and the hope for the future: "Break the bucolic theme; break it off, Muses! Now give me the goat and the bowl, to milk her and pour an offering to the Muses. Farewell a thousand times, Muses! sweeter song will I sing you hereafter" (150–53). This completes the pattern of balances. Dying is one unavoidable aspect of life not depicted on the cup, but it is the song's major subject. The cup offers a rich panorama showing several representative lives in the ongoing present; the song pays tribute to the single life of an outstanding figure from the past. The cup freezes a moment, the song tells of a process. The cup celebrates the little moments of daily life; the song commemorates a myth involving a man, nature, the pastoral society, and the deities.

Theocritus's poem offers no hope of rebirth or apotheosis for Daphnis. That would be introduced into the pastoral elegy by Menalcas's lament for Daphnis in Vergil's Fifth Eclogue. It offers instead the permanence embodied in what Spenser called "short time's endless monument," the finely wrought song. Truly, the cup and the song are each "epi to pleon," the maker's masterpiece, and by them a brief passage through time—of living, of dying—is caught by art. Art provides the memory. Art asks—indirectly through the image on the cup, directly through the lament itself—that nature and time grant an impossible pity that (here) art alone gives.

> For poetry makes nothing happen: it survives
> . . . it survives,
> A way of happening, a mouth.
> [W. H. Auden, "In Memory of W. B. Yeats," 36, 40–41]

It is not always just this, of course. For some elegists, following Vergil in Eclogue Five, the poem itself is the visionary path to an apotheosis.

> Candidus insuetum miratur limen Olympi
> sub pedibusque uidet nubes et sidera Daphnis.
> . . . "deus, deus ille, Menalca." [56–57, 64]

> [Daphnis in splendor marvels at the unfamiliar threshold of Olympus and sees beneath his feet the clouds and stars. . . . "A god, a god is he, Menalcas!"]

But at the very least the elegy holds the memory and the pity, suggesting that through the poem both will last beyond time, memorialized in the poem's compassion and hope.

> tu rostro de ultratumba bañe la luna casta de compasiva y blanca luz;
> y el Sátiro contemple, sobre un lejano monte,
> una cruz que se eleve cubriendo el horizonte,
> ¡y un resplandor sobre la cruz!
> [Rubén Darío, "Responso," 32–36][2]

> [And may the pure moon bathe your face beyond the tomb in white and tender light; and the satyr contemplate, on a distant peak, a cross that rises to cover the horizon, and radiance on the cross!]

Furthermore, even as it marks the death, it also commemorates the life, returning us to the simple details of mortal existence as the measure of the song, the death, and the life remembered.

> At last he rose, and twitched his mantle blue:
> Tomorrow to fresh woods and pastures new.
> [Milton, "Lycidas," 192–93]

The funeral elegy is so significant for the pastoral tradition because it permits the poet to speak of the natural cycle of life and death, to contain them both in a comprehensible system, and to establish a necessarily ironic relationship of values between them.

For Lycidas your sorrow is not dead,
Sunk though he be beneath the wat'ry floor.

[Milton, "Lycidas," 166–67]

Follow, poet, follow right
To the bottom of the night,
With your unconstraining voice
Still persuade us to rejoice.

[Auden, "In Memory of W. B. Yeats," 54–57]

The elegy is also the furthest, and perhaps the purest, expression of pastoral love, generosity, and union.

Daphnim ad astra feremus: amauit nos quoque Daphnis.

[Vergil, Fifth Eclogue, 52]

[Daphnis I shall exalt to the stars: me also Daphnis loved.]

So in Theocritus's First Idyll the splendidly wrought cup, in essence permanent, is given for a performance of the song, a performance that is ephemeral even though the song may be eternal in a way of its own. Thus Theocritus suggests how to value visual and verbal art, no doubt; but thus, too, he seems to suggest the worth of the elegiac tribute when set against narrative and descriptive art.

Like love, death is a topic especially appropriate to the pastoral because it is an experience that engrosses our attention, creating a realm of thought that seems to be separated from the flow of ordinary experience and outside of time. Yet it is neither outside of time nor detached from ordinary experience; rather, it forcibly reminds us of time's passing and makes us confront the world of nature and society around us.

Yes, thou art gone! and round me too the night
In ever-nearing circle weaves her shade.

[Arnold, "Thyrsis," 131–32][3]

Death calls forth pastoral irony in yet another way. It is a common experience, one of the two experiences we all share and therefore one of the two moments in time at which we seem to be without distinction or rank ("That sunk so low that sacred head of thine"—Milton, "Lycidas," 102). Yet that moment above all others is one that demands we say that this person was special, and that this death has made some mark on the landscape—both the internal landscape of the poet's heart and mind and the outer landscape of the natural world.

> Sus arbre sec s'en complaint Philomene;
>     L'aronde en faict cryz piteux et tranchans,
>     La tourterelle en gemit et en meine
>     Semblable dueil; et j'accorde à leurs chants.
> > [Clement Marot, "Eclogue sur le Trespas
> > de ma Dame Loyse de Savoye," 125–28]⁴

[In the barren tree Philomene complains; the swallow chirrups woeful, cutting cries; the turtle-dove moans and shows its sorrow; and I am one with their songs.]

As the pastoral elegy unites inner and outer nature, grief takes on an external presence. The speaker then can find a poetic path out of grief or a broader context for comprehending that grief. The poem concerns the human heart, the world we live in, and the truth about the future as it emerges from the interplay between the speaker and nature.

> spero che sovra te non avrà possa
> quel duro, eterno, ineccitabil sonno
> d'averti chiusa in così poca fossa;
>     se tanto i versi miei prometter ponno.
> > [Sannazaro, *Arcadia*, Eleventh Eclogue 154–60]⁵

[I do hope that the hard, impenetrable, eternal sleep will have no power over you, to trap you in so strait a ditch—if my verses can hold forth such a promise.]

> I am borne darkly, fearfully, afar;
> Whilst, burning through the inmost veil of
>     Heaven,
> The soul of Adonais, like a star,
> Beacons from the abode where the Eternal are.
> > [Shelley, "Adonais," 492–95]⁶

As a result of this tension between the great careless leveling by death and the compassionate commemoration of the dead by poetry, another irony emerges. Pathos is evoked by treating the departed as merely an innocent shepherd who has been victimized by pitiless death; but attention is demanded by treating the "shepherd" as much more than that—often, in fact, more than he or she could have been in real life. This can be true whether the poem is about Edward

King as "Lycidas" or about King Henri II as "Berger Henriot," king of the shepherds:

> Ce fut ce Henriot qui remply de bon heur
> Remist des Dieux banis le seruice en honneur,
> Et se monstrant des arts le parfait exemplaire,
> Esleua iusqu'au ciel le gloire militaire.
>
> [Ronsard, Eclogue I, 15–18][7]

[This was Henriot who, with good thoughts abundant, restored to dignity the service of the gods and, showing a perfect example of the arts, also raised military glory to the heavens.]

In so enlarging, by the magnifying power of grief, the actual scale of the life that is mourned, the poet turns biography and history into myth. This can prepare the way for the poet to speak as a seer whose vision and poetic ambition transcend the sheer act of mourning.

In Milton's "Epitaphium Damonis" we feel the full energy of that tension between the pastoral pathos and vatic ambition, and come to understand more clearly how it stimulates artistic creativity.[8] The poem was written about 1640 (three years after "Lycidas") in memory of Charles Diodati, from Milton's school days onward his one close friend. Diodati had died while Milton was touring in Italy, and the poem speaks of Milton's emotions upon returning to the familiar scenes from which his friend would always be absent. The elegy partly commemorates Diodati ("Damon") but even more markedly commemorates the poetic hopes of his mourner, "Thyrsis." For Thyrsis, though of the pastoral world, has been away from it; "Pastorem scilicet illum / Dulcis amor Musae Tusca retinebat in urbe" (13; "For love of the sweet muse kept that shepherd in the Tuscan city"). Returning, he feels most strongly death's violent and premature taking of Daphnis: *Praereptum* (7), "snatched away;" *tulerat . . . sub umbras* (11), "swept away to the shades;" *immiti rapuerunt fuere* (20), "pitilessly snatched you away to death." Consequently, though Thyrsis has returned

> Ast ubi mens expleta domum pecorisque relicti
> cura vocat, simul assueta seditque sub ulmo,           [14–15]

[When his mind was full, and care of the flock left at home called him back, and he settled under the familiar elm],

he can no longer fulfill his pastoral task. The refrain repeatedly dismisses his flock, "Ite domum impasti, domino iam non vacat, agni," ("Return home unfed, your master cannot care for you now, lambs"). The sorrowing shepherd begins the poem, therefore, at the junction of two times that embody change: the past, marked by Damon's death and the elegist's journey for the sake of his own art; and the future, which has not yet taken shape in his mind but clearly cannot be merely a continuation of anything he now feels or has felt in the past.

His poem must be more than a lament; it must be a poem. Both the dead man and his mourner have been artists, so the poet feels doubly obliged to his friend's memory as a friend and as a devotee of culture. Damon will be remembered, second only to Daphnis,

> Si quid id est, priscamque fidem coluisse,
>   piumque,
> Palladiasque artes, sociumque habuisse
>   canorum.                                              [33–34]

[So shall it be, if there is value in keeping the age-old faith and piety, and cultivating the arts of Pallas Athena, and having a poet for a friend.]

The agitated Thyrsis must struggle with his feelings of loss, negligence, and guilt in order to construct the double role of lover of the pastoral values and ambitious poet glad of challenges and fame. He is torn between what he left and lost, and what he found and gained:

> Ecquid erat tanti Romam vidisse sepultam?
> . . . . . . . . . . . . . . . . . . . . . . . . . .
> Ah! certe extremum licuisset tangere dextram,
> Et bene compositos placide morientis ocellos,
> Et dixisse, 'Vale! nostri memo ibis ad astra.'
>
>        Ite domum impasti, domino iam non vacat, agni.
> Quamquam etiam vestri nunquam meminisse pigebit
> Pastores Tusci, Musis operata iuventus,
> . . . . . . . . . . . . . . . . . . . . . . . . .
> Ipse etiam tentare ausus sum, nec puto multum
> Displicui, nam sunt et apud me munera vestra,
> Fiscellae, calathique, et cerea vincia cicutae.
> Quin et nostra suas docuerunt nomina fagos
> Et Datis et Francinus. . . .              [115, 121–26, 133–37]

[And was it so needful to see buried Rome . . . Ah, surely I could have touched your right hand at the end and closed your eyes in peaceful death, and said, "Farewell, remember me on your way to the stars." Return home unfed, your master cannot care for you now, lambs. And yet never shall I regret your memory, Tuscan shepherds, youths devoted to the Muses. . . .

I myself even ventured to compete, and think I did not greatly displease, for your gifts are still with me—baskets of rush and wicker, and pipes bound with wax. Even Dati and Francini taught their beechtrees my name . . . ]

Out of these discordances—the grief and piety for Damon (whose art of medicine, ironically, had failed to save him), the pain of his own imagined personal failure as a friend, the pride of his own artistic achievement amidst other shepherds worthy of note—Thyrsis declares a poetic ambition that necessitates going outside the limits of this pastoral world. "Vos cedite, silvae" (160), he declares; "make way, then, o woods." And this new movement also provides a new context for the refrain, which is repeated immediately after this line. Now we hear the voice of the would-be epic poet.

It is the confidence that comes with the assumption of a mightier voice that gives him access to a higher range of the imagination, with immediate conse-quences for his lament. Now the refrain will be echoed, rather than repeated, and echoed in significantly different form.

Nec tibi conveniunt lacrymae, nec flebimus ultra.
Ite procul, lacrymae.

[202–03]

[Tears are not right for you, they shall flow no more. Begone, my tears.]

Now Thyrsis can imagine Daphnis's bliss in heaven, to which he surely has been transported and which Thyrsis can now envision. The vision itself is not unusual, and some of the particular details recall Milton's "Lycidas." However, the diction is of a different literary mode, though still within the structure of traditional pastoral images.

Ipse, caput nitidum cinctus rutilante corona,
Laetaque frondentis gestans umbracula palmae,
Aeternum perages immortales hymenaeos,
Cantus ubi, choreisque furit lyra mista beatis,
Festa Sionaeo bacchantur et Orgia Thyrso.

[215–19]

[Your lustrous head circled with a brilliant crown, in your hands the joyful fronds of shady palms, you will join eternally in the immortal wedding where song and lyre mingle amid the passion of sacred dance, and the festal orgies revel under Sion's thyrsus.]

The brilliant play on the last word—the wand or "thyrsis" of bacchic revelry, here conceived as a divine staff of heavenly festivity, and the heavenly (rather than earthly) Thyrsis, Zion's celestial lord of song and comfort—demonstrates the artistically fused contraries on which the poem rests. It finally is and is not pastoral. It is a pastoral poem that is not confined to the pastoral world or to those pastoral attitudes toward experience that Theocritus explored at the birth of the tradition.

Much as "Lycidas" struggles against the limitations of conventional pastoral elegies, announces a religious vision, and ends with a narrator newly distanced from the pastoral singer of the elegy proper ("'I come . . . ' / Thus sang the uncouth swain"), so "Epitaphium Damonis" moves, at last concluding with the speaker distanced from the pastoral world he has known and cherished, though still feeling himself part of it. He is so distant that he can hand on his own pastoral name, in a way yielding up his only identity in the pastoral world; yet he is still so much a part of it that he can imagine it a fit way of referring to the divine. Though still "sub ulmo" ("under the elm"), he is far more distant from it now than he was while beyond the mountains and seas, visiting the "Pastores Tusci" (126) or even Rome, which for him was still the city to which Tityrus went. On the other hand, now Thyrsis can shed his guilt at having failed to comfort Daphnis, by writing for him in a way he (presumably) could not have done if he had been content to remain at home with his lambs. It was the desire to do more that permitted him to celebrate his pastoral friend properly.

Here we must recall that the writer of the pastoral is not a pastoral writer. The mute, inglorious Wordsworths produce no pastoral poems. Though perhaps pretending to be a pastoral character, the writer of a pastoral carries on the pretense through a persona. The writer is willing to take part in the fiction but is not bound to it in his or her own person. The pastoral created by this external author exists in all dimensions at once: horizontal space (the pastoral spot), vertical space (an environment connected with the realm of the deities, celestial or otherwise), time (a moment of peace or a link with the furthest past). It posits social structures, ethics, aesthetics. Therefore, the writer, who creates the pastoral from outside it, can stretch the genre in some dimensions beyond its customary limits. The writer, after all, responds simultaneously to the self-limiting energy of the coherent fictional universe and to the expanding energy of his or her own wider creative exploration.

In pushing the pastoral's limits, the artist expands the borders of the genre. Servius, the earliest annotator of Vergil, stated in the fourth century the narrow case that poems like the Fourth Eclogue were not truly pastoral; but for subsequent authors they became an inseparable part of the pastoral canon. So it must be. The conclusion to "Epitaphium Damonis" certainly violates strict pastoral decorum. But Milton's concluding evocation of singing and the rites of Bacchus, capped by the last word (with its reminiscences of Theocritean, Vergilian, and Miltonic pastoral names), suggests that Milton sees himself as not strictly breaking with the pastoral but pushing its limits as far as he can. And he does so under the sanction of pastoral piety and purity, the virtues that traditionally connect the pastoral world with the divine. Confident of Damon's salvation, and feeling moved by the mortal and artistic limitations of the pastoral world that he has known, he draws the pastoral motifs upward through another level of style and another form of myth-making. The lament becomes an engagement with the idea of death; the literary conquering of death, or at least accommodation with it, gives a new artistic life to the poet. In this way the writer—here Milton, but any writer as well—finds how the pastoral connects in some dimension with the outer circle of the writer's own mental world.

Without the elegy, nothing remains but the starkness of death. Hemingway's A Farewell to Arms—a work that in so many ways evokes the epic tradition ("arma virumque") and thereby challenges the traditional epic ethos—illustrates this when Frederic and Catherine's idyllic retreat ends with her death.

Following his escape from the military police, Frederic thinks, "Anger was washed away in the river along with any obligation" (323).[9] He is rejuvenated, emerging from his ordeal as a youth and a private person, no longer a military man: "I had the feeling of a boy who thinks of what is happening at a certain hour at the schoolhouse from which he has played truant" (245). He can try to avoid adult responsibilities, or at least redefine and so restrict them, though doing so involves some sophistry: the war becomes a schoolroom, his flight mere truancy, though he has no intention of forging a note from home and returning to the lessons. Henry—"such a silly boy" (251), Catherine persists in calling him—has left his experiences; they have not left him.

He is like a knight sojourning in a spot of blessed refuge. At first he has a fragile refuge in northern Italy with Catherine, his "girl," as she always is to him. But the encroaching outside world at last makes him a real refugee and ironically sends him to a seemingly more secure pastoral retreat. In Switzerland (where Catherine is in an advanced stage of pregnancy) these two, who imagine themselves as children, while away their time in adolescent sports and have "a fine life" (306).

The long idyllic moment in Switzerland is under emotional and physical pressure from the outside (which includes the anti-idyllic past of war and covert sex), as well as from the future product of past pleasure (a kind of negotium looming ahead). "I went back to the papers and the war in the papers" (310); "The only time I ever felt badly was when I felt like a whore in Milan" (Catherine, 294);

"What reason is there for her to die? There's just a child that has to be born, the by-product of good nights in Milan" (320). *Labor omnia vicit*, as Vergil observes in the *Georgics*: "labor conquers all." With a child comes a life of responsibility and work, the end of the idyll: "It makes trouble and is born and then you look after it and get fond of it maybe" (320). As is appropriate to the pastoral tone of this section, and generally appropriate to Hemingway's vision, the idyll ends not with the hard georgic effort of sustained life or with a grand epic voyage to the great and wonder-filled world outside, the new Hesperides ("we'll go to America, won't we darling? I want to see Niagara Falls. . . . The Golden Gate! That's what I want to see. Where is the Golden Gate?"). It ends instead with the death of the nymph.

This pastoral interlude marks the farewell to arms, not a brief respite or aberrant flight or seduction from arms. And though it closes with a death, there is no elegy, because the pastoral retreat has proven to be a deceptive refuge when confronted by life's processes. Any formal elegiac ritual of grief and compassion seems a futile gesture before the hard face of death: "But after I had got them out and shut the door and turned off the light it wasn't any good. It was like saying good-by to a statue" (332). In this skewed version of the pastoral, fruition (childbirth) merely confirms terminal mortality.

> hic inter densas corylos modo namque gemellos,
> spem gregis, a! silice in nuda conixa reliquit.
> [Vergil, First Eclogue, 14–15]

> [Here, just now, in the hazel thicket new-born twin kids, the hope of the flock—ah!—the ewe let fall onto the barren rock.]

Not only is the magnitude of Henry's inconsolability signified by the absence of the elegy, but so too is the poverty of the world in his eyes. For the idyll is short-lived, and what seemed a place for new life is merely another place for dying.

Death too is in Arcadia. Frederic Henry's silence implies that nothing of value can be said, except of course for the mere retelling of the story, the novel itself. Once again the innocent has fallen victim to death's brutal cruelty, has been overcome by that "duro, eterno, ineccitabil sonno" of which Sannazaro writes. There can be no formal elegy because essentially nothing else has been learned; there is nothing to be learned but the inevitability and the cruelty; therefore, there is nothing for the seer to see but the fact itself, and the appropriate response is to make the report. The telling of the story, with its earlier moments of recognition, complaint, and futile protest, replaces the poem of the swain complaining of the death of his nymph. The work's power lies in the death and in the telling. So the writer, through the elegy or whatever substitutes for the elegy, acknowledges the painful fragility of the pastoral moment and of life in its pastoral guise.

# 7

## Place and Time in the Pastoral

THE SPECIAL ASSOCIATIONS OF PLACE AND TIME IN PASTORAL LITERATURE ARE familiar to all readers.[1] Indeed, the pastoral is often thought of as synonymous with the secluded garden or the Golden Age, with the pure and honest country life that is so preferable to an artificial and corrupt courtly or urban society, or with a happier and more innocent past that has yielded to a decadent and turbulent present. Such motifs are so familiar and have so pervaded popular culture that they need no documentation. However, from examining how pastoral texts mark off space and time, we can see more clearly how pastoral literature creates its fictive enclave. Place includes both location (a particular geographic setting, like a meadow) and presence (a subjective impression of the qualities of an environment); similarly, time includes sequence, which consists of the orderly placement of moments in relation to one another through a day, year, lifetime, or the course of history, and duration, the subjective sensation of moments lasting or rushing by.

As we have seen in preceding chapters, pastoralism can express both the idealities and the imperfections of life. Freedom from worldly cares can also be escapist, and a life of leisure can be frivolous. Within "delicious solitude" (Marvell, "The Garden," 16) may lurk loneliness or helplessness. If the pastoral is nostalgic, in recapturing or celebrating the past it reveals life's evanescence. By intensifying emotional experiences, or by holding them in static tension, pastoral literature offers a heightened reaction to life's tensions. It is in this way that the pastoral resembles any lyrical art. Renato Poggioli has gone so far as to claim that "there is a pastoral cluster in any form of poetry."[2] While this remark is too broad to be helpful, it reminds us that, particularly through the emotion-charged depictions of space and time, pastoral images and attitudes have permeated all literature. A given text, of course, need not embody dialectical oppositions and ironies; many of the richest ones, however, do depend on them.

127

PLACE

The sense of a place has become important to pastoral art, though neither Theocritus nor Vergil was particularly concerned with depicting pastoral landscapes. Many later pastoralists were, and Longus and Ovid use place to a greater extent than the two lyric poets, who are generally more concerned with the landscape's effects on its inhabitants.[3] As in Vergil's First and Ninth Eclogues, the landscape's quality is denoted through the old associations and personal attachments expressed by the speakers, only occasionally stimulating a particularly detailed description:

> Certe equidem audieram, qua se subducere colles
> incipiunt mollique iugum demittere cliuo
> usque ad aquam et ueteres, iam fracta cacumina, fagos,
> omnia carminibus uestrum seruasse Menalcan.          [IX, 7–10]

> [Yet surely I had heard that, from where the hills stretch back and begin the gentle descent from the ridge, all the way to the water and the ancient beeches with their splintered tops, all of this Menalcas had saved with his songs.]

More often the specific location for a particular idyll or eclogue is noted, if at all, only in a passing phrase suggesting the barest sketch: "beside a spring" or "in the shade of the olive tree." Even the amoebean songs are not specifically about the landscape but are more likely about the produce it yields. Revealingly, one of Theocritus's most lavish descriptions of a pastoral landscape is put in the mouth of a city-dweller who, traveling to a harvest festival in the country, sees his surroundings with fresh eyes, not as his accustomed environment but as something that warrants particular observation. He and his friends

> . . . laid us down
> on soft beds of scented rushes and new-stripped
> vine-leaves, while high overhead rustled
> many a poplar and elm, and near at hand
> from the nymphs' cave splashed the holy water.
> On the shady boughs, the scorched cicadas carried
> their chirping labour on, and the tree frog croaked
> far off in the dense thorn brake.          [VII, 141–48]

This description (which continues for several more lines) reveals the detailed attentiveness of an outsider registering each nuance, rather than of a denizen intuitively screening out what is familiar from what might be unusual; indeed, it is an implicit inset. One can find such feelingly described pleasant spots in Tibullus or Horace, or in epics, more often than in the classical pastoral lyrics or the later poems that look to these lyrics as their ancestors. Vergil's exception that verifies the rule is the *locus amoenus* in his First Eclogue, described by Meliboeus as he is going into exile and lamenting the leaving behind of a landscape he will look upon no longer.

The pastoral place is defined by feelings of peace, contentment, belonging, and long association, as well as of easy possession. The shepherds, even when they serve masters, can rest under any congenial tree near any cooling spring; they may be tied to the landscape legally as well as emotionally, but they seem to possess it easily at the same time. In much pastoral poetry we sense the landscape more as a total physical surrounding than as a collection of particular details. The inhabitants fit into it naturally; they have not been placed deliberately within a specific, pictorial context. Sidney's landscape is, typically, sharply outlined but hard to see:

> In a grove most rich of shade,
> Where birds wanton musick made,
> May then yong his pide weedes showing,
> New perfumed with flowers fresh growing,
> Astrophill with Stella sweete,
> Did for mutuall comfort meete.[4]

To be sure, many pastoral landscapes are more richly described than this, but some restraints hold true. First, the pastoral landscape does not call attention to itself. Even if there is some distinguishing feature, or some element notable for its associations, it is not so distracting that it becomes the center of attention. The pastoral landscape discreetly balances its qualities; it exemplifies pastoral virtues. Second, the landscape is emotionally comfortable, or appropriate, for its inhabitants. It surrounds them with an unchallenging setting that may actually be a relief from life's troubles, or at least a reminder that such troubles as there are can be measured against the larger scale of nature.

> Hoch stand ich, neben mir der Linden Kamm,
> Tief unter mir Gezweige, Ast und Stamm;
> Im Laube summte der Phalänen Reigen,
> Die Feuerfliege sah ich glimmend steigen,
> Und Blüten taumelten wie halb entschlafen;
> Mir war, als treibe hier ein Herz zum Hafen,
> Ein Herz, das übervoll von Glück und Leid
> Und Bildern seliger Vergangenheit.
> [Annette von Droste-Hülshoff, "Mondesaufgang," 9–16][5]

[High I stood; close by me, the linden's crest; far below me, twigs, branch and trunk; amid the leaves the buzzing of moths began, I saw the fireflies rise aglow, and blossoms fluttered down as if half-asleep. To me it was as if a heart had reached its haven here, a heart filled with joy and sorrow and the image of happier times gone by.]

The narrator is surrounded by her environment as she stands on the balcony, awaiting the moonrise: *beside me, under me, the fireflies rising, the blossoms falling.* The heart's haven exists physically above the earth, lifted from the mundane associations of heavy experiences and yet still amid the pastoral landscape—indeed, encircled by it—in an idyllic space that seems set apart from the world but not from nature.

Third, the landscape may affect its inhabitants by its capacity to be interpreted. It may show life being renewed; the comforts in the workings of nature or the divinity; or perhaps the differences between human and vegetative life. Examples are Corydon's landscape in Vergil's Second Eclogue, which leads him to recognize his folly; the unchanged "green pastoral landscape" that Wordsworth sees again by the banks of the Wye; Colin Clout's "barren ground, whome winters wrath hath wasted" and which is an emblem of "My life bloud friesing with unkindly cold," of rejected passion or, by contrast, Maurice Scève's,

> Nouvelle amour, nouvelle affection,
> Nouvelle fleurs parmi l'herbe nouvelle:
> Et, jà passée, encor se renouvelle
> Ma primevère en sa verte action.[6]

[New love, new affection, new flowers amid new grass, and, though past already, again my spring renews itself in its green movement.]

Fourth, the landscape may suggest that somehow the human presence lingers on through the continuation of the natural scene that we have lived in and enjoyed and lived our lives as part of. "If you want me again look for me under your boot-soles," as Whitman says. Much as nature's influence holds onto us, we remain part of the landscape.

> Ô lac! rochers muet! grottes! forêt obscure!
> Vous, que le temps épargne ou qu'il peut rajeunir,
> Gardez de cette nuit, gardez, belle nature,
>   Au moins le souvenir!
> . . . . . . . . . . . . . . . .

Que le vent qui gémit, le roseau qui soupire,
Que les parfums légers de ton air embaumé,
Que tout ce qu'on entend, l'on voit ou l'on respire,
    Tout dise: Ils ont aimé!

[Lamartine, "Le Lac," 49–52, 61–64][7]

[O lake! Mute rocks! Grottoes! Dark forest! You that time spares, or can make young again, preserve that night, preserve—beauteous nature—at least the memory! . . . May the wailing wind, the sighing reed, the delicate perfumes of your balmy air, let all that is heard or seen or breathes, everything say: "They loved!"]

Lamartine's poem attempts to fuse silent time and mute nature to impress on the outer landscape a moment of bliss that the passage of life itself discards. The literal present evaporates, but the scene is constant and offers the hope that what is gone yet remains.

Pastoral space, therefore, exists for its emotional coloration. It defines a privileged spot marked off and enclosed from the world at large. It indicates how human life is integrated within nature, or how it sees in the natural world its proper field of reference. So in Vergil's Fifth Eclogue the apotheosis of Daphnis becomes significant because of its effects on the animate world.

ergo alacris siluas et cetera rura uoluptas
Panaque pastoresque tenet Dryadasque puellas.
nec lupus insidias pecori nec retia ceruis
ulla dolum meditantur; amat bonus otia Daphnis.          [58–61]

[Delight then enlivens the forests and fields, Pan as well as the shepherds and the Dryad maidens. The wolf makes no plots against the flock; nets are not set for the deer; good Daphnis loves peacefulness.]

The pastoral setting may be characterized in particular by the presence or memory of friends or relatives, because continuity with the past is important to the pastoral. The pastoral historical sense is personal, based on remembered songs, friends, and lovers, local gods and nymphs, passed from person to person as a direct legacy, often as a reward for some particular artistic performance.

Vergil's Ninth Eclogue laments the disruption of that sort of pastoral life by tracing out its artistic consequences. Dealing with the same land confiscations referred to in the First Eclogue, this one speaks of the plight of those who remain to see their former property in the hands of the stranger who threw them out and are bullied about by an ex-soldier who cares nothing for them or their ways. Menalcas's songs were not enough to win a reprieve from the government order, and the pastoral herdsmen have not the strength to oppose the new owners. Moeris tells Lycidas,

> . . . carmina tantum
> nostra ualent, Lycida, tela inter Martia quantum
> Chaonias dicunt aquila ueniente columbas.
> quod nisi me quacumque nouas incidere lites
> ante sinistra caua monuisset ab ilice cornix,
> nex tuus hic Moeris nec uiueret ipsa Menalcas.             [IX, 11–16]

> [Our songs have as much power, Lycidas, against Mars's tools as they say Charmian doves do when the eagle arrives. Had I not somehow ended this new dispute, cautioned by a raven in a hollow tree on the left, neither your Moeris would be alive nor even Menalcas.]

Lycidas is indignant that there should be not only death in Arcadia but the threat of murder as well and, even worse, the threat of murder against the pastoral singers.

> Heu, cadit in quenquam tantum scelus? heu, tua nobis
> paene simul tecum solacia rapta, Menalca!
> quis caneret Nymphas?

> [Alas, can anyone conceive such an outrage? Alas, you yourself as well as the solace you give nearly taken from us, Menalcas! Who would sing of the nymphs?]

This last question, as well as the danger that gave rise to it, prompts a series of fragmented quotations of partially remembered songs, a poignantly abortive version of the traditional pastoral song contest. Neither man is able to get beyond five lines of a composition, so that the eclogue is like a dream of Arcadian fragments, both characters having trouble with recollections disrupted by time and the change in the land, which has become hostile. Moeris laments,

> Omnia fert aetas, animum quoque. saepe ego longos
> cantando puerum memini me condere soles.
> nunc oblita mihi tot carmina, uox quoque Moerin
> iam fugit ipsa; lupi Moerin uidere priores.             [IX, 51–59]

> [Time carries away everything, even a mind. Often as a boy, I remember, my singing laid the sun to rest. Now I have forgotten all my songs; Moeris's voice itself is gone. The wolves saw Moeris first.]

The last line is a proverbial explanation for the loss of one's vocal ability, but in view of the story Moeris has told earlier, it is also a figurative explanation of the violent effect brought about by the land's new ownership. The processes of change, in time and place, whittle away one's connection with the past and one's own identity. They cast gloom over the present and future.

Lycidas tries to perk up their spirits by suggesting that they rest and sing some songs; but Moeris, who has the last word, replies that they should be about their tasks and leave singing for a better time. They seem stranded in present woes, the past receding and slaking off, the future indeterminate. The pattern of discontinuity and inconclusiveness in this eclogue's structure coincides with the threat to the herdsmen's rights to the landscape.

To appreciate the contrast we might consider the model pastoral song performed by Theocritus's Lycidas in Idyll VII, wherein he describes his vision of a delightful pastime.

> . . . Two shepherds shall pipe to me,
> one of Acharnae, one of Lycopas, and Tityrus
> nearby will sing of how, when Daphnis the herd
> loved Zenea once, the hills around
> groaned, and the oaks that grow on Himera's banks
> mourned him, the while he wasted like the snows
> below rearing Haemus, Athos, Rhodope
> or remotest Caucasus lying. And he shall sing
> of the goatherd enclosed in a great coffer, alive,
> by his wicked master's presumption: the snub-
>     nosed bees
> fed him from bland flowers, hieing from the meadow
> to the fragrant cedar chest, for the Muse had honied
> nectar spilt on his lips. O bless'd Comatas!          [75–87]

Vergil's eclogue has long been known as a reworking of material from this idyll; and here we can see one important thematic revision. In contrast to Vergil's herdsmen, this Lycidas can imagine a world in which he is surrounded by song, in which pastoral musicians can spin their melodies and lyrics of pastoral deities and the legends surrounding them. One of those songs, interestingly, would tell of how the favor of the gods saved the goatherd-poet Comatas from his resentful master in honor of his sweet singing; indeed, Comatas's sweet voice makes his own salvation possible. His story, then, is part of the inherited material of the pastoral world, an element of both pastoral history and the pastoral landscape.

That landscape, no matter how specific and local, is at the same time universal and aboriginal. So Vergil, who came from northern Italy and spent many of his adult years in Naples and Rome, nonetheless sees fit to address the pastoral muses at the beginning of his Fourth Eclogue as "Siciledes Musae," Sicilian Muses, after Theocritus, who may have been born and raised in Syracuse but who did much of his writing in Alexandria and set many of his idylls on Cos. In "Lycidas" Milton similarly addresses the Arcadian Arethuse and Alpheus, the river Mincius (from Vergil's Seventh Eclogue), and the "Sicilian Muse," while also referring to places in the British Isles. Similarly, in Julio Herrera's sonnet "La vuelta de los campos," the Spanish country town seems to bear its literary generic heritage as part of its landscape:

> Dos mozas con sus cantaros se deslizan apenas.
> Huye el vuelo sonambulo de las horas serenas.
> Un suspiro de Arcadia peina los matorrales . . .
>
> [Two lasses bearing water jugs sidle by. The sleepwalking flight of the quiet hours passes on. A sigh from Arcadia brushes the copse . . . ][8]

Not only is the pastoral feeling inescapable; the pastoral tradition is inescapable. It becomes part of the way in which we perceive or (as here) imagine the world. Herrera knows that this imagined scene is not just generally idyllic. It is quite specifically pastoral, an Arcadian vision, so much so that the air itself seems to blow from Arcadia. Fittingly, Herrera, a Uruguayan, did not know firsthand the landscape that he portrays as "Arcadian." No matter. He too has lived in Arcadia.

> We cannot help but live in Arcadia in some place, at some time.

> We are talking now of summer evenings in Knoxville, Tennessee in the time that I lived there so successfully disguised to myself as a child.[9]

In this passage, the opening of James Agee's "Knoxville, Summer of 1915," several temporal elements of the idyllic experience come together: the traditional season of classical pastoral, summer; the romantic time, evening; childhood (even as a "disguise," recognizing that the idyll is a sort of artifice, a pretense in which one willingly believes and which one successfully enjoys). The physical setting is complemented by the presence of the tightly knit family, adding coherence and stability to the temporal setting. Here they take their ease, with the narrator conscious of their comforting, sheltering beings, and of the life of art and familial tenderness that seems to surround him. In the midst of gentle nature, they also belong to nature and seem quite as reassuring as the world around him that all is peaceful and loving.

> On the rough wet grass of the back yard my father and mother have spread quilts. We all lie there, my mother, my father, my uncle, my aunt, and I too am lying there. . . . They are not talking much, and the talk is quiet. . . .

The stars are wide and alive, they seem each like a smile of great sweetness, and they seem very near. All my people are larger bodies than mine . . . with voices gentle and meaningless like the voices of sleeping birds. One is an artist, he is living at home. One is a musician, she is living at home. One is my mother who is good to me. One is my father who is good to me.

At home: this is the dominant impression of the pastoral environment. The author creates a temporal or spatial setting that will satisfy, or at least have the potential to satisfy, the desire to be at home. To pastoral characters, nature is a friend (indeed, an occasionally moody one) whose company and qualities, particularly generosity, they enjoy, and with whom they feel an easy equality. This is so even when feeling at home only means, as it sometimes does, that one's sorrows are regrettably natural.

> My sheepe are thoughts, which I both guide and serve,
> Their pasture is faire hills of fruitlesse love:
> On barren sweetes they feede, and feeding sterve,
> I waile their lot, but will not other prove.
>
> [Sidney, *Arcadia*, "Dorus His Comparison" 1–4]

Even in this expression of sorrow the quiet verse implies the complacent acceptance that goes with a sense of inevitability. Such emotions may be long-lasting, even if sequentially limited, and may merge with other feelings as well. Agee, for instance, feels the pain that comes with realizing that his loving family that guards his pastoral life cannot tell him who or what he is. But still the experience stands as specially gratifying, the time remembered as specially privileged. The idyll may be imperfect, but the pastoral definition of time and place attests to clearly sensed values. Pastoral art records our longing for a life bounded by friendliness and goodness, at once contained, enclosed, and at the same time infinite.

What matters most is the emotional quality of the experience, not how it comes about. Almost by way of reply to Horace's Alfius, for whom pastoral means possession, Marge Piercy finds comfort with her lover under someone else's beech tree, refuge from the likes of Alfius.

> Our soil utters threats of a creditor,
> our trees mutter complaints and grocery lists.
> Only the woods of strangers murmur
> sensually of velvet beds on the night. . . .[10]
>
> ["In Search of Scenery"]

Off one's own turf, the "arching" tree in this summer night completes the lovers' ideal landscape, "gracious, compliant."

## TIME

For several reasons, Theocritus's ideal pastoral time of day is noon, and so it is through much of pastoral literature. Obviously the midday Mediterranean heat would make noon appropriate for resting, socializing, singing, or thinking one's private thoughts. Rosenmeyer points out the relevance of some literary and intellectual contexts. For one, the combination of sun and shade at noontime perfectly balances these natural influences; further, as a midpoint in the day's progress, noon is an appropriate time to reflect and seek inspiration; for these reasons it is also conventionally an appropriate time to meet deities. In general, Rosenmeyer observes, there is in the noon stillness "a core of suspended energy" available for creative use.[11] Whatever the reason, the observation in Idyll VI that when Damoetas and Daphnis sit down to begin their song contest it is summer and noon echoes down through pastoral literature in such passages as Coleridge's

> And thus, my Love! as on the midway slope
> Of yonder hill I stretch my limbs at noon.
> ["The Eolian Harp," 34–35][12]

Mallarmé's faun also stretches out his afternoon reverie from the "silence du midi."

By contrast, the descent of evening, especially in earlier pastorals, may be ominous. Vergil's First Eclogue ends in the shadows from the mountains beyond which Meliboeus must trudge into exile: "maioresque cadunt altis de montibus umbrae" ("and from the mountain-tops longer shadows fall"). The Tenth Eclogue closes the volume on an even more troubled note.

> surgamus; solet esse grauis cantatibus umbra,
> iuniperi grauis umbra; nocent et frugibus umbrae.
> ite domum saturae, uenit Hesperos, ite capellae.     [75–78]

> [So let us rise: the shade is bad for singers, the juniper's deep shade; shade is also bad for crops. Home, now; Hesperus comes. Home, now, well-fed, my little goats.]

The sense of encroaching gloom and unfolding dangers is caught wryly by Marvell at the end of "Upon Appleton House," where fast-approaching night makes the world seem grotesquely topsy-turvy, defying rational laws. Like the salmon-fishers who return home carrying their boats over their heads, "And like the Antipodes in shoes, / Have shod their heads in their canoes," (771–72)[13] making of themselves a cross between human and lower creatures, "rational amphibii," so night approaches, prompting the hurried exclamation, "Let's in: for the dark hemisphere / Does now like one of them appear" (775–76).

However, while shepherds and tutors take their rest in the middle of the day, most of us who live in more hectic surroundings must wait. Particularly from the eighteenth century onward there has been a strong tradition of twilight and nighttime pastorals, as writers have sought a time that more closely approximates the qualities that Theocritus could find in the noon-hour. As Anne Finch, Countess of Winchilsea, writes,

> When in some River, overhung with Green,
> The waving Moon and trembling Leaves are seen;
> When freshen'd Grass now bears it self upright,
> And makes cool Banks to pleasing Rest invite,
> . . . . . . . . . . . . . . . . . . . . . . . . . . . . .
> In such a *Night* let Me abroad remain,
> Till Morning breaks, and All's confus'd again;
> Our Cares, Our Toils, our Clamours are renew'd,
> Or Pleasures, seldom reach'd, again pursu'd.
>
> [9–12, 47–50][14]

The night virtually creates an enchanted landscape—alive, vital, yet refreshingly restful—in contrast to day's frantic futility.

There is less consensus on the pastoral times of the year, though there is a general, subjective sense of how the time should feel. It is not so much the time of year itself as the associations of a particular time of year within a given culture. Most pastoral literature takes place during summer, when the real shepherd's work is likely to be easy. Nature's richness, bursting forth without human effort at cultivation, can be enjoyed during the long, clear days; the heat promotes languor and detachment from the outside world; the cool shade is particularly inviting; and the summer may bring a change in the day's occupation.

> From his sixth year, the Boy of whom I speak,
> In summer, tended cattle on the hills;
> But, through the inclement and the perilous days
> Of long-continuing winter, he repaired,
> Equipped with satchel, to a school, that stood
> Sole building on a mountain's dreary edge.
>
> [Wordsworth, "The Excursion," I, 118–23][15]

So the ideal life may be expressed in the young Milton's terms:

> Thither all their bounties bring,
> That there eternal summer dwells.
>
> [Milton, A Mask Presented at Ludlow Castle, 987–88]

Of course, summer can be uncomfortable too.

> solstitium pecori defendite: iam uenit aestas
> torrida, iam lento turgent in palmite gemmae.
>
> [Vergil, Eclogue VII, 47–48]

[Protect my flocks from the heat of the solstice; now comes sultry summer; now buds swell on the bending vine.]

Therefore the ideal pastoral climate may offer the best of summer without its scorching heat. As Arnold celebrates a perfect moment in "Thyrsis,"

> This winter-eve is warm,
> Humid the air! leafless, yet soft as spring,
>     The tender purple spray on copse and briers!
>     And that sweet city with her dreaming spires,
> She needs not June for beauty's heightening.          [16–20][16]

Such a season, unnatural and intense, seems to have descended from outside of time, perfect in its dreaming ideality.

Of course, Spenser, Pope, and Clare have no trouble finding bucolic material for the winter months as they traverse their fictive pastoral years. Further, Whittier's "Snow-Bound," subtitled "A Winter Idyll," treats the pleasures appropriate to winter in pastoral fashion. For Whittier, in the midst of winter's rage the family hearth offers warmth and comfort. It is a pastoral refuge, in its way, from the terrors of destructive nature.

> Shut in from all the world without,
> We sat the clean-winged hearth about,
> Content to let the north-wind roar
> In baffled rage at pane and door. . . .
> The mug of cider simmered slow,
> The apples sputtered in a row,
> And, close at hand, the basket stood
> With nuts from brown October's wood.[17]

In this passage the homestead is an island of natural delights; here nature's bounty from milder seasons can be enjoyed in loving surroundings, and they seem all the more gratifying by contrast with the howling wind outside. For English poets the quintessential pastoral months are May and June; but Keats (for example) writes about a pastoral autumn, and Milton sees as perfect pastoral seasons not only "eternal summer" but also the combination of spring and autumn that holds in prelapsarian paradise.

Though there are four seasons in the pastoral world, there seem to be three seasons of life: childhood, late adolescence, and old age. There is no middle age. For some writers—Traherne, Wordsworth, Lewis Carroll, Milne—the child's attitude toward life seems ideal because it is harmonious with its environment. Once these clouds of glory dissipate, or Christopher Robin has to spend too much of his day at school, or Alice grows as mature as her sister, something is lost. Then we are to imagine a new pastoral state attesting to a different level of pastoral experience. The young shepherds must be old enough to fall in love, which they do with heady energy, emotional exuberance, naiveté, and vulnerability. They lack the complete, selfless unity with their surroundings which they once enjoyed unconsciously, though they may feel self-consciously that they share nature's moods. Still inexperienced, they are not yet wise.

Beyond this stage lies another span of silence until we meet them again in old age. The old pastoral characters (like Vergil's Tityrus—*fortunate senex*—or Philemon and Baucis in Ovid's *Metamorphoses* and Goethe's *Faust*, or Shakespeare's Corin) most clearly exemplify the complacent, philosophic acceptance of life, as well as the stable, familial, and religious values that characterize the quiet and sanctity of the pastoral environment. Usually they want only to be left alone, in peaceful semiretirement. These stages may be combined in the lamented shepherd of the pastoral elegy, usually one who, dying in the prime of life, may pass on to a more sublime understanding of the creative force within life, in a heavenly pastoral landscape still full of vitality but now divine and eternal: "The fieldes ay fresh, the grasse ay greene" (Spenser, "November," 189).

Spenser's "February" effectively sets the pastoral contrast between youth and age in a dialogue between Cuddie, the young cowherd, chafing under the duress of a long winter that he feels is sapping his vitality, and the old shepherd Thenot, who urges that he be stoical in the face of the changing seasons that are beyond mortal control. Thenot asks,

> Must not the world wend in its commun course
> From good to badde, and from badde to worse,
> From worse vnto that is worst of all,
> And then returne to his former fall? [11–14]

Perhaps derived from the passage in Vergil's First Georgic, "sic omnia fatis / in peius ruere ac retro sublapsa referri" (199–200); "So according to fate's laws all things quickly regress and are carried away from their goals"), this—as well as the Latin passage—ends in the conclusion that steadfast work is the only possible defense against "Winters wracke" and the inevitable deterioration of all things.[18] Vergil, in the lines immediately preceding those just quoted, warns of the dangers that follow from ignoring this elementary but painful prudence; and he does so in terms that might explain why Thenot, in answering Cuddie's apparently reasonable complaints about winter, calls the other a "laesie ladde" (9), though nothing in Cuddie's opening speech shows extraordinary sloth.

> uidi lecta diu et multo spectata labore
> degenerare tamen, ni uis humana quotannis
> maxima quaeque manu legeret.                              [197–99]
>
> [I have seen seeds, though carefully selected and watched with greatest care,
> still degenerate, unless every year the choicest ones were chosen by hand.]

The "uis humana" provides, along with the good will of the gods, the only protection against that inevitable decline; and at this point in his poem that "power" is represented not by Cuddie's animal spirits but by Thenot's prudence and determination. Human constructive and creative power finds its voice in his declaration that "euer my flocke was my chiefe care" (23).

All this is beyond Cuddie. Proud of his youth and arrogant in his lustiness, he sees in the "foolish old man" only a brain "emperished . . . Through ruste elde." Cuddie compares himself and Thenot with the herds they tend, noting that his own bullock is young, warm-blooded, virile, and healthy, while Thenot's sheep are aged, cold, listless, and weak. As emblems of the men, the animals become paradigms of the antithesis between spring and winter, youth and age. Thenot, who suffers by Cuddie's comparison, insists, however, that the outward show is not everything, for outward emblems are susceptible of different interpretations. While Cuddie's descriptions of the herds are accurate, they are not sufficient to account for all the elements in human life. Something is gained with age, something Cuddie does not yet understand.

Cuddie's comical reaction to Thenot's fable is predictable: "Here is a long tale, and little worth." Indeed, although the general drift is beyond misapprehension, we too may feel that the story rather imperfectly fits the poem's situation. Spenser does not seem to point the moral here as sharply as he might, because the young man's vigor does after all have a positive value. It represents a directness, a forcefulness of life that Thenot (through no fault of his own) lacks; and the month of February is, after all, hardly the time to argue against youth, liveliness, and love. But Cuddie's attitude is vulnerable, and Spenser permits his antagonist to score some telling points against him. As there is no point in blaming the old man for being old, so the young man merits no particular admiration for being young and acting it.

But the debate does not end in a draw between equals whose virtues and failings cancel each another out. Rather, Spenser seems to recognize that the debate between spring and winter, youth and age, is not an abstract and self-sufficient issue. It reflects contrasting notions of the attitudes appropriate to life in this difficult world, and by the structure of this eclogue he implies how he balances the opposing values. Though Spenser can remain sufficiently detached to permit Cuddie's mocking retort at the end, still it is Thenot who is allowed to tell his tale, and the disparaging rejoinder is all that Cuddie can muster by way of reply. There are obvious limits to the old man's wisdom, but his fable at least constitutes the power to assimilate and communicate knowledge. Love, which has bewitched Cuddie, seems not to have done much for his brain.

The pastoral emphasis on the extremes of youth and age, or infancy and death, in the cycle of an individual life corresponds with its concentration on the golden or Edenic age in the world's infancy, the messianic or Golden Age that awaits in the future, or the paradisial eternity of heaven. The Golden Age that will come again in Vergil's Eclogue IV, bringing a spring that is also a harvesttime, indicates by its circularity that the pastoral era is our natural one, from which we have unfortunately been separated but to which we will return. Milton, at the beginning of *Paradise Regained*, sees a double form of return.

> I who erewhile the happy garden sung,
> By one man's disobedience lost, now sing
> Recover'd Paradise to all mankind,
> By one man's firm obedience fully tried
> Through all temptation, and the Tempter foil'd
> In all his wiles, defeated and repuls't,
> And Eden rais'd in the waste wilderness.                    [I, 1–7]

Here the two paradises are the heavenly paradise awaiting the faithful as their reward and the spiritual Eden raised by the Son through his defense of both himself and the faith in his battles with temptation. One significant consequence of this circular movement is to cancel time's effects, creating the illusion of unending duration, in itself a pastoral fiction. Ovid's description of the Golden Age casts it as a time when "ver erat aeternum" (I, 107; "spring was eternal"); but even here it is not simply spring, because it is a time of constant, spontaneous fruition as well as constant renewal, the autumn harvest joined to spring.

> mox etiam fruges tellus inarata ferebat,
> ne renovatus ager gravidis canebat aristis.
> flumina iam lactis, iam flumina nectaris ibant,
> flavaque de viridi stillabant ilice mella.                     [I, 109–12]

[Soon the untilled earth brought forth its fruits, and the unturned field quickened with growing wheat; rivers flowed with milk, rivers flowed with nectar, and golden honey dripped then from the trees.]

This is not a climate of extremes or finalities. That presumably is why the Golden Age is vernal rather than aestival, despite summer's continuing importance in pastoral poetry. The pastoral year is dominated by those moments of renewal and gratification that, when combined, make time satisfy itself.

The notion of making time pause, even stop, or circle back to the beginning (stretching duration, in other words) is basic to the pastoral instinct for enclosure. Being absorbed in a moment of blessed, privileged time means being settled into an emotionally comfortable experience. Whether attained or not, the desire for that is at the heart of the pastoral. For the pastoral, time is a concommitant of emotion. For this reason, nostalgia is often an important temporal quality of pastoral literature. Nostalgia subverts the passage of time. Through it, a supposedly golden past is recoverable by the imagination; and it does not much matter whether that past is one's own childhood, an earlier era, or even the first days of the human race itself. Time is compressed, so that the pastoral age seems endless. For instance, Colin Clout in Spenser's "June" can say, in apparent homage (as E. K. points out) to Chaucer, dead for a century and three-quarters, "The God of shepheardes Tityrus is dead, / Who taught me homely, as I can, to make" (81–82). No matter that Chaucer and Vergil (and his character Tityrus) are conflated in the name, and time compressed. All pastoral poets and characters know and remember one another; their eras and worlds overlap. Therein lies one of the special graces of the pastoral universe. It is cozy and timeless, at least in its ideal constructions. Its temporal and spatial continuity is sustained by art, which gives the pastoral world shape, duration, moment, and meaning.

These emotional qualities of the pastoral senses of place, sequence, and duration are expressed effectively in the opening passages of Emlyn Williams's autobiography, George, where the author describes himself as a boy in Wales, stretched out on the grass on an April morning, taking stock of himself in both space and time.

The bleat of a sheep. A bird called, careless, mindless. Eighteen inches from my eye, a tawny baby frog was about to leap. It waited.

Everything waited: the hymn had ceased, the bird was dumb and suspended. "I was born November the 26th 1905 and the world was completed at midnight on Saturday July the 10th 4004 B.C."—our Bible stated the year at the top of page one, the rest I felt free to add—"and has been going on ever since, through Genesis Revelation the six wives of Henry the Eighth the Guillotine and the Diamond Jubilee right until this minute 10 A.M. Sunday April the 14th 1912, when the world has stopped. The sun will not set tonight, or ever again, and I am the only one who knows."

No sound: the spool of time has run down, the century is nipped in the bud. I shall never grow up, or old, but shall lie on the grass forever, a mummy of a boy nestling in the middle of it with a nameless warmth like the slow heat inside straw. This is the eternal morning.[19]

For a moment the world is imaginatively locked at a place in time, as is the boy, locked also in space, in the idyllic moment when nothing can or should change. He becomes a part of the pastoral world ("like the slow heat inside straw") that surrounds him, and in fact triggers his reverie as the sounds of the sheep and bird ("careless, mindless") hang in the silence, and the frog crouches, poised and unmoving. The morning of this day, and of his youth, both filled with warmth, bring to a climax the rush of human history and the individual experience of existence. Within him, he spontaneously recreates the Golden Age. Time stops in this moment. And then the moment is over. The frog jumps; someone calls to George; he must straighten his Sunday clothes and run back to town. The natural passage of time and the requirements of a society that lives according to its own sense of the temporal proprieties and responsibilities reassert themselves. History returns with a rush, and with a metaphysical puzzle for the pastoral dreamer who has imagined the world halted for an instant into an ideally arranged picture. "The sun did set, and by the time it rose next morning the *Titanic* had been sunk. If the world *had* stopped, they would not have drowned; I thought about it for days."

At the instant when the boy feels and expresses to himself, "This is the eternal moment," reality (in the form of a very real frog who is beyond his imagination's power to control) asserts itself, much as Theocritus's shepherds must rush off to tend their sportive goats, and Vergil's to find shelter against the evening. Quickly he is called away to the somewhat less pastoral civilization of Sunday rites, then to an outside world jarringly real and contact with the insistent assault of a history far more vivid and resonating than the schoolbook landmarks speeding into the past. The pastoral moment is short-lived. Duration is a trick of the mind, and only memory and imagination retain the pastoral experience as if alive.

In the face of death, the desire to "seize the day" is a longing for a pastoral refuge in time, place, or action, to find what comforts one can in moments sheltered from slings and arrows or out of the hearing of time's wingéd chariot. As Horace writes in his Soracte Ode (I, ix), urging Thaliarchus to warm himself with plenty of firewood, good wine, and lovers,

> quid sit futurum cras, fuge quaerere et
> quem fors dierum cumque dabit, lucro
>     adpone, nec dulcis amores
>         sperne puer neque tu choreas,
> donec virenti canities abest
> morosa.                                    [13–18]

[What the future may bring, don't think about; and what fate gives you daily, mark as profit. Never spurn sweet love or dancing while you are young, while crabbed age is still far off from your springtime.]

Even if we know that the pastoral experience is but a passing moment doomed by time's flow, by the inevitable onset of cares and the resulting estrangement from life's basic pleasures, still it is valuable, and may be all the more precious when we recognize its evanescence. "Quid aeternis minorem / Consiliis animum fatigas?" ("Why weary your overburdened soul with never-ending planning?"), Horace asks in II, ii, 11–12. Life's worthwhile questions, he implies, are essentially rhetorical. Life goes through changes, so we always need relief from the relentless pace of events.

> cur non sub alta vel platano vel hac
> pinu iacentes sic temere et rosa
>     canos odorati capillos,
>         dum licet, Assyriaque nardo
> potamus uncti?                              [13–17]

[Why not indulge ourselves, lying beneath a plane tree or this tall pine, our gray hairs scented with roses, pomaded with Assyrian nard?]

Death, the great leveler, makes us all pastoral characters, and therefore the knowledge that death must come should make our earthly pastoral world that much more precious to us. Enjoyment cannot be taken away, only prevented by time and the fates from returning.

cedes coemptis saltibus et domo,
villaque flavus quam Tiberis lavit,
    cedes et extructis in altum
      divitiis potietur heres.
divesne prisco natus ab Inacho,
nil interest an pauper et infima
    de gente sub divo moreris,
      victima nil miserantis Orci:
omnes eodem cogimur, omnium
versatur urna serius ocyius
    sors exitura et nos in aeternum
      exilium inpositura cumbae.         [Odes, II, iii, 17–28]

[You will yield up your purchased groves and your home, and your country house, washed by the yellow Tiber; you will yield them up. And the wealth you piled high will pass to an heir. Rich, descended from ancient Inachus, that doesn't matter. Or poor, and from the dregs of society, a sacrifice for the pitiless netherworld. All of us are collected there. Sooner or later fate tumbles everything out of the urn, and we must take our places on the boat to eternal exile.]

This, after all, is the doom that makes us all merely bucolic swain, pitifully vulnerable like Meliboeus to the turns of fate and the hard ways of gods and mortal demigods. It is the threat of endless exile from the land of milk and honey, with all that we loved and enjoyed and possessed left behind, all protection and all privileges at once removed. There is this too: against the marmoreal chill of death, life on this bountiful earth, filled with moments of small yet important pleasures, is itself pastoral.

# 8

## Pastoral Society and Ethics

PASTORAL SOCIETY IS PREDOMINANTLY MALE. WOMEN, NYMPHS, AND GODDESSES are frequently mentioned and may be dramatically important, but within pastoral poems they rarely speak. Even in the romances and in Renaissance pastoral dramas, where shepherdesses appear fairly often, they are usually outnumbered. Also, women writers seldom use pastoral literary motifs in the literal, traditional ways in which male writers do.

One cannot be sure, however, what conclusions to draw from such observations. Verisimilitude might explain the predominance of male shepherds, given that real sheep-tending was more usually done by men and boys. But, more important, the number of female authors during the centuries in which pastoral literature flourished is very small, and the presumptive audience was predominantly male. (Also, in many periods the prohibition against women on the stage confined women's roles to boys and consequently restricted the sheer number of female speaking roles.) We should notice further that the pastoral's thematic characteristics might be appropriate to the traditional ways of life and thought for most women, but for that very reason it would be an unlikely and unattractive choice for those who were sufficiently unconventional to present themselves as writers.

This is not to say that there are no conventional pastoral works by women: Mary Sidney, Countess of Pembroke, for instance, wrote a completely traditional pastoral dialogue for one of Queen Elizabeth's pastoral entertainments. But a woman's perspective can make significant and enlightening changes in our view of the generic tradition. Lady Mary Wroth, another member of the Sidney family, wrote a long love lament, "A Sheephard who no care did take," rather similar to the numerous other poems, like Spenser's "January" eclogue, about a shepherd pining for a disdainful woman; but Wroth allows the shepherdess to speak for herself as well, and so to tell of her own pain; more unusually, her shepherdess expresses compassion for the shepherd, while not yielding her experience to his needs.

> If I do tye you, I release
> The bond wherein you are,
> Your freedome shall not find decrease,
> Nor you accuse my care.
> The paine I have is all my owne,
> None can of it beare part,
> Sorrow my strength hath ouerthrowne,
> Disdaine hath killed my heart.[1]

Aphra Behn, though she seems as much at home within the metaphoric tradition of pastoral poetry as does any other Restoration writer, will sometimes use pastoral erotic motifs in riotously comical ways by treating the woman's role in erotic encounters with a boldness that alters the dynamic relationships and the significance of the pastoral love tryst.

Two texts, the first by Behn, will suggest the challenges that women writers face from traditional pastoral imagery and ideas.

> I love to see the Amorous *Swains*
> Unto my Scorn their Hearts resign:
> With pride I see the Meads and Plains
> Throng'd all with *Slaves*, and they all mine:
> Whilst I the whining Fools despise,
> That pay their Homage to my Eyes.[2]

Here the poet takes on the role of the familiar figure from pastoral poetry, the cruel, tyrannical shepherdess, mistress of the sighing swain's heart, playing her role to the hilt while at the same time reducing the shepherd's role to its absurdity. Is the mistress of the poet's heart inevitably a "Phyllis" or "Amyranth" or "Amaryllis"? Very well, then, here she is, surveying all those who have sworn their devotion in identical terms to what might as well be the same Phyllis, devoid of face or substantive identity. Is the poet's Phyllis always fickle and proud? Very well, then, here is the fickle and proud Phyllis delighting in her power. Looked at the other way around, not just from an opposing set of values but from the vantage point of the ostensible subject of pastoral courtships, the spectacle is preposterous.

The other text is from Annette von Droste-Hülshoff's poem "Am Turme," in which the tower where she stands to gaze at the seashore and watch the waves play while a ship bobs offshore, becomes a pedestal on which she has been unwillingly placed, and from which she resentfully gazes at the world denied her by gender.

> Seh auf und nieder den Kiel sich drehn
> Von meiner luftigen Warte;
> O, sitzen möcht ich im kämpfenden Schiff,
> Das Steuerruder ergreifen
> Und zischend über das brandende Riff
> Wie eine Seemöve streifen.[3]                     [19–24]

[I watch from my lofty tower as the keel rises and falls. Oh, that I might sit on that striving ship, gripping the rudder and riding over the surf-churning reef, like a skimming seagull.]

Her "luftige Warte" is an airy tower that is also an imposed, lofty point of view that sets her "above" what she sees and therefore prevents her from enjoying it. Not only is she sequestered from masculine activities; she is also denied the pleasure of the natural elements themselves. Seeing the waves cavorting on the beach, she longs to join them,

> Und jagen durch den korallenen Wald
> Das Walross, die lustige Beute!                   [15–16]

[And hunt through the coral woods the walrus, the jolly quest.]

The inevitable conclusion challenges oppressive actuality with imagination:

> Wär' ich ein Mann doch mindestens nur,
> So würde der Himmel mir raten;
> Nun muss ich sitzen so fein und klar,
> Gleich einem artigen Kinde,
> Und darf nur heimlich lösen mein Haar
> Und lassen es flattern im Winde!                  [27–32]

[Were I a man, even the least important, then heaven would grant my wish. Now I must sit, so refined and serene, like a well-behaved child, and only secretly loosen my hair and let it blow in the wind!]

To be like a simple child, and so protected from the turbulent tossing of life's seas, might be one vision of a pastoral life to someone who otherwise sees no shelter from the world's mutability, unpredictable dangers, and relentless pace. To Droste-Hülshoff, however, it is merely a symbol of frustration and confinement. Under such circumstances the pastoral fiction will seem far less compelling than the heroic.

Regardless of the cause, masculine predominance in the pastoral literary society has several consequences. One is the development of homosexual romantic and erotic relationships, which are usually accepted as if they were normative, or at least quite as normal as heterosexual. In Theocritus, explicit banter about homosexual intercourse is merely part of the natural landscape of desire. Though it might seem—and be—crude, coarse, and even violent, such material is treated as if it were as natural as the coupling of ram and ewe. Some of the most intense emotional relationships in pastoral literature are homosexual, and the intensity seems to be heightened by the general absence of sexual gratification.

Writing largely of male social conversation, male relationships based on love (or desire) for one another, and male love of art, the pastoral writer allows men to express a range of emotions not traditionally ascribed to men or publically expressed by men in literature or society. Without female characters to take on "feminine" functions, emotions, and values, the male characters can behave in atypical ways. Indeed, insofar as the pastoral posits a set of values opposed to such more familiar masculine pursuits as physical competition, the force of arms, stolid devotion to labor, and the accumulation of wealth and wide fame, pastoral literature expresses the conventionally "feminine" part of the human temperament. This may be one reason why the pastoral lyric, from Vergil onward, has been taken to be a minor genre appropriate for the young writer, as if not sufficiently serious for the adult male author. It may also help to explain why the generic pastoral poem becomes so artificial, so safely encased within predictable gestures, and yet so widespread: the desire to express the ideas remains, along with suspicion that they are improper; consequently, artificial expression serves as a social cover, making the poem seem to be merely a conventional or playful exercise and not the expression of seriously held desires or beliefs.

Scarcity of women contributes to the feeling of containment that is so important to pastoral experience. Social roles and relationships seem more tightly limited when the characters are of the same sex. They also seem more artificial, as if this were a world consciously constructed so as to limit the possibilities for social interactions and developments. There are, for all practical purposes, no marriages in the pastoral world and few possibilities of marriage, though there are of course many romantic and erotic relationships, most of which tend to be inconclusive or ungratifying in some way. As in *Daphnis and Chloë*, marriage is likely to come outside the pastoral frame, though the characters may remember their experiences in the pastoral world with sufficient fondness to pretend to pastoralism. When marriage comes, it is as an ending (in *As You Like It*, for instance), suggesting that the pastoral life is indeed a way of life prior to responsibilities, precluding the complicated social arrangements, formal legal or religious laws, and pragmatic concerns that come with familial responsibilities. These would limit the fictional image of total freedom so important to the pastoral ethos. The shepherd's style will be cramped if a spouse and children are waiting at home.

For the male writer, the pastoral's appeal is at least partly erotic, sometimes barely sublimated. In Ovid's versions of such essential stories as that of Apollo and Daphne or Pan and Syrinx, the pastoral world is a place of temptation for the divine wanderers and of danger for the mortal inhabitants, who may be "saved" only by being transformed into parts of the landscape. They become objects for the gods to play with; and if in this way they divert the erotic energies that would have destroyed them, they are also denied mortal fulfillment. They become exemplars of virtues and find their immortality not amongst the stars but amid the plants and trees they loved; yet in this way they are also accessible to their would-be ravishers, whose sublimated passion finds other than sexual ways of making them objects. So, Daphne for example:

> hanc quoque Phoebus amat, positaque in stipite dextra
> sentit adhuc trepidare novo sub cortice pectus,
> complexusque suis ramos ut membra lacertis
> oscula dat ligno: refugit tamen oscula lignum.
> cui deus "at quoniam coniunx mea non potes esse,
> arbor eris certe" dixit "mea. Semper habebunt
> te coma, te citharae, te nostrae, laure,
>     pharetrae."                                                    [I, 553–58]

[After that, Apollo still loved her; and touching his hand to the trunk, he felt the breast's movement yet beneath the bark, and he clasped the knotty limbs as though they were arms. He kissed the wood; the wood shrank back from his kiss. The god said, "Since now you cannot be my spouse, you shall surely be my tree. So the laurel shall bedeck my hair, my lyre, and my quiver."]

Or, with Syrinx and Pan,

> Panaque, cum prensam sibi iam Syringa putaret,
> corpore pro nymphae calamos tenuisse palustres;
> dumque ibi suspirat, motos in harundine ventos
> effecisse sonum tenuem similemque querenti.
> arte nova vocisque deum dulcedine captum
> "hoc mihi conloquium tecum" dixisse "manebit."
> atque ita, disparibus calamis compagine cerae
> inter se iunctis, nomen tenuisse puellae.                         [I, 705–12][4]

[And Pan, who thought he now embraced Syrinx, instead of the nymph's form held the marshy reeds. At that he sighed, and breath moving through the stalk made a slender sound, like a sigh; and charmed by the sweetness of this new art, the god said, "Such colloquy still remains to me." At which he joined together the different-sized reeds with wax and called them, bound, by the maiden's name.]

These stories seem particularly revealing because they deal with the creation of the principal attributes of the two gods who are so important to pastoral life and art. Apollo and Pan do not love their nymphs any the less for finding that they have become mere bits of the landscape; indeed, their passion continues and the lovers find that, unlike the vulnerable but elusive women, the flora that they have become are more accessible, though admittedly accessible in a different way. They cannot be conquered sexually, but they can be possessed—indeed ravished—in a different fashion. At the same time, the laurel and the syrinx become inseparably linked with the devoted gods. These stories suggest metaphoric explorations of our love for the pastoral and our use of the pastoral; but from the double perspectives of god and nymph, pursuer and pursued, we face the real significance of pastoral powerlessness and attractiveness. We understand that we change what we love and try to possess; that such passion binds together the one who desires and the object of desire; that when desire becomes objectified in the pastoral environment it is both easier to possess and harder to gratify; and that when passion becomes destructive and then sublimated through art, the result both reduces the object of passion and eternalizes it. We also see that human desires and pastoralism are locked in tension, fused by a paradox: we cannot gratify our most burning desire, but we easily find delight all around us. Ovid's stories, filled with poignant drama, aesthetically balance the ironic antitheses of the pastoral experience without the commitment to moral judgment implicit and explicit in the poetry of, for instance, Spenser, Horace, and Vergil.

So, though the pastoral world itself may be pure, it can also be erotically alluring. Simplicity may be so uncommon that it is provocative. Some people, like Calidore and Florizel, feel compelled to possess it (just as, Coridon and Colin Clout woefully note, others may feel repelled by it). One finds this motif in, for example, Saint Georges's scenario for Adam's ballet *Giselle*, in which the prince has disguised himself as a peasant and has taken up residence in a cottage so as to woo and wed the country girl Giselle, though he happens to be engaged to a beautiful princess. In Lessing's *Emilia Galotti* (I, 5) the prince offers a revealing definition of the qualities he sees in Emilia's portrait: "Liebreiz und Bescheidenheit" ("allurement and unpretentiousness"). One can imagine that Emilia's fiancé, in wanting to retire to the country with her, has recognized the same qualities and been moved to accept her values, the second of which is antithetical to those of the urbane court. The prince, however, wants to possess her and what she represents while also absorbing her into his world, an impossibility that proves destructive to Emilia. Calidore, after all, remains among the shepherds largely because of his attraction to Pastorella, whose name implies that she embodies in her beauty and simplicity the highest attraction of pastoral life. A lover complaining helplessly against the indifference or cruelty of someone all-powerful (because that person is capable of causing pain without being vulnerable to pain) is in an essentially pastoral condition of vulnerability and isolation. Why not, then, pretend to be a shepherd for the purpose of writing about grief?

The pastoral life is associated with desire and love at least partly because those emotions most closely express the author's longings for both leisure and naturalness, two qualities only palely imitated by the profession of writing. We long for the pastoralism that we do not possess, though we may believe we love it. As Goethe's Faust says in his palace as he prepares to turn Mephisto loose against Philemon and Baucis, who will not sell him their little cottage,

So sind am hartsten wir gequält,
Im Reichtum fühlend, was uns fehlt.[5]

[For this is the torment hardest to take:
to sense, amid riches, what we lack.]

The rareness, the fragility, the vulnerability of pastoral existence, like those of a delicate flower, seem to stimulate the inclination to pick, to possess, though perhaps the attempt to possess may prove destructive. The pastoral world is alluring partly because it is beautiful in itself, partly because it embodies what we do not have. Whether it means to or not (and sometimes it does indeed mean to), it tells us of our poverty. In this spirit Shakespeare's Henry VI pauses in the midst of battle to think that "it were a happy life / To be no better than a homely swain," (*3 Henry VI*, II, v, 21–22). Its security amid its deficiencies and defenselessness reminds us of how poor and insecure we really are amid our comforts and defenses. No wonder that the pastoral lover so often sighs for a coy, aloof, heartless shepherdess or shepherd.

The shepherd is likely obsessed with one emotion and one person. This is appropriate to the pastoral tendencies toward intensification and stasis. Fittingly, a pastoral society is small and tightly knit. We may feel that there are many shepherds within a pastoral realm or region, but few actually speak or receive notice; there is no real populace. Further, though tightly knit, pastoral society is loosely organized. It may be inherently well ordered, but it is hardly governed. Masters may be somewhere about to oversee the work, but they always remain out of sight and hearing. There may be a ruler, but high status is most often reserved for the artist (whose ability to sing and play is the mark of the real aristocrat within pastoral society) or for the one aged shepherd who seems to speak for the entire pastoral culture and who wisely understands its virtues through long years spent in a timeless landscape that never changes and so is comprehensible.

As in any small, close society, everyone knows everyone else in the pastoral world. The pastoral society and its literary tradition are like a small family or community in which one continually meets and talks about the same people. Here the same names come up repeatedly in the different poems within a volume, and they are passed on (like the name Lycidas) from generation to generation. As significant allusions develop through repetition, the resemblances and relationships emerge like inherited traits or family characteristics in a namesake. When pastoral characters gather, their conversation is filled with recollections of previous meetings, mutual friends, shared experiences and private jokes.

Vergil's Fifth Eclogue effectively suggests pastoral social life and social structure.

> Cur non, Mopse, boni quoniam conuenimus ambo,
> tu calamos inflare leuis, ego dicere uersus,
> hic corulis mixtas inter consedimus ulmos? [1–3]

> [Since we have met here, Mopsus—two good men, you at playing the light pipes, I at reciting verses—why not sit together here, where hazels and elms mingle?]

Menalcas's definition of goodness obviously begins with artistic, and especially lyric, ability; their having separate but complementary skills serves as reason enough for them to spend their time together. The offhand opening to the conversation implies that they know one another well, yet here their association derives principally from considerations of craftsmanship rather than any other grounds of friendship.

Mopsus consents by deferring to the other as his senior: "Tu maior; tibi me est aecum parere, Menalca" (4) ("You are senior, I yield precedence to you, Menalcas"). Not only is this polite; it also signifies that the natural order of life establishes the social hierarchy. Menalcas, however, replies with an artistic compliment: "Montibus in nostris solus tibi certat Amyntas" (8) ("In our hills only Amyntas rivals you"). Amyntas never appears in the eclogues, but he has been mentioned previously in passing; he is one of the well-known pastoral figures whose significant identity seems to come from how characters refer to him rather than from anything inherently significant in him. Mopsus's response perhaps pays tribute to Menalcas's skill, but it also indicates that conceit goes along with that ability: "Quid, si idem certet Phoebum superare canendo?" (9) ("Who, him who is determined to outsing Phoebus?"). A few lines later Mopsus, warming to the contest, is ready to meet the best; he will perform something he composed recently, and "tu deinde iubeto certet Amyntas" (15) ("then you can tell Amyntas to take on the challenge").

It is clear from the conversation that Menalcas did not mean to slight Mopsus, nor is the latter offended at Menalcas for ranking him below the famous Amyntas. A compliment was intended, and it is taken as a compliment, even though Mopsus feels it overvalues his absent rival. Indeed, Menalcas quickly realizes his slip, and generously repairs it.

> Lenta salix quantum pallenti cedit oliuae,
> puniceis humilis quantum saliunca rosetis,
> iudicio nostro tantum tibi cedit Amyntas.               [16–18]

[As the bending willow gives way to the green olive, as the lowly wild nard to the bed of crimson roses, so in our judgment Amyntas must yield to you.]

Menalcas, though the elder, twice urges Mopsus to begin and thereby set the pattern for the songs. Although this could be strategic (some chess players prefer to play black), it seems gracious. While they sing, "pascentis seruabit Tityrus haedos" (12) ("Tityrus will watch the grazing kids"). Tityrus never appears again in this poem. We remember him vividly from the First Eclogue and the subsequent reference to him in the Third. He is an old friend, grateful himself for favors and willing to help out while his colleagues seek some harmless diversion; his presence assures us that all is well with this cozy, familiar company.

Mopsus, eager to try out the fresh material, accepts Menalcas's invitation to go first. He sings a beautiful dirge for Daphnis which is eloquently praised by the other herdsman,

> nec calamis solum aequiperas sed uoce magistrum:
> fortunate puer, tu nunc eris alter ab illo.               [48–49]

[Not only in piping but in singing too you are your master's equal. Fortunate lad, you now succeed him.]

This is the highest praise Menalcas could give in this circumstance. It also reminds us of how the pastoral world cherishes closeness in emotional, social, and temporal matters. Mopsus now stands in the direct line of Daphnis, his teacher and predecessor. In this almost timeless world, the gift of song is passed to succeeding generations as if directly from the master's throat.

Next, however, comes Menalcas's turn. His is an interesting situation because he has to take up the artistic challenge set by the first singer, which means singing a song related to the material previously presented. In this case the subject, and its emotional content, will restrict Menalcas to a similarly pious treatment, but one that will not seem to challenge the delicacy of Mopsus's emotion-laden rememberance of Daphnis. Menalcas's solution is to offer an old piece of his as a sort of gift for Mopsus because of his love for Daphnis.

> nos tamen haec quocumque modo tibi nostra uicissim
> dicemus, Daphninque tuum tollemus ad astra,
> Daphnin ad astra feremus; amauit nos quoque Daphnis.
>
> [50–53]

[Yet I will try what I can to repay you with what I say, and your Daphnis raise to the stars. Daphnis I shall exalt to the stars. Daphnis also loved me.]

His song, that is, will be an apotheosis of Daphnis—your Daphnis, he points out, though he also claims Daphnis's love. He is therefore offering a vision of Daphnis that will please the singer who has just paid tribute to this pastoral god, turning the contest into an exchange of artistic and spiritual gifts that center on mutual devotion to one of the central deities of the pastoral world, himself once a beautiful herdsman, still alive in the remembrance of his successors. Mopsus takes the offering with the full generosity of the intention, expressing first his gratitude for what Menalcas proposes; then his praise again for Daphnis, the subject of the song (Menalcas has not, for instance, chosen to salute a different deity); and last his respect for the song, which he has not yet heard but which has apparently acquired a reputation in this close-knit society.

> An quicquam nobis tali sit munere maius?
> et puer ipse fuit cantari dignus et ista
> iam pridem Stimichon laudauit carmina nobis.          [54–56]

[Could we get any greater gift? The boy himself deserved a song, and this song Stimichon long ago praised.]

In addition to these internal patterns of social coherence, there is, of course, the external. Mopsus's song, lamenting the passing of Daphnis and concluding with his epitaph, is a Theocritean elegy, considering only Daphnis's early existence and the sorrowful effects of his passing in the natural world; as such, it can be seen as a direct descendant of Thyrsis's lament for Daphnis in Theocritus's First Idyll. Menalcas's contribution is Vergil's addition to the pastoral legend of Daphnis, providing not only a reassuring, dramatically imagined vision of Daphnis in heaven but also a similarly reassuring view of Daphnis's divine effect on the pastoral world:

> sub pedibusque uidet nubes et sidera Daphnis.
> ergo alacris siluas et cetera rura uoluptas
> Panaque pastoresque tenet Dryadasque puellas.

> [Beneath his feet Daphnis sees the clouds and stars. Delight then enlivens the forests and fields, Pan as well as the shepherds and the Dryad maidens.]

Furthermore, the continuing religious rites of Daphnis's devotees promise continued peace and plenty. "Sis bonus o felixque tuis" (65), Menalcas sings and prays ("Be good and gracious to your own"), much as Milton's "uncouth swain" will respond to his vision of Lycidas in heaven,

> Now, Lycidas, the shepherds weep no more;
> Henceforth thou art the genius of the shore,
> In thy large recompense, and shalt be good
> To all that wander in that perilous flood.

"Quae tibi, quae tali reddam pro carmine dona" (81), Mopsus excitedly exclaims ("what is there for you, what could I give you for such a song?"). Before he can answer properly, Menalcas hastens to give him a present:

> Hac te nos fragili donabimus ante cicuta;
> haec nos "formonsum Corydon ardebat Alexin,"
> haec eadem docuit "quoium pecus? an Meliboei?"     [85–87]

> [First I shall give you this fragile reed. This taught me "Corydon loved beautiful Alexis" and this very one "Whose flock is that, Meliboeus?"]

The reed pipe is said literally to have taught these songs, as if to emphasize that nature is the real source of human creativity, for the music and the meaning are within nature. Furthermore, the phrases Menalcas mentions are (roughly) the opening lines of the Second and Third Eclogues. In the biographical context, then, Vergil identifies himself with Menalcas and encouragingly passes on to a follower his poetic style and vision.

Within the fictive world, however, something else is taking place. At the end of the Fifth Eclogue, Menalcas reminds us of the continuity of pastoral art and experience. By referring to his own artistic past and thereby tying together some detached incidents within this pastoral culture through his artistic participation in them, he makes that culture more coherent and more compact. Further, Menalcas's recollections turn the pastoral "world" into a fictional one. The

Second Eclogue, Corydon's monologue prefaced with a brief introduction by an unidentified speaker, now appears as an artifice, not a report of a real bit of pastoral drama. Menalcas calls to mind art's omnipresence. When Mopsus then gives him a beautiful shepherd's crook, which Antigenes often asked for unsuccessfully (though, he says, Antigenes deserved love), he attests to the superiority of art and spiritual love (expressed mutually by Menalcas's song) to eros.

The mention of Antigenes, like that of Amyntas and some others who are only alluded to in the poem, implies a larger network of friendships and acquaintances; but these figures appear only on the imagistic horizon of the poem, so as to be gestured toward for some particular purpose. They do not so much expand the range of the poem as define its real limits. Mopsus, for example, has chosen not to take up the first topics Menalcas suggests, the passionate Phyllis or the praiseworthy Alcon or the naughty Codrus; they warrant mentioning only so they can be rejected as subjects, in favor of a more worthy topic. That they are there, of course, affirms that the pastoral world is not necessarily solitary or lonely, but rich and varied in its characters. However, we are not asked to become involved with more than two or three at a time; and the poem uses those two or three with dramatic and thematic sharpness.

To be sure, pastoral characters are not always considerate of one another. In Theocritus's idylls they can become downright insulting. Even Menalcas, in the Third Eclogue, engages in some sharp bantering and trading of accusations with Damoetas. Indeed, one charge Damoetas levels against him is a fit of jealous spite against Daphnis:

Aut hic ad ueteres fagos cum Daphnidos arcum
fregisti et calamos, quae tu, peruerse Menalca,
et, cum uidisti puero donata, dolebas
et, si non aliqua nocuisses, mortuus esses.                              [12–15]

[Or here by the old beeches when you smashed Daphnis' bows and arrows. When you saw them given to the lad, you malicious Menalcas, you were miserable, and if you hadn't done something destructive you would have dropped dead.]

If we are to accept this unanswered charge as somehow "true," then Menalcas's performance in the Fifth Eclogue (at the end of which he himself refers specifically to the earlier poem) must be seen partly as expiation for Daphnis and partly as a show of affection for the grieving Mopsus; and it is all the more touching for that. It reveals the emotional range possible within pastoral's private relations. Though

pastoral characters may feel resentful and harbor grudges, their actions are restrained by unlegislated limits of behavior. If shepherds become violent or passionate, their outlets are confined to dirty tricks against inanimate objects, to sexual
taunting or attempts at seduction, to battles on the field of song, and to private,
gnawing despair. That despair is most dangerous, both to the herdsman and to the
flock and land he is supposed to tend.

An unsympathetic outsider, however, may see something base or under-
handed in country behavior. A pseudonymous sixteenth-century poem, after
satirizing urban trickery, moves on to rustic misdeeds.

> And to the Country then I goe,
>    to liue in quiet state.
> There did appear no subtile showes,
>    but yea and nay went smoothly:
> But Lord how Country-folks can glose,
>    when they speake most soothly. . . .
> There was no open forgerie,
>    but vnder-handed gleaning:
> Which they call Country pollicie,
>    but hath a worser meaning.[6]

Although the usual pastoral type visible to the outsider is the innocent rustic who
may be corrupted, cheated, or seduced by the city slicker, there is also the common
image of the sly, deceptively simple native who fleeces the tourists; "Arcades
ambo," Byron writes (ironically quoting "Arcadians both" from Vergil's Second
Eclogue), "id est, blackguards both." In an antipastoral work the victim would
simply leave the country and return to the more open environment of the city,
with all its obvious faults. But the sixteenth-century poem stays within the
pastoral tradition by posing a pastoral solution. The speaker, a woodsman, returns
to the forest, where "liue I quietly alone" in a rather sober and melancholy private
pastoral refuge.

Usually, however, pastoral characters will seem vulnerable before outsiders.
Their moral shortcomings are revealed first in their failure to fulfill their responsibilities within their culture. Because pastoral society assigns no pressing obligations and few real responsibilities (those being only casual and sporadic), the
shepherd's neglect of those duties is an especially onerous failing, particularly since
it victimizes not only the master but also the flock, which, like the shepherd, is
highly vulnerable and unable to do very much for itself. As Spenser writes,

criticizing a clergy that does not take its obligations seriously (but also recording a basic pastoral principle),

> Thilke same bene shepeheards for the Deuils
>   stedde,
> That playen, while their flocks be vnfedde.

> ["May," 43–44]

The plaint is echoed in "Lycidas"—"The hungry sheep look up, and are not fed" (125)—and is also found in the classical pastoral, in addition to the Bible. In Theocritus's Idyll IV, for instance, Battus continually tries to irk Corydon by accusing him of mismanaging his herd.

> "Do you perhaps milk them all in the evening,
>   on the quiet?"
> "Poor beasts that they are! They've not done
>   too well for a herdsman."
> "Just look at that heifer! Nothing but skin
>   and bones!
> You don't feed her on dewdrops, do you, like a
>   cicada?"
> "That bull, the ruddy one, 's not got much
>   substance either."

The charge of outright dishonesty occurs elsewhere in pastoral literature. It is "realistic" but also attests to some laxity of conduct that accompanies, in the absence of clear authority, governance by natural principles and the general presumption of goodliness. As Flannery O'Connor's Mrs. Hopewell says to the rascally itinerant Bible salesman when he complains that she rejects his sales pitch out of snobbery toward "country people," "'Why,' she cried, 'good country people are the salt of the earth!'"[7] They appear infrequently, but the pastoral tradition includes renegades and cagey scoundrels, whose crimes, appropriate to their rank and environment, involve sneakiness and trickery, the small-scale private vices, petit larceny rather than grand theft, all the tribe of Autolycus.

Apart from these occasional instances of crudity or villainy, pastoralism has some inherent qualities that can become defects. The spiritual defenses of the pastoral world may break down in the face of a force the shepherds lack the means or the courage to resist. So, in Vergil's Ninth Eclogue, the usurping soldier will win his argument against the natives because he has raw violence on his side. Similarly, in Book VI, canto x, of The Faerie Queene, when an improbable tiger attacks Pastorella, the first would-be rescuer is Calidore's rival, a herdsman who has long wooed her:

> . . . but when he saw the feend,
> Through cowherd feare he fled away as fast,
> Ne durst abide the daunger of the end.　　　　　　　　　　[stanza 35]

Spenser's punning *cowherd* sets the issue squarely. The mild and sheltered pastoral life has not prepared Coridon, or any other pastoral character, for true heroism when faced with nature's unaccustomed savagery. Later, the entire pastoral enclave is devastated by a band of savage people, brigands more numerous and more resourceful than the tiger; and though Calidore can rescue Pastorella from the tiger, she and her friends must undergo suffering and sorrow before he can save her from the villains against whom the pastoral world has not been able to protect itself. Those outlaws themselves represent a darker side of the forest. It is, after all, only a short step from the bucolic society that lacks the martial knowledge and moral strength to defend itself from evil to the outlaw society that preys in barbaric and cowardly fashion on the weak. Victor and victim, though dissimilar in so many ways, are dangerously isolated from civil values. In the pastoral culture, the absence of a strong authority is a blessing that makes pastoral freedom possible, but also a danger that makes pastoral vulnerability inevitable. The privateness, independence, and lack of adventurousness are grounds for both praise and blame.

Because pastoralism takes shape in oppostion to the usual values and forces of society at large, it can be better or worse. The pastoral setting need not be rustic, merely a refuge. In Stendhal's novels it is a prison or some other spot that might seem undesirable if not for the greater unpleasantness of the outside world. There are pastoral spots, like Armida's garden in *Jerusalem Liberated*, that seduce characters from their public responsibilities. And there are also potentially pastoral spots that an author or character insists on seeing ironically, not accepting the myth of idealization. Lermontov's Pechorin, in *A Hero of Our Time*, describes Taman antipastorally as "the worst little town of all the seacoast towns in Russia," and there, fittingly, he is lured by a gypsy girl into a moonlight tryst in a rowboat, only to find that she means to drown him.[8] It is also fitting that Pechorin, to some degree a romantic in spite of himself, ends up blaming himself for having inadvertently upset the cozy, sheltered life of these people. "What business did fate have to land me in the peaceful midst of *honest smugglers*? Like a stone thrown into the smooth water of a spring, I had disrupted their peace, and like a stone, had very nearly gone to bottom myself!" The intruder somehow suspects that normal ethical judgments are insignificant when placed beside the value of the autonomy that the pastoral culture maintains. Yet even if Pechorin has not quite conquered his sympathy for the gypsies, we have seen enough to distrust this sentimentality, as did Lermontov, who once complained in a letter from the Caucusus that he found himself unable to have sex with the peasant girls "because they stink."[9] Shakespeare's Touchstone seems close at hand, with his country wench, Audrey, "an ill-favor'd thing, sir, but mine own," whom he must remind to "bear your body more seeming."

In "The Gypsies" Pushkin similarly, but more terrifyingly, develops the image of a rustic society living independent of social moral conventions and perceived by more conventional standards as immoral and licentious. To a civilized man who, like Calidore, finds the life of the gypsies attractive and erotic, the consequences of the deep cultural divergence prove completely destructive, though the gypsy society eventually continues in its old ways, unruffled by outside intrusion, the clash of passions, and even murder. Freedom from authority and conventionality can seem appealing. But there may be a price to pay for the pastoral world's separation from discipline and cultivation. Further, for some of us, the gap between pastoral society and our more familiar society may simply be too great to close. When we try to enter the other, our illusions of what that pastoral society ideally might or ought to be cannot be reconciled with the actual implications of that way of life. The pastoral world remains independent, even independent of our fantasies. When human voices wake us, we may drown.

The pastoral also merges with some of our myths of the jolly outlaw, like Robin Hood or Gay's Macheath. These characters are pastoral in several ways. They may represent a low social class, but they are proud of their values. They operate independently of social conventions, which they often see as false or elitist; they are at least likeable, perhaps good-hearted, and sometimes (like Robin Hood) believe that they are redressing social and economic injustices; furthermore, they often serve the satirist's function by deflating authority.

As Sidney's comments suggest, there is a strong satirical tradition in pastoral literature, usually sanctioned formally by Vergil's First Eclogue but often far more specific and more allegorically detailed than Vergil's poem. The pastoral satirist can claim several strategic rhetorical advantages. For one, his or her social position permits the satirist to speak candidly, having nothing to lose and being uninterested in seeking gain. For another, the pastoral character can claim to see through artifices and facades, having common sense and simple nature as guides. And finally, invulnerable to fashions and newfangled notions, he or she can claim to speak from a long tradition of virtue and honesty. Shepherds in Theocritus and Vergil criticize one another's behavior as tenders of their animals; later pastoralists extend the implications of that pastoral role. They are critics and tenders of a flock of readers, much like spiritual ministers, and so have their own pastoral roles to perform. When Mantuan uses his pastoral eclogues to write in detail about internal disagreements among the Carmelites, or Boccaccio to address contemporary political issues (as in his Seventh Eclogue, a veritable shouting match in which "Daphnis," the emperor Charles, denounces "Florida," the city of Florence, for consorting with the Germans), they are expanding the satirical roles of the shepherds.

The pastoral speaker, keeping within the implied limits of characterization, can be blunt, knowing nothing of subtlety or discretion. Of course, we also understand that we are to take the criticism from whence it purportedly comes: if it is crude or offensive to anyone, it comes from a fictive character who has not claimed to be anything other than a plain-dealing peasant, speaking perhaps for the "common man" or "general appearance," but in that case certainly not for people of greater discernment and refinement.

Insofar as the shepherd has public moral responsibilities, they are those of the casual philosopher, critic, or satirist. They are discharged by simply declaring or showing the merits of pastoral life, by word more than deed, and by calling attention to behavior that falls short of these pastoral ideals. Through usually peaceful and even lyrical protest, and through the clear articulation of a set of values based on love, friendship, empathy with nature, compassion, and simple satisfactions, the shepherd indicates what is right. There need be no particular requirement to do much, if anything at all, beyond expressing some limited comforts. As in Tityrus's response to Meliboeus, politeness demands something; and yet the principle of containment seems so powerful that he can barely express any but the most meager practical and short-term assistance to Meliboeus— scarcely an offer of help, much less a crusade on his behalf or even an earnest effort to try to find him a refuge from his misery.

To Sidney, defending the supposedly frivolous pastoral in the course of his defense of poetry, the pastoral (as exemplified by Vergil's First Eclogue) contained the moral capacity for addressing the social and political problems of a hierarchical society, because of its sympathetic treatment of the pains and pleasures of the lowest classes:

> Is the poor pipe disdained, which sometime out of Meliboeus' mouth can show the misery of people under hard lords or ravening soldiers? And again, by Tityrus, what blessedness is derived to them that lie lowest from the goodness of them that sit highest. . . ?[10]

If we look behind Sidney's schematizing, we can see the assumption that the pastoral world itself is a locus of honesty and goodness, deserving at least compassion, and in its most troubled moments deserving respectful attention for its revelations of candid observations.

The tutelary moral significance of the pastoral world is found repeatedly in those texts that emphasize the simplicity, modesty, and peacefulness of the pastoral life. In most instances this means life in the woods, subsisting on what nature and a few simple human (perhaps divinely taught) skills (like cheese-making and beekeeping) can offer. But again, it is not only the setting but even more the attitude that counts. Let us consider George Orwell's *Keep the Aspidistra Flying*, in which the protagonist, Comstock, a poet from a lower-middle-class family, is determined to sink into abject poverty because he sees it as the only possible refuge from the drearily predictable life of "success": a "good" job, a family, a respectable home with a potted aspidistra in the window. During most of the novel we are made to feel that, no matter what his and our common sense has to say, Comstock is engaged in a defiantly quixotic, morbidly heroic attempt to preserve his assaulted integrity.

> . . . he had taken an oath against marriage long ago. Marriage is only a trap set for you by the money-god. You grab the bait; snap goes the trap; and there you are, chained by the leg to some "good" job till they cart you off to Kensal Green. And what a life! Licit sexual intercourse in the shade of the aspidistra. Pram-pushing and sneaky adulteries. And the wife finding you out and breaking the cut-glass whiskey decanter over your head.[11]

Marital sex in the shade of the houseplant, baby-tending, and secret dalliances are, of course, Comstock's interpretation of the bourgeois idyll. He revises the bountiful pastoral refuge into a mocking enclosure of a different sort: a trap. Amaryllis and Rosalind are now simply one's own faithful but not infinitely complacent spouse. Tityrus's spreading beech tree has become a potted aspidistra, and the verdant meadow, Kensal Green. Sheep-tending in the hills is replaced by a nine-to-five; song contests give way to baby-tending, and country courtships to furtive affairs; the hand-carved wooden wine goblet is now a luridly menacing cut-glass whiskey decanter. What he grasps at in place of this corrupted idyll is barren and dismal; but his effort is a spectacular attempt to detach himself from the business of the world, from an *otium* that has become corrupted by the values of *negotium*, and to find some form of self-containment that will permanently satisfy his pathetic egoism. In place of the pastoral idyllic statement, "I live on my own terms and am thankful to have the little that I need," he offers a corollary: "I live on my own terms and am thankful to have little that I need." Thus Comstock attempts to reinvent the pastoral. Its original terms have become debased, and in their stead one must insist on new ones for oneself, even if those new terms compel one away from the idyll and toward the cave of hard primitivism. In the end, he fails—which is to say that he yields to the modern version of the pastoral, precipitated by a tryst with his sweetheart on a rural outing that proves a success in spite of Comstock.

In this work we can see a peculiarly involuted mingling of pastoral motifs and pastoral attitudes. The monologue quoted above reveals how contemporary life parodies pastoral images. His response, so vigorous in its denials, is a different form of pastoral: a kind of self-containment that functions within his life very much like a more conventional form of the pastoral, giving it a nucleus of direction or focal point of meaning and values, though it is imagistically contrary to the conventional pastoral world.

The notion of containing one's desires and expectations and thereby finding pleasure is expressed well in the unruffled lines of Sir Edward Dyer's "My Mind to Me a Kingdom Is." Dyer's poem is devoid of explicitly pastoral imagery, but it is pastoral in mode, because it is a compendium of rhetorical assertions and thematic contrasts that fill sixteenth-century pastoral poems and cascade like autumn leaves in anthologies of pastoral verse such as *England's Helicon*. His comments on economics—"Though much I want that most would have, / Yet still my mind forbids to crave"—(5–6) and political power—"I press to bear no haughty sway, / I wish no more than may suffice, / I do no more than well I may"—(19–21) celebrate the dignified freedom of one whose mind is its own pastoral world.[12] In Dyer's scheme of things, the mind is like the pastoral poet's ideally perceived nature: "Look, what I want my mind supplies." He then draws the inevitable analogy between pastoral and royal senses of satisfaction: "Lo! thus I triumph like a king, / My mind content with anything" (23–24).

The attractive image of the pastoral, perhaps Edenic, world as a place not only of a pleasant but also of a moral life permeates the popular and artistic imagination of our culture. Joni Mitchell's song, "Woodstock," expresses the idea in the particular terms of the late 1960s and its social, political, and artistic movements.

> I came upon a child of God
> He was walking along the road
> And I asked him, where are you going
> And this he told me

I'm going on down to Yasgur's farm
I'm going to camp out on the land
And try an' get my soul free
    We are stardust
    We are golden
    And we've got to get ourselves
    Back to the garden[13]

Mitchell's poem takes up many pastoral motifs, including the notion that those who live in the pastoral world are favored of heaven and live within holy laws of purity. Adhering to the right principles of nature, they are both divine ("stardust") and royal ("golden"), though they may become artificially separated from the pastoral world and so must strive to return to it. Though the destination is a farm, in this instance the farm is not a place of georgic labor but, rather, a modern version of the song contest; a rock-and-roll concert. We remember the distances between electronically amplified hard rock and shepherds' songs set to the melodies of a reed pipe; but both in their way are "popular" music, that is, music of common folk. Camping out on the land, like taking to the pastoral woods, is the path to spiritual freedom from a complex and oppressive society.

In literature written by people undergoing or trying to initiate great social or cultural changes, the pastoral ideal may stand as a future promise, as in Horace's Epode 16, or Micah (4 : 4): "But they shall sit every man under his vine and under his fig tree; and none shall make them afraid." However, in feminist, third-world, and "minority" writings, the pastoral is less likely than the heroic to stand as an image of the original Golden Age. Pastoralism—basically passive, tolerant, sheltered, vulnerable, and suffering—is at best an equivocal model for an audience whose problems are bound up with these qualities. It is true that pastoral visions of the past can attractively depict ecological soundness, communal cooperation, friendly competition, moral wholesomeness, and uncommercial artistry. On the other hand, the pastoral attitude toward power, though perhaps subversive, is not the substance of constructive rebellion. As Frederic Henry observes, so many soldiers "were beaten to start with. They were beaten when they took them from their farms and put them in the army. That is why the peasant has wisdom, because he is defeated from the start" (179). That sort of peasant wisdom has to be thrown off, or at least regarded as a front for quieter and more dangerous knowledge. The pastoral, even Edenic, description of the black college campus in Ralph Ellison's *Invisible Man* simultaneously covers and reveals the truth about accommodation with white society. The Lewis Allan song recorded by Billie

Holiday helps us also remember that, for some, the landscape itself ceases to be visualizable as purely pastoral when it becomes a landscape of exploitation and oppression.

> Southern trees bear a strange fruit
> Blood on the leaves and blood at the root
> Black bodies swinging in the Southern breeze
> Strange fruit, hanging from the poplar trees.
>
> Pastoral scene of the gallant South
> The bulging eyes, the twisted mouth
> Smell of magnolias, sweet and fresh
> Then the sudden smell of burning flesh. . . .[14]

Rulership and even leadership are generally inimical to pastoralism. Of governance, as Gonzalo says in *The Tempest*, "no name of magistrate. . . . No sovereignty" (II, i, 149, 156). Even when there are titular monarchs, as in Sidney's *Arcadia*, their pastoral involvement means that they will not show monarchical authority or power.

As we learn from Tityrus, pastoral joy can depend on a good and powerful ruler's benevolence, or at least on the appearance of this. Juan del Encina's *Imitacion de las eglogas de Virgilio*, dedicated to Isabella and Ferdinand, blends translations of Vergil with moralistic elaborations, allegories, and verbal embellishments designed to transform Vergil's poems into tributes to the two monarchs. Marie-Antoinette, by playing shepherdess with scented sheep at Versailles, implies her interpretation of the condition of France as well as her mode of dealing with experience.

Many pastoral works take up the royal desire to pretend to pastoralism, or the pastoral desire to make the monarch "one of us." The poems of Theocritus and Vergil that are either explicitly or implicitly political allegories reflect these desires. For example, if we think of Menalcas in Eclogue Five as Vergil and consider the temporal and personal suggestions about Daphnis, then it is appropriate to recognize the elegy for Daphnis as an elegy for the assassinated Caesar. The progress entertainments for Queen Elizabeth as she toured noble country houses lavishly used pastoral images and allegories in their tributes to her, as did poets such as Spenser; nor was this a phenomenon confined to English treatments of their queen. We recognize its potency still today in politicians who try to cultivate "the common touch" or proclaim themselves "average citizens," "homemakers," or representatives of "the little guy."

These various treatments express several different ideas. Rulers long for the simple life, recognizing that it is good and knowing how unpleasant their own circumstances really are, though they might seem ideal to those who are ignorant of the joys of true simplicity or the woes of wealth and power. The ruler, at least fictionally, feels a kinship with everyone, even the least notable, and is not too proud to let that be said. Furthermore, the ruler shares the people's values, principally the pastoral values of righteousness, candor, and modesty of desires. The state (they also imply) is idyllic, ruled—for example, in Marot's "Eglogue au Roy"—by a king who is Pan himself, or a shepherdess queen who is the daughter of Pan and an Arcadian nymph. Like a shepherd, the ruler can remain apart from the ambitious concerns of others. Consciously or not, these texts may also suggest that being a ruler is idyllic. For if one set of definitions of living the pastoral life is, "being content with what you have because you have all that you need, and being able to live as you please," then a monarch can be treated as a quintessentially pastoral figure, just as a shepherd or shepherdess can be depicted as a monarch within the world of pastoral games, and just as a real monarch or royal offspring can find a proper place within pastoral society.

Such tropes are possible because pastoralism is so easily associated with moral perfection, and in particular with the ideal original state of life. In the blessed time of the Golden Age, Hesiod claims, people lived easy lives, but they behaved themselves. Ovid elaborates,

> aurea prima satast aetas, quae vindice nullo, / sponte sua, sine lege, fidem rectumque colebat. / poena metusque aberant, nec verba minantia fixo / aere ligabantur, nec supplex turba timebat / iudicis ora sui, sed erant sine vindice tuti.
>
> [*Metamorphoses*, I, 89–93]

Golding's faithful and resonant translation deserves quoting:

> Then sprange up first the golden age, which
>     of it selfe maintainde
> The truth and right of every thing unforct
>     and unconstrained.
> There was no feare of punishment, there was no
>     threatning lawe
> In brazen tables nayled up, to keepe the folke
>     in awe.
> There was no man would crouch or creepe to
>     Judge with cap in hand,
> They lived safe without a Judge, in everie
>     Realme and lande.[15]

The Book of Genesis tells us not only that our ancestors first lived in a garden, but also that Abel was a shepherd, Cain, a tiller of the ground. The not inconsiderable amount of Hebraic pastoral imagery reaches its climax in that passage which is also crucial for the development of Christian moralistic eclogues, Ezekiel 34, which begins with God instructing the prophet to denounce "the shepherds of Israel" for glutting themselves while neglecting their flocks and ends, "And ye my sheep, the sheep of My pasture, are men, and I am your God, saith the Lord God." In Christian scriptures shepherds are the ones to whom the angels announce the birth of Christ, who himself is often represented as the lamb of God or shepherd of his human flock.

The notion of the pastoral world as inherently innocent, free from the corruptions of worldly society, accords with ideas about the Golden Age and Eden; it also leads to fantasies about desert islands, the Blessed Isles that Horace writes of in his Epode 16, Tahiti, and of course what F. Scott Fitzgerald called at the end of The Great Gatsby "the fresh green breast of the new world." Writing in 1752 that "Westward the Course of Empire Takes Its Way," George Berkeley foresaw "another golden age" in a part of the world not yet "Barren of every glorious theme,"

> In happy Climes, the Seat of Innocence,
>   Where Nature guides and Virtue rules,
> Where Men shall not impose for Truth and Sense
>   The Pedantry of Courts and Schools.[16]

Berkeley's new world joins the ideals of Tasso and Guarini into a perfect fusion of nature and virtue: in these "happy Climes"

> The Force of Art by Nature seems outdone,
>   And fancied Beauties by the true.

Flourishing nature therefore yields not only bounty but also Truth, which is nature elevated and refined into a pure principle.

In two famous, complementary choruses from the Italian Renaissance, the pastoral Golden Age is differently interpreted as providing a golden rule for human behavior.[17] To Tasso in his Aminta, nature originally taught, "S'ei piace, ei lice," that is, "if it is pleasing, it is lawful." By contrast, Guarini directly replies in Il Pastor Fido, "Piaccia, se lice," "it pleases, if it is lawful." Each passage argues for the restoration of these rules to the world from which they have been removed or driven. They offer very different ways to think about pastoral excellence and, taken together, indicate the variety within pastoral concepts of morality. On the one hand, nature is delightful when unfettered by social artifices; on the other hand, ingrained morality is easily gratifying to those who possess it.

The moral issues so differently framed by Tasso and Guarini are worked out dramatically by Milton in his *Mask Presented at Ludlow Castle (Comus)*. The motto for the masque is "Eheu quid volui misero mihi! floribus austrum perditus." From Vergil's Second Eclogue, this is Corydon's self-accusatory realization that his passion for Alexis has led him to neglect the real riches of properly cultivated and well-ordered nature. In the masque the healthy corrective to Corydon's plight is found in the thinking of the Lady, who rejects Comus's enticements to sensuality. Time is short, he reminds her; and the bountiful giver of nature pours out its gifts to be enjoyed, not neglected while they waste. After all, he insists,

> If all the world
> Should in a pet of temperance feed on Pulse,
> Drink the clear stream, and nothing wear but
> Frieze,
> Th' all-giver would be unthank't, would be
> unprais'd. [720–23]

Comus's diction emphasizes the austerity of the life he ridicules by playing on the homophone *freeze* and the homonym *pulse*. The Lady's reply is ecologically sound. Nature teaches respectful, economical distribution of resources, so that justice is well served, each good person having all that is needed, without want or excess.

> If every just man that now pines with want
> Had but a moderate and beseeming share
> Of that which lewdly-pamper'd Luxury
> Now heaps upon some few with vast excess,
> Nature's full blessing would be well-dispens't
> In unsuperfluous even proportion. [768–73]

What she imagines is a universal pastoral economy.

This open conflict between Comus and the Lady over the right understanding of nature repeats the implied conflict between the Attendant Spirit and Comus, both of whom appear at times as shepherds. Having made known in his opening lines his celestial origins and his mission on earth, the Spirit announces that his mission depends on his taking

> . . . the weeds and likeness of a swain
> That to the service of this house belongs,
> Who with his soft pipe and smooth-dittied song
> Well knows to still the wild winds when they roar,
> And hush the waving woods, nor of less faith. [84–88]

A complex allegory is at work here. This role is being taken by the musician Henry Lawes, tutor to the children who are the main characters in the masque. Lawes appears as a divinely appointed guardian masquerading as a pastoral character who faithfully serves the household with his art (as, of course, Henry Lawes does in real life). The "swain" is further depicted as a type of Orpheus, the supreme pastoral artist and master of harmony and nature. So these pastoral fictions have several layers to them.

The Attendant Spirit accepts the roles as accommodations to human myths and methods of understanding. His own view of mortal life's pastoral condition is rather more critical than one might presume from his own assumption of shepherd's weeds. He comes, he says, from a clear and serene region

> Above the smoke and stir of this dim spot
> Which men call Earth, and with low-thoughted care
> Confin'd and pester'd in this pinfold here,
> Strive to keep up a frail and feverish being.          [5–8]

Here human life seems meanly rustic. It lacks spiritual or philosophical elevation. The vile, unimaginative self-enclosure, as if in an animal pen, parodies pastoral ideals of enclosure and modesty. Pastoral life may seem to unenlightened humanity an ideal of virtue; it is used in this way by the Spirit for its imagistic power. From a celestial perspective, however, it is a poor substitute for real virtue.

Immediately upon the Spirit's departure, Comus arrives with his crew of beast-visaged mortals, his "herd," as he calls them. He follows the patterns of the lower celestial world, the visible heavens, called forth by "The Star that bids the Shepherd fold" (93). He sees cosmic order from the distorting perspective of the pinfold where he lives, the son of Circe and Bacchus, with his human herd. But Comus also understands the symbolic import of the pastoral, much as the Spirit does. As the Lady approaches, he scatters a magical powder that will change her perception of him: "I shall appear some harmless villager / Whom thrift keeps up about his country gear" (166–67).

His ruse works, and Comus ("good shepherd," the Lady calls him with rich, unknown irony) offers her shelter in the pastoral terms that he has mastered, in "a low / But loyal cottage" (319–20).

The Lady, in turn, has a complex view of the possibilities within the pastoral setting. Earlier she expressed the fear that the music she heard (actually that of Comus and his crew)

> . . . was the sound
> Of riot and ill-manag'd merriment,
> Such as the jocund flute or gamesome pipe
> Stirs up among the loose unletter'd hinds,

When for their teeming flocks and granges full
In wanton dance they praise the bounteous Pan,
and thank the gods amiss.                                        [171–77]

Out of context this may seem merely snobbish and parochial, though its accuracy
within the play-world implies she understands the larger world. On the other
hand, her reply to Comus's offer also accepts the moralistic myth of pastoral
innocence.

Shepherd, I take thy word,
And trust thy honest offer'd courtesy,
Which oft is sooner found in lowly sheds
With smoky rafters, than in tap'stry halls
With courts of princes, where it first was nam'd,
And yet is more pretended.                                       [321–26]

There are many ironies entailed here. To begin with, the Lady is of course being
tricked, so that her speech, resonant and self-assured as it is, sounds naive and
flawed in its premise. Yet of course she is taken in by pretended innocence,
hypocrisy (which only God can perceive); and she indeed is being taken to a
tapestried hall where courtesy is merely pretended. Finally, the masque is being
performed in the tapestried halls on her own familial estate, where her parents
presumably exemplify that rare and true courtesy that can yet be found in the
pastoral courts of princes. The Lady's double vision of the pastoral moral world is
quite consonant with her experience of the pastoral physical world. She was left
alone in the woods when her brothers, with whom she was traveling, saw that she
was tired and settled with her "Under the spreading favor of these pines," and
then went off to find "berries, of such cooling fruit / As the kind hospitable woods
provide." Their failure to return has left her vulnerable "In the blind mazes of this
tangled wood." So her world appears deeply ambiguous, filled with images and
experiences in need of some conceptual framework to be correctly understood and
acted upon, susceptible to double and conflicting interpretations, at once reassuring and threatening, at once a place of losing and a place of finding, of wantonness
and courtesy, of the music of Orpheus and of Pan.

After the Lady's rescue, she, her brothers, and the Spirit, still in shepherd's
guise, "travel" to her father's castle—that is, the very place where the masque is
being performed, to join in a celebration. As the Spirit prepares us for the country
dances that will precede the more stately courtly dances of the three children, he
explains,

All the swains that there abide,
With jigs and rural dance resort.

> We shall catch them at their sport,
> And our sudden coming there
> Will double all their mirth and cheer.                    [951–55]

At the beginning of the next scene he ends these country dances with the arrival of the noble youths, announcing,

> Back, shepherds, back, enough your play,
> Till next sun-shine holiday;
> Here be without duck or nod
> Other trippings to be trod
> Of lighter toes, and such court guise
> As Mercury did first devise
> With the mincing Dryades
> On the lawns and on the leas.                              [958–65]

One of the interesting aspects of this second speech is that in it the Spirit seems to replace one form of pastoralism with another, more elegant and more divine but still pastoral in its qualities. Indeed, these speeches, so appreciative of the attractive qualities of rural pleasures, posit for the pastoral a hierarchy that is as much esthetic as social and ethical. Through its tone of voice, as well as its literal instructions, the repeated "back, . . . back" puts these shepherds literally in their places, both as dancers and as members of this society. There is nothing here about the moral qualities of the pastoral experience. This scene seems to give us a third possibility, between the extremes suggested by the Lady's scorn of the "unletter'd hinds" and her praise of the "lowly sheds" of courtesy. Those two extremes admit of no resolution and indeed are left unresolved here; nor is either explicitly refuted. True, the work seems to present the pastoral world appreciatively at last, but the earlier suspicions and criticism are left unanswered. Instead, we are invited to understand that the pastoral experience is a limited but enjoyable one in and of itself. It is, we see, accessible to a variety of interpretations, all true in their own way and all justified in literary pastorals. Inherently the pastoral is neither good nor bad but can be made the embodiment of our conceptions of goodness and evil. In a wider perspective, a far-ranging view of the actualities and possibilities of life, the pastoral world is merely a vibrant but limited world. It must move back in the presence of the greater refinements of the court, of civilized culture.

But also, the realm to which the Spirit returns is itself a kind of pastoral world, reminding us that the image of goodness and perfection remains the pastoral image, even if it must be a transcendent version of the pastoral, superior to the inferior versions to be found in our "pinfold," where shepherds in their ignorance are likely to think that anything is lawful if it pleases and consequently praise the gods amiss:

> Up in the broad fields of the sky:
> There I suck the liquid air
> All amid the Gardens fair
> Of Hesperus, and his daughters three
> That sing about the golden tree:
> Along the crisped shades and bow'rs
> Revels the spruce and jocund Spring,
> The Graces and the rosy-bosom'd Hours
> Thither all their bounties bring,
> That there eternal summer dwells.                    [980–88]

Gray's "Elegy Written in a Country Churchyard" works through a number of pastoral motifs, particularly those concerning society and action and worldly success; and it records the virtues of lives led in solitude or away from public notice, cut off from the possibilities of great triumphs as well as great evils; but the narrator's emotional reaction to the story that he imagines unfolding before him is "the passing tribute of a sigh," an appropriately pastoral reaction to what he imagines as "sober wishes" of those departed.[18] The passing sigh recalls the passed lives, much as "the curfew tolls the knell of parting day." And though one may appropriately feel melancholy when confronted with the signal that marks the completed span of time, summing up the day in the fading chimes, so too one can feel melancholy in gazing at those gravestones that record the passing of other spans of time, the summing of lives in "Their name, their years, spelt by the unlettered Muse" and the sober lines "That teach the rustic moralist to die." Yet the emotion is a quiet response of natural sympathy, a grieving for oneself.

> For who to dumb Forgetfulness a prey,
>     This pleasing anxious being e'er resigned,
> Left the warm precincts of the cheerful day,
>     Nor cast one longing lingering look behind?                    [85–88]

Gray strikingly sets forth here the mild and gentle antitheses that mark his pastoral expression of mortality. Mortal existence is "pleasing" (though "anxious") and earthly life "warm" and "cheerful." The enemy is mere oblivion. Our response to pleasure past, summed up in the last line above, is brief, silent, intense, but cognizant of the inevitable passing. There is no space here for lamentations, for heroic rhetoric, grandeur, self-dramatization, defiance, or protest. Pastoral vulnerability is particularly poignant because in the pastoral world the compensations for mortality are slight; but instead of this being cause for heightened rage, it is met by a pastoral response that seems infectious. The very landscape seems to breed the quiet acceptance of the passage of time, the homeward journey to rest and quietness in the full and pious acceptance of nature and divine order.

> Perhaps in this neglected spot is laid
>     Some heart once pregnant with celestial fire;
>     Hands that the rod of empire might have swayed,
>     Or waked to ecstasy the living lyre.                    [45–48]

In such an observation are the seeds of protest against the waste and frustration; and indeed the next stanza moves toward such a protest.

> But Knowledge to their eyes her ample page
>     Rich with the spoils of time did ne'er unroll;
>     Chill Penury repressed their noble rage,
>     And froze the genial current of the soul.                [49–52]

Here we are on the verge of the extended pastoral satire against social corruptions, misplaced values, or social inequities. Instead the next stanza takes the poem in a different direction, back toward the pastoral view of natural sympathies and the acceptance of limitations as part of nature's order.

> Full many a gem of purest ray serene,
>     The dark unfathomable caves of ocean bear:
>     Full many a flower is born to blush unseen,
>     And waste its sweetness on the desert air.               [53–56]

The equation of human life with mineral and vegetable life breaks the movement toward protest; protest implies a social standard for conduct and for the course of one's fortunes. Rather, the poem asserts that the natural standard is the correct one: we are part of nature and must accept, though perhaps with some unavoidable sorrow, nature's principles, according to which those who are in harmony with her live out the cycle of their lives faithful to her equitable laws. For what is not alive in this world? "The lowing herd wind slowly . . . The plowman homeward plods . . . the beetle wheels . . . The moping owl does to the moon complain. . . ." While the dead "sleep," life continues with "The breezy call of incense-breathing morn," and over their coffins "heaves the turf." Is not all of nature animate, at least as much so as those who live? And is not the earth, the very ground, alive? No wonder this vibrant, changing but timeless pastoral world should suggest that our being on this earth and our having been on it is enough, must be enough. No wonder that this suggestion should carry with it a tempering of human emotions even in the face of social injustices and the hard absoluteness of death.

Coleridge's "Reflections on Having Left a Place of Retirement," however, leads to a rather different judgment of our social responsibilities, though it values nonetheless the lively tranquillity of the pastoral scene.

> Low was our pretty Cot: our tallest Rose
> Peep'd at the chamber-window. . . .
> Thick Jasmins twined: the little landscape round
> Was green and woody, and refresh'd the eye.
> It was a spot which you might aptly call
> The Valley of Seclusion! [1–2, 6–9]¹⁹

A wealthy town merchant passing by gazes longingly but sadly on all he sees, "And sigh'd, and said, it was a Blessed Place. And we *were* bless'd." Even a climb to a neighboring peak, affording a panorama stretching to the Channel Isles and the ocean, merely intensifies the sense of peace.

> No *wish* profan'd my overwhelmed heart.
> Blest hour! It was a luxury,—to be! [41–42]

Yet the speaker turns from this charmed landscape of retirement to a harsh world of struggle where outrages and cruelty must be endured. Pastoral life does not end for him (as it does for so many characters in pastoral literature) with a devastating intrusion by the outside world or with natural longings for worldly success. He leaves because his native sense of justice overrules his love of pastoral pleasures.

> Ah! quiet Dell! dear Cot, and Mount sublime!
> I was constrain'd to quit you. Was it right,
> While my unnumber'd bretheren toil'd and bled,
> That I should dream away the entrusted hours
> On rose-leaf beds, pampering the coward heart
> With feelings all too delicate for use? [43–48]

In pastoral seclusion people can pity but avoid those "unnumber'd bretheren" while "Nursing in some delicious solitude. . . . Their slothful loves and dainty sympathies!" (58–59). Coleridge's speaker now sees the pastoral world from the outside; but unlike the "wealthy son of Commerce" who visits it from the urban world and therefore envies its "Blessed" condition, he has been inwardly moved to join "the bloodless fight / Of Science, Freedom, and the Truth in Christ" (62–63). He wants to transcend the private and petty self-indulgence of pastoral life.

However, that is not the last word. For the poem concludes by showing how deeply he has been touched by his early experiences and in what way the pastoral experience remains a valid ideal. Now, in the large and troubled world to which he has gone, he still finds pastoral images as refreshing and necessary as Wordsworth's daffodils, though Coleridge's vacant and pensive mood comes after more strenuous exertion and tussling with the world's ways.

> Yet oft when after honourable toil
> Rests the tir'd mind, and waking loves to dream,
> My spirit shall revisit thee, dear Cot!  [64–66]

Mentally returning to the cottage means more than escaping from daily troubles; it means recovering an image of perfection that affords a standard for life. It thereby renews his commitment to social justice.

> Ah!—had none greater! And that all had such!
> It might be so—but the time is not yet.
> Speed it, O Father! Let they Kingdom come!  [70–72]

The vision of the world from the moutaintop offers far more than a dramatic landscape of visual beauty. "It seem'd like Omnipresence! / God, methought, had built him there a Temple . . ." (38–39). If this is a temple, then it is a holy spot marked off from profane life. But profane life is most in need of such a temple, the rich as well as the poor (as Thoreau was to notice in *Walden*). True, Coleridge does not imply (as Thoreau often does) that the rich suffer equally with the poor. Like the Lady in Milton's *Comus*, he senses that

> If every just man that now pines with want
> Had but a moderate and beseeming share
> Of that which lewdly-pamper'd Luxury
> Now heaps upon some few with vast excess,
> Nature's full blessings would be well dispens't
> In unsuperfluous even proportion.  [768–73]

It is not simply a matter of economy, of course. The final appeal to eschatology signifies that the pastoral world—which means not just rustic existence but the harmonious union of the natural and the human—is an image of the perfect world to come. That will come for all only when we are spiritually ready to accept it.

One can, Coleridge suggests, sufficiently limit one's vision so as to live within the pastoral world and neither notice nor worry that not everyone yet has the privilege of living there. The danger of pastoralism is isolationism. Not only does it breed complacency, it also encourages the belief that nothing can be done about the larger troubles of life. However, once one becomes conscious of the

world in which others toil without significant reward, pastoralism seems insuffi-
cient. One needs to enter the world of strife, yet seek, as Michael says to Adam
near the end of *Paradise Lost*, "A paradise within thee, happier far" (XII, 587). In
Coleridge's view, the paradise one has known must remain in the mind as a model
of what must be created for others. Only when that ideal is achieved can one
comfortably return to Eden.

Though the pastoral view of society and social justice may find deep
emotional expression, as with other emotions these are restrained by various
techniques, most often, however, by some emotional balancing or rechanneling.
In Vergil's First Eclogue, for example, our sense of the injustice done to Meliboeus
is balanced by Tityrus's joyful gratitude, implying that since political and social
forces are beyond our comprehension and control, those who are helpless can only
emotionally respond to experience. In "Lycidas" the vigorous denunciation of
current abuses is redirected into a prophecy that seems to promise revenge or
rectification, but one so cryptic that its literal meaning remains uncertain. Instead
of a direct call for action from above or below, there is a confident statement that
something is surely going to be done:

> But that two-handed engine at the door
> Stands ready to smite once, and smite no more.                    [130–31]

As tempting as it is to search for something that will fit this description, this
mysterious passage works in the poem because it is quite in keeping with the
pastoral reaction to indignation against injustice. Whatever ought to be done, it is
beyond us to do it, and even beyond us to propose what to do. We can protest and
hope, like the Pilot of the Galilean lake or the herdsmen in Vergil's Ninth
Eclogue. We can lament and thank, like those in his First, or Milton's "uncouth
swain."

In the image of the recumbent singer (i.e., a poet), Vergil finds the image
for the pastoral itself: a poem about poetry, yes, but not a mere elaboration of
craft. In a controlled context that does not pretend to be literally explicit in
contemporary terms but is still open to artistically regulated influences from the
external world, the poet attempts to learn what poetry can teach and achieve,
finding through the process of creation the justification for what he or she does.
And although this is to some extent true of all art, it is especially true of the
pastoral because of its self-conscious fascination with the processes and varieties of
song, and its formalistic obsession with the material of its own generic past.

At times, in moments of simple pastoral, the expression itself seems
enough. In complex pastorals, each form of expression explores a possible way of
understanding. The world of aesthetic discriminations permits each voice to prove

its own excellence, secure in the controlling artist's knowledge that style, meaning, and ethics are not divisible. That control, encompassing not only the varieties of pastoral but also the varieties of antipastoral, has as its purpose the expression and comprehension of life's variety. It thereby takes us to the limits of the pastoral world.

In the pastoral, then, we find struggles and disappointments and emotional turbulence, as well as bliss, lifted into art. These emotions are expressed through and contained by art, which thereby implies through its success its own value and the value of the shaped, formalized, structured response to experience that the pastoral manifests. We see, that is, the significance of containment, metaphor, and irony. As Theocritus writes about the Cyclops' wooing song, "In this way did Polyphemus shepherd his love with song / and he found a readier cure than if he had paid hard cash." Art can even sublimate eros, if not actually cure it or solve the problems it creates. What results is not directly "engaged" literature. Neither is it necessarily amoral or morally neutral. Often invested with a strong moral commitment, pastoral literature addresses that commitment through feelings and beliefs, as a shared emotional devotion or as a vision. Insofar as pastoral literature tries to change anything, it works not through a pattern of exemplary fictive action or a prescription for societal reform, but rather through expressions of human feelings. Like the poor, it "shall never cease out of the land," for what it speaks of is common to our humanity. Without the pastoral, we would not be what we are.

# Notes

## INTRODUCTION

1. "The Song of the Happy Shepherd," in *The Collected Poems of W. B. Yeats* (New York: Macmillan, 1960), p. 8.
2. *The Eclogues of Alexander Barclay*, ed. Beatrice White, Early English Text Society, no. 175 (Oxford: Oxford University Press, 1928), p. 219.
3. *The Works of Michael Drayton*, ed. J. William Hebel (Oxford: Oxford University Press, 1941), 2:345.
4. Petrarch, *Epistolae varie* 42 (August 1347), in *Francisci Petrarcae epistolae de rebus familiaribus et variae*, ed. Giuseppe Fracassetti (Florence: Felicis LeMonnier, 1859), 3:411. See also Petrarch's *Bucolicum carmen*, trans. and ed. Thomas G. Bergin (New Haven: Yale Univsersity Press, 1974), especially pp. 225–26, where this letter is cited.
5. George Puttenham, *The Arte of English Poesie*, ed. Edward Arber (London: Edward Arber, 1906), book 1, chap. xviii, pp. 52–53.
6. *The Poems of Alexander Pope*, ed. John Butt (New Haven: Yale University Press, 1963), p. 120.

## CHAPTER 1

1. Among the discussions of pastoral poetry's origins, special mention must be made of that by Thomas C. Rosenmeyer, *The Green Cabinet: Theocritus and the European Pastoral Lyric* (Berkeley: University of California Press, 1969), chap. 2.
2. Homer, *The Iliad*, trans. Richmond Lattimore (Chicago: University of Chicago Press, 1962), pp. 391, 125, and 131–32, respectively.
3. John Milton, *Complete Poems and Major Prose*, ed. Merritt Y. Hughes (New York: Odyssey Press, 1957). I have generally modernized the capitalization and use of italics.
4. Hesiod, *Theogony*, trans. D. Wender (Harmondsworth: Penguin, 1973), pp. 23–24.
5. Quotations from the Hebrew Bible follow *The Holy Scriptures* (Philadelphia: Jewish Publication Society, 1917). Those from the New Testament follow the Authorized Version.
6. *The Geneva Bible* (1560), facs,. repr. ed. Lloyd E. Berry (Madison: University of Wisconsin Press, 1969). Hallett Smith, *Elizabethan Poetry* (Cambridge, Mass.: Harvard University Press, 1952), p. 3, emphasizes the importance of David as a shepherd-poet as he surveys the Elizabethan fondness for the pastoral genre.

7. *The Poems of Theocritus*, trans. Anna Rist (Chapel Hill: University of North Carolina Press, 1978). All Theocritus's quotations are from this translation. References to the Greek text are from *Theocritus*, ed. and trans. A. S. F. Gow (Cambridge: Cambridge University Press, 1952).

8. The text of *The Shepheardes Calendar* is that of *The Works of Edmund Spenser: A Variorum Edition*, ed. Edwin Greenlaw et al., (Baltimore: The Johns Hopkins University Press, 1943), vol. 1, *The Minor Poems*, ed. Charles Grosvenor Osgood and Henry Gibbons Lotspeich. Subsequent quotations from *The Fairie Queene*, Book VI, come from this edition, the relevant volume edited by Osgood Greenlaw, Frederick Morgan Padelford, Ray Heffner, James C. McManaway, Dorothy Mason, and Brents Stirling (1938).

9. *The Poems of Sir Philip Sidney*, ed. William A. Ringler, Jr. (Oxford: Clarendon Press, 1962), p. 39 (from *The Countess of Pembroke's Arcadia*, Second Book).

10. Vergil, *Eclogues*, ed. Robert Coleman, Cambridge Greek and Latin Classics (Cambridge: Cambridge University Press, 1977).

11. My discussions of Theocritus throughout are indebted to A. S. F. Gow, *Theocritus*; Anna Rist, *Poems of Theocritus*; and Gilbert Lawall, *Theocritus' Coan Pastorals* (Washington, D.C.: Center for Hellenic Studies, 1967). These have been valuable for the literary and historical context, as well as for their considerations of the poems as works of art.

12. Andrew Marvell, *Complete Poetry*, ed. George deF. Lord (New York: Random House, 1968), pp. 48−50.

13. *The Odyssey of Homer*, trans. Richmond Lattimore (New York: Harper & Row, 1967).

14. Miguel de Unamuno, *Obras completas*, ed. Manuel Garcia Blanco (Madrid: Escelicer, 1966), 6:511−12.

## CHAPTER 2

1. Harold E. Toliver, *Pastoral Forms and Attitudes* (Berkeley: University of California Press, 1971), p. 3.

2. Johann Peter Uz, "Der Weise auf dem Lande," last stanza; in *Deutsche Dichtung im 18. Jahrhundert*, ed. Adalbert Elschenbroich (Munich: Hanser, n.d.), p. 74. According to the editor, this may have been composed as a satire; but it has some straight-faced cousins.

3. All Shakespearean quotations are from *The Riverside Shakespeare*, ed. G. Blakemore Evans (New York: Houghton Mifflin, 1974).

4. *The Selected Poems of Federico García Lorca*, ed. Francisco García Lorca and Donald M. Allen (New York: New Directions, 1955), pp. 2−6, my translation.

5. *The Collected Poems of Wallace Stevens* (New York: Alfed A. Knopf, 1965), p. 193.

6. *George Herbert and the Seventeenth-Century Religious Poets*, selected and ed. Mario A. Di Cesare (New York: W. W. Norton, 1978), p. 25

7. Voltaire, *Mélanges*, ed. Jacques van den Heuvel (Paris: Gallimard, 1961), pp. 202−06.

8. Leconte de Lisle, *Poèmes choisis*, ed. Edmond Eggli (Manchester: University of Manchester Press, 1973), pp. 17–18.
9. *The Works of George Peele*, ed. A. H. Bullen (London, 1888), vol. 1.
10. Christopher Marlowe, *The First Part of Tamburlaine the Great*, in *The Complete Plays*, ed. T. B. Steane (Baltimore: Penguin, 1969).
11. All Horace's quotations are from *Q. Horatii Flacci opera*, ed. Friedrich Klingner (Leipzig: Teubner, 1970).
12. Eduard Fraenkel, *Horace* (Oxford: Oxford University Press, 1957), pp. 42–53.
13. Quoted in *The Penguin Book of English Pastoral Verse*, ed. John Barrell and John Bull (London: Allen Lane, 1974), p. 230.
14. Albius Tibullus, *Carmina*, ed. F. W. Lenz and G. C. Galinsky, 3d ed. (Leyden: Brill, 1971). There is a pointed analysis of Tibullus's pastoralism by Charles Fantazzi, "Virgilian Pastoral and Roman Love Poetry," *American Journal of Philology* 87 (1966):188–91.
15. Raymond Williams, *The Country and the City* (New York: Oxford University Press, 1973), pp. 9–12.
16. Mary Shelley, *The Last Man*, ed. Hugh J. Luke, Jr. (Lincoln: University of Nebraska Press, 1965).

## CHAPTER 3

1. Luis de Góngora, *Poems of Góngora*, ed. R. O. Jones (Cambridge: Cambridge University Press, 1966).
2. Conrad Aiken, *Brownstone Eclogues* (Bloomington: Indiana University Press, 1962), p. 34.
3. Friedrich Schiller, *Samtliche Werke*, ed. Jost Perfahl (Munich: Winkler, 1968), vol. 1.
4. Gotthold Ephraim Lessing, *Lessings Werke*, ed. Julius Petersen and Waldemar v. Olshausen (Berlin: Bong, 1925), vol. 2; quotations are from II, iv, 13–14 and I, vi, 15–16, respectively.
5. "A Sun Bath—Nakedness," *Specimen Days* (Boston: David R. Godine, 1971), p. 71.
6. *The Poems of Sir Philip Sidney*, (*The Countess of Pembroke's Arcadia*, First Book), p. 13.
7. Flannery O'Connor, *Three by Flannery O'Connor* (New York: Signet, n.d.).
8. *Poems of Robert Browning*, ed. Donald Smalley (Boston: Houghton Mifflin, 1956), p. 15.

## CHAPTER 4

1. Richard Wagner, *Tannhäuser*, ed. Max Hochkofler (New York: Eulenberg, 1961).
2. Luiz Vaz de Camoëns, *The Lusiads*, trans. William C. Atkinson (Harmondsworth: Penguin, 1952), p. 216.
3. William Wordsworth, *Selected Poems and Prefaces*, ed. Jack Stillinger (Boston: Houghton Mifflin, 1965), pp. 108–11.

4. "Ces jours me sont si doux en ce beau lieu champêtre," *The Penguin Book of French Verse;* 2:117.

5. Eduard Mörike, *Werke,* ed. Gerhart Baumann and Siegfried Grosse (Stuttgart: J. G. Cotta'sche, 1961), 1:112–14.

6. In addition to the discussions of "April" in the Spenser items cited in the Bibliography, see also: Thomas H. Cain, "The Strategy of Praise in Spenser's 'Aprill,'" *Studies in English Literature* 8 (1968):45–58; Louis Adrian Montrose, "'Eliza, Queene of Shepheardes,' and the Pastoral of Power," *English Literary Renaissance* 10, no. 2 (1980):153–82; and Elkin Calhoun Wilson, *England's Eliza* (Cambridge, Mass.: Harvard University Press, 1939), pp. 126–66, which provide general background on Elizabethan applications of the royal pastoral motif.

## CHAPTER 5

1. Vergil's First Eclogue is one of the most widely discussed classical poems. In addition to the works on Vergil cited in the Bibliography, the following are especially significant analyses: Charles Paul Segal, "*Tamen Cantabitis, Arcades*—Exile and Arcadia in Eclogues One and Nine," *Arion* 4 (1964):237–66; and John B. Van Sickle, "Studies of Dialectical Methodology in the Virgilian Tradition," *Modern Language Notes* 85 (1970):884–928. Both deal with the relations between this poem and larger artistic patterns in the volume.

2. Sir Philip Sidney, *An Apology for Poetry,* ed. Geoffrey Shepherd (London: Nelson, 1965), p. 133.

3. Erwin Panofsky, "Et in Arcadia Ego: Poussin and the Elegiac Tradition," *Meaning in the Visual Arts* (Garden City, N.Y.: Doubleday, 1955), p. 300.

4. Alfonso Traina, "La chiusa della prima ecloga virgiliana (vv. 82–3)," *Lingua e Stile* 3 (1968):52, my translation.

5. Eleanor Winsor Leach, *Vergil's "Eclogues": Landscapes of Experience* (Ithaca, N.Y.: Cornell University Press, 1974), p. 137.

6. Traina, "La chiusa," p. 52, my translation.

7. See, for example, William Empson's analysis of Shakespeare's sonnet "They that have power to hurt and will do none" in *Some Versions of Pastoral* (Norfolk, Conn.: New Directions, 1960), pp. 85–111.

8. *The Works of John Suckling,* ed. Thomas Clayton (Oxford: Clarendon Press, 1971), *The Non-Dramatic Works,* pp. 79–84.

9. *The Complete Poetry of Robert Herrick,* ed. T. Max Patrick (New York: W. W. Norton, 1968), p. 367 (no. H-864).

10. Vergil, *Opera,* ed. R. A. B. Mynors, Oxford Classical Texts (Oxford: Clarendon Press, 1972, rev. ed.).

11. Torquato Tasso, *Gerusalemme liberata,* ed. Anna Maria Carini (Milan: Feltrinelli, 1961).

12. Wayne C. Booth, *A Rhetoric of Irony* (Chicago: University of Chicago Press, 1974), pp. 176–78.

13. Christopher Marlowe, *The Complete Poems and Translations*, ed. Stephen Orgel (Harmondsworth: Penguin, 1971), p. 209.
14. Sir Walter Raleigh, "The Nymph's Reply," in Marlowe, *Complete Poems*, p. 212.
15. Babette Deutsch, *Coming of Age: New and Selected Poems* (Bloomington: Indiana University Press, 1959), p. 56.

## CHAPTER 6

1. W. H. Auden, *Collected Shorter Poems, 1927–1957* (New York: Random House, 1967), p. 141.
2. Rubén Darío, *Poesías completas*, ed. Alfonso Méndez Plancarte (Madrid: Aguilar, 1954), pp. 667–68.
3. *The Poems of Matthew Arnold*, ed. Kenneth Allott, 2d ed. rev. by Miriam Allott (London: Longman, 1979), p. 537.
4. Clement Marot, in *The Pastoral Elegy: An Anthology*, ed. Thomas Perrin Harrison (Austin: University of Texas Press, 1939), pp. 134–45, my translation.
5. Iacopo Sannazaro, *Opere*, ed. Enrico Carrara (Turin: Unione Tipografice-Editrice, 1963), p. 192.
6. Percy Bysshe Shelley, *Shelley's Poetry and Prose*, ed. Donald H. Reiman and Sharon B. Powers (New York: W. W. Norton, 1977), pp. 392–406.
7. Pierre de Ronsard, "Eclogue One," *The Pastoral Elegy*, p. 153.
8. Significant essays on the structure and themes of "Epitaphium Damonis" include those by A. S. P. Woodhouse, "Milton's Pastoral Monodies," *Studies in Honor of Gilbert Norwood* (Toronto: University of Toronto Press, 1952), pp. 261–78; and Ralph W. Condee, "The Structure of Milton's 'Epitaphium Damonis,'" *Studies in Philology* 62 (1965):577–94.
9. Ernest Hemingway, *A Farewell to Arms* (New York: Charles Scribner's, 1957).

## CHAPTER 7

1. Helpful discussions of time and place in pastoral literature, principally classical, include Adam M. Parry, "Landscape in Greek Literature," *Yale Classical Studies* 15, no. 1 (1957):3–29; Bernard F. Dick, "Ancient Pastoral and the Pathetic Fallacy," *Comparative Literature* 20, no. 1 (1968):27–44; Zoja Pavlovskis, "Man in a Poetic Landscape: Humanization of Nature in Virgil's *Eclogues*," *Classical Philology* 66 (1971):151–68; Charles Segal, "Landscape into Myth: Theocritus' Bucolic Poetry," *Ramus* 4, no. 2 (1975):115–39; and especially Thomas G. Rosenmeyer, *The Green Cabinet: Theocritus and the European Pastoral Lyric* (Berkeley: University of California Press, 1969), pp. 86–91, 179–205.
2. Renato Poggioli, *The Oaten Flute* (Cambridge, Mass.: Harvard University Press, 1975), p. 41.
3. See, for example, the comments by Bernard F. Dick, "Ancient Pastoral and the Pathetic Fallacy," *Comparative Literature* 20, no. 1 (1968):27–44.

4. *The Poems of Sir Philip Sidney* (*Astrophil and Stella*, Eighth Song), p. 217.
5. Annette von Droste-Hülshoff, *Droste-Hülshoffs Werke*, ed. R. Walbinder (Berlin: Aufbau-Verlag, 1969), pp. 179–80.
6. Maurice Scève, *The Penguin Book of French Verse: 2*, p. 18.
7. Alphonse de Lamartine, *Oeuvres poétiques*, ed. M. F. Guyard (Paris: Gallimard, 1963), p. 38.
8. Julio Herrera y Reissig, *The Penguin Book of Spanish Verse*, ed. J. M. Cohen (Harmondsworth: Penguin, 1960), p. 342, my translation.
9. James Agee, *A Death in the Family* (New York: McDowell, Obolensky, 1957), pp. 3–8.
10. Marge Piercy, *Stone, Paper, Knife* (New York: Alfred A. Knopf, 1983), p. 93.
11. Rosenmeyer, *The Green Cabinet*, p. 89.
12. Coleridge, *Selected Poetry*, p. 57.
13. Marvell, *Complete Poems*, p. 88.
14. "A Nocturnal Reverie," *The Poems of Anne, Countess of Winchilsea*, ed. Myra Reynolds (Chicago: University of Chicago Press, 1903), pp. 268–70.
15. Wordsworth, *Selected Poems*, pp. 25–26.
16. *Matthew Arnold*, p. 537.
17. John Greenleaf Whittier, *The Poetical Works of Whittier*, ed. Horace E. Scudder (Boston: Houghton Mifflin, 1975), pp. 400–01.
18. Vergil, *Opera*. For a discussion of some thematic distinctions between pastoral and georgic poetry, see Andrew V. Ettin, "Milton, T. S. Eliot, and the Virgilian Vision: Some Versions of Georgic," *Genre* 10, no. 2 (1977):233–58.
19. Emlyn Williams, *George: An Early Autobiography* (New York: Random House, 1961).

## CHAPTER 8

1. Lady Mary Wroth, *Pamphilia to Amphilanthus*, ed. G. F. Waller, Salzburg Studies in English Literature, Elizabethan Renaissance Studies 64 (Salzburg: Universität Salzburg, 1977), p. 110.
2. Aphra Behn, "Song," *By a Woman Writt: Literature from Six Centuries by and about Women*, ed. Joan Goulianos (Baltimore: Penguin, 1974), p. 88.
3. *Droste-Hülshoffs Werke*, pp. 68–69.
4. Ovid, *Metamorphoseon, Liber I*, ed. A. G. Lee (Cambridge: Cambridge University Press, 1953).
5. Johann Wolfgang von Goethe, *Goethes Poetische Werke* (Stuttgart: J. G. Cotta'sche, 1959), vol. 5; Faust, part 2, act 5, lines 11251–52.
6. *England's Helicon, 1600–1614*, ed. Hyder Edward Rollins (Cambridge, Mass.: Harvard University Press, 1935), vol. 1, no. 140.
7. Flannery O'Connor, "Good Country People," in *Three by Flannery O'Connor*, p. 250.
8. Mihail Lermontov, *A Hero of Our Time*, trans. Vladimir Nabokov (New York: Doubleday, 1958), "Taman." The italicized phrase in the longer quotation is also italicized in the Russian.

9. Letter of January 16, 1836, quoted by Janko Lavrin, "Some Notes on Lermontov's Romanticism," *Slavonic and East European Review* 36, no. 1 (1957):72.
10. Sidney, *Apology*, p. 116.
11. George Orwell, *Keep the Aspidistra Flying* (London: Secker and Warburg, 1962).
12. Edward Dyer, "My Mind to Me a Kingdom Is," *Tudor Poetry and Prose*, ed. J. William Hebel et al. (New York: Appleton-Century-Crofts, 1953), p. 123.
13. Joni Mitchell, "Woodstock," in *The Norton Introduction to Literature: Poetry*, ed. J. Paul Hunter (New York: W. W. Norton, 1973), p. 85.
14. Quoted by Michelle Russell, "An Open Letter to the Academy," in *Building Feminist Theory: Essays from "Quest"* (New York and London: Longman, 1981), pp. 104–05.
15. *Ovid's Metamorphoses: The Arthur Golding Translation*, ed. John Frederick Nims (New York: Macmillan, 1965), p. 6.
16. "Verses by the Author on the Prospect of Planting Arts and Learning in America," *The Works of George Berkeley*, ed. A. A. Luce and T. E. Jessop (London: Thomas Nelson, 1955), 7:373.
17. Peter V. Marinelli, *Pastoral* (London: Methuen, 1971), pp. 25–27, has a good comparison of these two opening choruses.
18. *The Complete Poems of Thomas Gray*, ed. H. W. Starr and T. R. Hendrickson (Oxford: Clarendon Press, 1966), pp. 37–43.
19. Samuel Taylor Coleridge, *Selected Poetry and Prose*, ed. Donald A. Stauffer (New York: Random House, 1951), pp. 58–60.

# Bibliography

In the last two decades there has been an increased interest in thinking and writing about pastoral literature. To some extent, contemporary involvement with the pastoral is part of a general rethinking about literary history and—like the rediscovery of the Metaphysicals and subsequently of baroque literature as a whole—is an attempt to derive critical and literary stimulation from forms that a previous literary generation had dismissed as old-fashioned and played-out. Surely, however, some of the impetus must come from an impulse that is indeed pastoral—namely, from a desire for a literary form which seems safe and predictable, and which constructs a pattern of life similarly safe and predictable. In contrast to the indeterminacy of contemporary society and contemporary art, pastoral literature offers a well-marked field for exploration. Events happen in pastoral literature, but there are no "happenings" of the sort that comprise a concert by John Cage or (generally) the front page of a newspaper. It gives no comfort to the student of history, literary and otherwise, to notice that there was also interest in the pastoral during the 1900s and 1930s.

Along with affection for the pastoral may go some curiosity as to how it was possible to think and write in such a way and what it must have felt like to do so. That curiosity is captured nicely in the preface to a work curious in itself, the "translation" (which is to say, translation joined with running commentary) of Vergil's *Eclogues* and *Georgics* by David R. Slavitt. Describing how he set upon his task, Slavitt writes, "The poems made almost no sense. They were a babble of unconvincing shepherds. . . . Finally, I worked out a desperate kind of attack, which was to ask of each *Eclogue*: If you were ever a living, breathing poem, what could you conceivably have been about?" It comes as a jolt that he should write this way, because his response is so startlingly modern. Dr. Johnson might concur that the shepherds are "unconvincing," but it would not have seemed to him that the poems "made almost no sense." What comes of Slavitt's engagement with these texts is, of course, a Vergil who is, like Jan Kott's Shakespeare, "our contemporary." Nonetheless, Slavitt's wrestling with the poems on two levels simultaneously, as translator and as interpreter, reminds us of how far we are from them and yet how accessible to us they still remain.

Through more literal translations, classical pastoral poetry has become more immediately available to a generation with small Latin and less Greek. While

A. S. F. Gow's handsome bilingual edition with extensive textual commentary remains indispensible for a close study of Theocritus, general reading of the Idylls has been facilitated by the more recent translations by Barriss Mills, Anthony Holden (who includes Moschus and Bion), and Anna Rist. During this same period Vergil's Eclogues have been translated by C. Day-Lewis, William Berg, A. J. Boyle, and Paul Alpers (the latter three providing bilingual editions, as did E. V. Rieu in his popular earlier translation). Rist's, Berg's and Alpers's translations are accompanied by detailed critical analyses. These versions, furthermore, have benefited from editorial work by Gow on Theocritus and by R. A. B. Mynors, Michael Coleman (with extensive annotations), and Boyle on Vergil.

Criticism on classical pastoral poetry has also been lively. Our understanding of Theocritus has profited particularly from the interpretations by Rist and Gilbert Lawall, while Thomas G. Rosenmeyer has been instrumental in redefining Theocritus's pertinence to the whole tradition of lyric poetry. (David M. Halperin's attempt to distinguish Theocritus's "bucolic poetry" from later "pastoral poetry" appeared too late for me to use in this study.) Significant work on Vergil's pastoral poetry has come from Friedrich Klingner, Eleanor Winsor Leach, Brooks Otis, Jacques Perret, Viktor Pöschl, Michael C. J. Putnam, Charles Segal, Bruno Snell, and John B. van Sickle, as well as Alpers, Boyle, and Coleman. An issue of the journal *Ramus*, edited by Boyle and devoted to classical pastoral poetry, contains several valuable essays by these and other classicists. The works of Jean-Marie André and Gordon Williams are also important to understanding the cultural and literary context of Roman pastoral literature. The study of primitivism by Arthur O. Lovejoy and Franz Boas is suggestive.

For the history of pastoral literature, the older surveys by W. W. Greg, Enrico Carrara, Irene Behrens, and Mia Irene Gerhardt remain useful, as do the more specialized studies by Hector Genouy, Alice Hulubei, Jacques Marsan, and Hallet Smith. Michael O'Loughlin has traced into the Renaissance some Roman traditions about the retired life. Harry Levin has dealt with the Golden Age in the Renaissance, touching partly on pastoral texts. A. Bartlett Giamatti has studied the pastoral garden-inset in epic poetry, while Terry Comito has ranged more widely in investigating ideas about the garden in Renaissance culture. W. Leonard Grant and Helen Cooper have expanded our knowledge and understanding of the breadth of pastoral literature between Vergil and the late Renaissance, and of changes in emphasis during that period. Ellen Zetzel Lambert has studied the major elegies from Theocritus to Milton. Dorothy Schuchman McCoy shows pastoral periphrasis to be a valuable index to period stylistics. Harry Berger, Jr., has published some provocative and important examinations of the nature and meaning of Renaissance pastoralism. J. E. Congleton's survey of critical theories of pastoral poetry extends from the Renaissance to the early Romantics in England and on the Continent but centers on neoclassical doctrines. Richard Feingold considers pastoral and georgic motifs in eighteenth-century English poetry, and David Wagenknecht writes on Blake's pastoralism. Finally, Erwin Panofsky's analysis of the "Et in Arcadia Ego" theme in literature and the visual arts remains a landmark for our understanding of this pervasive pastoral idea.

As for the pastoral writers of the English Renaissance, a list of all of the helpful critical articles would be massive. In addition to those already cited, critics who have written at length on nature and pastoral poetry include Donald Cheney, Humphrey Tonkin, and Nancy Jo Hoffman on Spenser; Patrick Cullen on Spenser and Marvell; Richard Mallette on Spenser and Milton; Frank Kermode, Richard Cody, Thomas McFarland, and Andrew Young on Shakespeare; Donald M. Friedman on Marvell; and John R. Knott, Jr., William G. Madsen, and Louis Martz on Milton.

Special mention should also be made of Frank Kermode's anthology of English Renaissance pastoral texts, and of John Barrell and John Bull's selection of English pastoral writings from Googe to Yeats, which includes brief historical essays on changes in emphasis in pastoral literature of various periods.

Several specialized works dealing with the pastoral elements in more recent literature suggest the continuation of the tradition. Particular mention should be made of works by Herbert Lindenberger, Michael Squires, Lawrence Poston, and Madeline Moore; and studies in American literature by Annette Kolodny, R. W. B. Lewis, John F. Lynen, Lucinda Hardwick MacKethan, Leo Marx, Lewis P. Simpson, and Henry Nash Smith. Semiotic approaches can be found in essays by Marc Eli Blanchard and Michael Riffaterre. David R. Thuente has surveyed criticism of pastoral narratives.

There have been a few lively works combining close readings of individual texts with theories about the nature of pastoral literature. All of these works take us at least to the end of the nineteenth century or into the twentieth. Peter V. Marinelli's brief handbook provides a useful starting place for exploring the main motifs. Laurence Lerner finds the main pastoral motif to be nostalgia in its various forms. Raymond Williams probes the tensions between pastoral fictions and English social conditions. Harold Toliver concentrates on the ways that works by authors (mostly British and American) from Vergil to Wallace Stevens represent their attitudes toward artistic and social values. Renato Poggioli, who died before completing his work on the pastoral, left behind some influential published essays that were collected along with his uneven, unpublished writings into a suggestive, though skeletal, book. Ranging widely across European literature, Poggioli was attempting to trace out the main pastoral motifs as they seemed to emerge into prominence in selected literary texts at various points in history. William Empson's controversial work, first published in 1935, remains the most challenging—both the most important and least helpful book on the pastoral. Concentrating on motifs but not working within the historian's framework, Empson chooses totally improbable texts but brings to bear on them a highly sophisticated and profound understanding of how pastoral literature functions and what it is about. Finally, much interest in the pastoral was stimulated by Northrop Frye's brief but suggestive remarks in his *Anatomy of Criticism*.

Aside, of course, from the ongoing reinterpretation of the major texts, more work needs to be done on the historical changes in pastoral literature considered in the light of other literary, cultural, and social changes; on the connections between pastoralism in literature and in the other arts; on modern versions of pastoral motifs and techniques, particularly in films; and on the sociology of pastoral literature.

Some interesting recent attempts at modern pastoral literature are Diane Ackerman's first book of poems, *The Planets*; Guy Davenport's collection of stories, *Eclogues*; and Gilbert Sorrentino's novel *Blue Pastoral*. These are overt reminders that the pastoral mode is still with us. The landscape of pastoral literature spreads out broadly. Undeniably, there are monotonous stretches in it, and stubble; and every now and then someone has stuck a painted fawn next to a pink plaster flamingo on a machine-mowed lawn. Yet there is so much more. In ways that we are only recently beginning to understand, pastoral literature has defined and shaped our experiences in life. Who can doubt that it will continue to do so?

The following list includes writings by the authors mentioned in the foregoing survey, as well as other secondary works cited in the Notes.

Ackerman, Diane. *The Planets: A Cosmic Pastoral*. New York: Morrow, 1976.

Alpers, Paul. *The Singer of the "Eclogues": A Study of Virgilian Pastoral*. Berkeley: University of California Press, 1979.

André, Jean-Marie. *L'Otium dans la vie morale et intellectuelle romaine des origines à l'époque augustéene*. Paris: Presses Universitaires de France, 1966.

Barrell, John, and Bull, John, eds., *The Penguin Book of English Pastoral Verse*. London: Allen Lane, 1974.

Berg, William. *Early Virgil*. London: Athlone Press, 1974.

Berger, Harry, Jr. "The Ecology of the Mind." *The Centennial Review* 8 (1964): 36–78.

———. "The Renaissance Imagination: Second World and Green World." *The Centennial Review* 9 (1965).

———. "Mode and Diction in *The Shepheardes Calender*." *Modern Philology* 67 (1969): 140–49.

———. "Conspicuous Exclusion in Vermeer: An Essay in Renaissance Pastoral." *Yale French Studies* 47 (1972): 234–65.

Blanchard, Marc Eli. "*Daphnis and Chloe*: The Story of Mimesis," pp. 111–26; and "Pastoral Style, Pastoral Self," 167–80. In *Description: Sign, Self, Desire*. The Hague: Mouton Publishers, 1980.

Cain, Thomas H. "The Strategy of Praise in Spenser's 'Aprill.'" *Studies in English Literature* 8 (1968): 45–48.

Carrara, Enrico. *La poesia pastorale*. Milan: Dr. Francesco Vallardi, n.d. [1905].

Cheney, Donald. *Spenser's Image of Nature: Wild Man and Shepherd in "The Fairie Queene."* New Haven: Yale University Press, 1966.

Cody, Richard. *The Landscape of the Mind: Pastoralism and Platonic Theory in Tasso's "Aminta" and Shakespeare's Early Comedies*. Oxford: Clarendon Press, 1969.

Coleman, Robert, ed. Vergil, *Eclogues*. Cambridge Greek and Latin Classics. Cambridge: Cambridge University Press, 1977.

Comito, Terry. *The Idea of the Garden in the Renaissance*. New Brunswick, N.J.: Rutgers University Press, 1978.

Condee, Ralph W. "The Structure of Milton's 'Epitaphium Damonis.'" *Studies in Philology* 62 (1965): 577–94.

Congleton, J. E. *Theories of Pastoral Poetry in England 1684–1798*. Gainesville: University of Florida Press, 1952.

Cooper, Helen. *Pastoral: Medieval into Renaissance*. Ipswitch, England, and Totowa, N.J.: D. S. Brewer and Rowman & Littlefield, 1977.

Cullen, Patrick. *Spenser, Marvell and the Renaissance Pastoral*. Cambridge, Mass.: Harvard University Press, 1970.

Davenport, Guy. *Eclogues: Eight Stories*. Berkeley, Calif.: North Point Press, 1981.

Day-Lewis, Cecil, trans. *The Eclogues, Georgics and Aeneid of Virgil*. London: Oxford University Press, 1966.

Dick, Bernard F. "Ancient Pastoral and the Pathetic Fallacy." *Comparative Literature* 20, no. 1 (1968): 27–44.

Durr, Robert Allen. "Spenser's Calendar of Christian Time." *ELH* 24 (1957): 269–98.

Empson, William. *Some Versions of Pastoral*. Norfolk, Conn.: New Directions, 1950. Originally published as *English Pastoral Poetry*, 1935.

Feingold, Richard. *Nature and Society: Later Eighteenth-Century Uses of the Pastoral and Georgic*. New Brunswick: N.J.: Rutgers University Press, 1978.

Friedman, Donald M. *Marvell's Pastoral Art*. Berkeley: University of California Press, 1970.

Frye, Northrop. *Anatomy of Criticism*. Princeton: Princeton University Press, 1957.

Genouy, Hector. *L'Elément pastoral dans la poésie narrative et le drame en Angleterre, de 1579 à 1640*. Paris: Didier, 1928.

Giamatti, A. Bartlett. *The Earthly Paradise and the Renaissance Epic*. Princeton: Princeton University Press, 1966.

Gow, A. S. F., ed. and trans., *Theocritus*. 2 vols. Cambridge: Cambridge University Press, 1952.

Grant, W. Leonard. *Neo-Latin Literature and the Pastoral*. Chapel Hill: University of North Carolina Press, 1965.

Greg, W. W. *Pastoral Poetry and Pastoral Drama*. London: A. H. Bullen, 1906.

Halperin, David M. *Before Pastoral: Theocritus and the Ancient Tradition of Bucolic Poetry*. New Haven: Yale University Press, 1983.

Hamilton, A. C. "The Argument of Spenser's *Shepheardes Calendar*." *ELH* 23 (1956): 171–268.

Harrison, Thomas Perrin, ed., and Leon, Harry Joshua, trans. *The Pastoral Elegy: An Anthology*. Austin: University of Texas Press, 1939.

Hoffman, Nancy Jo. *Spenser's Pastorals: The Shepheardes Calendar and "Colin Clout."* Baltimore: The Johns Hopkins University Press, 1977.

Holden, Anthony, trans. *Greek Pastoral Poetry*. Harmondsworth: Penguin Books, 1974.

Hulubei, Alice. *L'Eclogue en France au XVIe siècle*. Paris: Librairie E. Droz, 1938.

Kermode, Frank, ed. *English Pastoral Poetry: From the Beginnings to Marvell, An Anthology*. New York: Norton, 1952.

————, ed. "Introduction." Shakespeare, *The Tempest*. Arden edition. 6th ed. Cambridge, Mass.: Harvard University Press, 1958.

Knott, John R., Jr. *Milton's Pastoral Vision: An Approach to Paradise Lost*. Chicago: University of Chicago Press, 1971.

Kolodny, Annette. *The Lay of the Land: Metaphor as Experience and History in American Life and Letters*. Chapel Hill: University of North Carolina Press, 1975.

Lambert, Ellen Zetzel. *Placing Sorrow: A Study of the Pastoral Elegy Convention from Theocritus to Milton*. Chapel Hill: University of North Carolina Press, 1976.

Lawall, Gilbert. *Theocritus' Coan Pastorals: A Poetry Book*. Washington, D.C.: Center for Hellenic Studies, 1967.

Leach, Eleanor Winsor. *Vergil's "Eclogues": Landscapes of Experience*. Ithaca, N.Y.: Cornell University Press, 1974.

Lerner, Laurence. *The Uses of Nostalgia: Studies in Pastoral Poetry*. New York: Schocken Books, 1972.

Levin, Harry. *The Myth of the Golden Age in the Renaissance*. Bloomington: Indiana University Press, 1969.

Lewis, R. W. B. *The American Adam: Innocence, Tragedy and Tradition in the Nineteenth Century*. Chicago: University of Chicago Press, 1955.

Lindenberger, Herbert. "The Idyllic Moment: On Pastoral and Romanticism." *College English* 34 (1972): 335–51.

Lovejoy, Arthur O., and Boas, Franz. *Primitivism and Related Ideas in Antiquity* Baltimore: The Johns Hopkins University Press, 1935.

Lynen, John F. *The Pastoral Art of Robert Frost*. New Haven: Yale University Press, 1960.

MacCaffrey, Isabel Gamble. "Allegory and Pastoral in *The Shepheardes Calender*." *ELH* 36 (1969): 88–109.

McCoy, Dorothy Schuchman. *Tradition and Convention: A Study of Periphrasis in English Pastoral Poetry from 1557–1715*. The Hague: Mouton, 1965.

MacKethan, Lucinda Hardwick. *The Dream of Arcady: Time and Place in Southern Literature*. Baton Rouge: Louisiana State University Press, 1980.

Madsen, William G. "The Idea of Nature in Milton's Poetry." In *Three Studies in the Renaissance*, pp. 181–283. Yale Studies in English 138. New Haven: Yale University Press, 1958.

Marinelli, Peter V. *Pastoral*. Critical Idioms Series. London: Methuen, 1971.

Marsan, Jules. *La Pastoral dramatique en France à la fin du XVIe et au commencement du XVIIe siècle*. Geneva: Slatkine Reprints, 1969. Original ed., Paris, 1905.

Martz, Louis L. *Poet of Exile: A Study of Milton's Poetry*. New Haven: Yale University Press, 1980.

Marx, Leo. *The Machine in the Garden: Technology and the Pastoral Ideal in America*. New York: Oxford University Press, 1964.

————. "Pastoral Ideals and City Troubles." *Journal of General Education* 20 (1969): 251–71.

————. "Susan Sontag's 'New Left' Pastoral: Notes on Revolutionary Pastoralism in America." *TriQuarterly* 23/24 (1972): 552–75.

Mills, Barriss, trans. *The Idylls of Theokritos*. West Lafayette, Ind.: Purdue University Press, 1963.

Montrose, Louis Adrian. "'Eliza, Queene of Shepheardes,' and the Pastoral of Power." *English Literary Renaissance* 10, no. 2 (1980): 153–82.

Moore, Madeline. "Some Female Versions of Pastoral: *The Voyage Out* and Matriarchal Mythologies," pp. 82–104. In *New Feminist Essays on Virginia Woolf*, ed. Jane Marcus. Lincoln: University of Nebraska Press, 1981.

Mynors, R. A. B, ed. *P. Vergili Maronis Opera*. Oxford Classical Texts. Rev. ed. Oxford: Clarendon Press, 1972.

O'Loughlin, Michael. *The Garlands of Repose: The Literary Celebration of Civic and Retired Leisure, The Traditions of Homer and Vergil, Horace and Montaigne*. Chicago: University of Chicago Press, 1978.

Otis, Brooks. *Virgil: A Study in Civilized Poetry*. Oxford: Oxford University Press, 1964.

Panofsky, Erwin. "The Early History of Man in Two Cycles of Paintings by Piero di Cosimo." In *Studies in Iconology*. Oxford: Oxford University Press, 1939, chap. 2.

————. "Et in Arcadia Ego: Poussin and the Elegiac Tradition." In *Meaning in the Visual Arts*, chap. 7. Garden City, N.Y.: Doubleday, 1955.

Parry, Adam M. "Landscape in Greek Literature." *Yale Classical Studies* 15, no. 1 (1957): 3–29.

Pavlovskis, Zoja. "Man in a Poetic Landscape: Humanization of Nature in Virgil's *Eclogues*." *Classical Philology* 66 (1971): 151–68.

Perret, Jacques. 2 ed. *Virgile*. Paris: Editions du Seuil, 1959.

Poggioli, Renato. *The Oaten Flute: Essays on Pastoral Poetry and the Pastoral Ideal*. Cambridge, Mass.: Harvard University Press, 1975.

Pöschl, Viktor. *Die Hirtendichtung Virgils*. Heidelberg: Carl Winter, 1964.

Poston, Lawrence. "Three Versions of Victorian Pastoral." *Genre* 13 (1980): 305–36.

Putnam, Michael C. J. *Virgil's Pastoral Art*. Princeton: Princeton University Press, 1970.

Rieu, E. V., trans., Virgil, *The Pastoral Poems*. Harmondsworth: Penguin, 1954.

Riffaterre, Michael. "Système d'un genre descriptif." *Poetique* 9 (1972): 15–30.

————. "Interpretation and Descriptive Poetry: A Reading of Wordsworth's 'Yew-Trees.'" *New Literary History* 4 (1973): 229–56.

Rist, Anna, trans. *The Poems of Theocritus*. Chapel Hill: University of North Carolina Press, 1978.

Rosenmeyer, Thomas G. *The Green Cabinet: Theocritus and the European Pastoral Lyric*. Berkeley: University of California Press, 1969.

Segal, Charles. *Poetry and Myth in Ancient Pastoral: Essays on Theocritus and Virgil*. Princeton: Princeton University Press, 1981.

Simpson, Lewis P. *The Dispossessed Garden: Pastoral and History in Southern Literature*. Athens, Ga.: University of Georgia Press, 1975.

Slavitt, David R., trans. *The Eclogues and Georgics of Virgil*. Garden City, N.Y.: Doubleday, 1972.

Smith, Hallett. "Pastoral Poetry: The Vitality and Versatility of a Convention." In *Elizabethan Poetry*. Cambridge, Mass.: Harvard University Press, 1952, chap. 1.

Snell, Bruno. "Arcadia: The Discovery of a Spiritual Landscape." In *The Discovery of the Mind*, trans. T. G. Rosenmeyer. Oxford: Oxford University Press, 1953, chap. 13.

Sorrentino, Gilbert. *Blue Pastoral*. Berkeley, Calif.: North Point Press, 1983.

Squires, Michael. *The Pastoral Novel: Studies in George Eliot, Thomas Hardy and D. H. Lawrence*. Charlottesville: University Press of Virginia, 1974.

Stewart, Stanley. *The Enclosed Garden: The Tradition and the Image in Seventeenth-Century Poetry*. Madison: University of Wisconsin Press, 1966.

Thuente, David R. "Pastoral Narratives: A Review of Criticism." *Genre* 14 (1981): 247–67.

Toliver, Harold E. *Pastoral Forms and Attitudes*. Berkeley: University of California Press, 1971.

Tonkin, Humphrey. *Spenser's Courteous Pastoral*. Oxford: Oxford University Press, 1972.

Traina, Alfonso. "La chiusa della prima ecloga virgiliana (vv. 82–3)," *Lingua e Stile* 3 (1968): 45–57.

van Sickle, John B. "The Unity of the Eclogues: Arcadian Forest, Theocritean Trees." *Transactions of the American Philological Association* 98 (1967): 491–508.

———. "Studies of Dialectical Methodology in the Virgilian Tradition." *Modern Language Notes* 85 (1970): 884–928.

Wagenknecht, David. *Blake's Night: William Blake and the Idea of Pastoral*. Cambridge, Mass.: Harvard University Press, 1973.

# Index

197